MINDREADING

*An Integrated Account of Pretence,
Self-Awareness, and
Understanding Other Minds*

SHAUN NICHOLS
and
STEPHEN P. STICH

CLARENDON PRESS · OXFORD

OXFORD

UNIVERSITY PRESS

Great Clarendon Street, Oxford OX2 6DP

Oxford University Press is a department of the University of Oxford.
It furthers the University's objective of excellence in research, scholarship,
and education by publishing worldwide in

Oxford New York

Auckland Cape Town Dar es Salaam Hong Kong Karachi Kuala Lumpur
Madrid Melbourne Mexico City Nairobi New Delhi Shanghai Taipei Toronto

With offices in

Argentina Austria Brazil Chile Czech Republic France Greece
Guatemala Hungary Italy Japan Poland Portugal Singapore
South Korea Switzerland Thailand Turkey Ukraine Vietnam

Oxford is a registered trade mark of Oxford University Press
in the UK and in certain other countries

Published in the United States
by Oxford University Press Inc., New York

© Shaun Nichols and Stephen P. Stich, 2003

British Library Cataloguing in Publication Data

Data available

Library of Congress Cataloging in Publication Data

Data available

ISBN 978-0-19-823610-8 (pbk.)

Typeset by Newgen Imaging Systems (P) Ltd., Chennai, India
Printed in Great Britain
on acid-free paper by
Biddles Ltd., King's Lynn, Norfolk

ACKNOWLEDGEMENTS

We began working on this book in 1995, and in the intervening years we have benefited from the comments and conversation of many people including Luca Bonatti, Peter Carruthers, Gregory Currie, Martin Davies, Catherine Driscoll, Luc Faucher, Jerry Fodor, Trisha Folds-Bennett, Christopher Frith, Gary Gates, Rochel Gelman, Tim German, Alvin Goldman, Alison Gopnik, Robert Gordon, Paul Harris, Chris Jarrold, Barbara Landau, Alan Leslie, Angeline Lillard, Brian Loar, Ron Mallon, Dominic Murphy, Josef Perner, Philip Robbins, Richard Samuels, Brian Scholl, Eric Schwitzgebel, Jonathan Weinberg, and Robert Woolfolk. Our warm thanks to all of these friends and colleagues. No doubt there are others who should be on our list, but aren't because our memories are all too fallible. We hope they will accept our thanks anonymously.

Work on the book was supported by a National Endowment for the Humanities Fellowship for University Teachers (FA-33344-95) to Stephen Stich, a National Research Service Award Postdoctoral Fellowship from the National Institutes of Health to Shaun Nichols (PHST32MH19975) as well as by internal grants at Rutgers University and at the College of Charleston. The Rutgers University Center for Cognitive Science provided Nichols with a home away from home for two years, and provided both of us with a stimulating and congenial environment. For all of this support, we are very grateful.

Some portions of the book are drawn from work we published while the book was evolving. Chapters 2 and 4 are expanded and substantially revised versions of previously published articles (Nichols and Stich 2000, 2002). We've also borrowed bits here and there from a few other articles (Nichols 2001, 2002; Stich and Nichols 2003). We are grateful to the publishers for permission to use this material. We are also grateful to Ronald Resnick for permission to use images from his change-blindness demonstration in figure 3.2.

Seven years is a *long* time to be at work on a book—a lot longer than we thought it would take when we began, and a lot longer than our publisher bargained for. But during all this time our editor, Peter Momtchiloff, has greeted the delays with encouragement and aplomb. Thanks, Peter. We hope you *still* think it was worth the waiting for.

Finally, and above all, we would like to thank our families – Heather, Sarah, and Julia, and Jude, Jonah, and Becca. It is hard to imagine doing this work at all without their love, support, and patience. We dedicate this work to them, with gratitude and affection.

OXFORD COGNITIVE SCIENCE SERIES

MINDREADING

OXFORD COGNITIVE SCIENCE SERIES

General Editors
MARTIN DAVIES, JAMES HIGGINBOTHAM, PHILIP JOHNSON-LAIRD,
CHRISTOPHER PEACOCKE, KIM PLUNKETT

Published in the series

Reference and Consciousness
John Campbell

Concepts: Where Cognitive Science Went Wrong
Jerry A. Fodor

Ways of Seeing
Pierre Jacob and Marc Jeannerod

Context and Content
Robert C. Stalnaker

Seeing Reason: Diagrams and Languages in Learning to Think
Keith Stenning

Face and Mind: The Science of Face Perception
Andy Young

CONTENTS

1

Introduction

[I]t occurred to me that I could improve my parents' opinion of me by using my new [telepathic] faculty to help out with my schoolwork—in short, I began to cheat in class. That is to say, I tuned in to the inner voices of my schoolteachers and also of my cleverer classmates, and picked information out of their minds. I found that very few of my masters could set a test without rehearsing the ideal answers in their minds—and I knew, too, that on those rare occasions when the teacher was preoccupied by other things... the solutions could always be found in the precocious, prodigious mind of our class genius, Cyrus-the-great. My marks began to improve dramatically—but not overly so, because I took care to make my versions different from their stolen originals; even when I telepathically cribbed an entire English essay from Cyrus, I added a number of mediocre touches of my own. My purpose was to avoid suspicion; I did not, but I escaped discovery. Under Emil Zagallo's furious, interrogating eyes I remained innocently seraphic; beneath the bemused, head-shaking perplexity of Mr. Tandon the English master I worked my treachery in silence—knowing that they would not believe the truth even if, by chance or folly, I spilled the beans. (Salman Rushdie, *Midnight's Children*, 169)

In Salman Rushdie's *Midnight's Children*, the main character, Saleem Sinai, discovers that he can read other people's minds. In this passage, Saleem recounts how he exploited his mindreading abilities to improve his performance in school. But there are really two extraordinary kinds of mindreading going on here. One of them, telepathy, is extraordinary because it is supernatural and mythic; the other kind of mindreading is extraordinary because it is so pervasive, powerful, and important in real life that it is taken for granted. Rushdie leads us to marvel at Saleem's supernatural abilities. But a very natural and quotidian sort of mindreading plays an equally important role in this passage. Saleem began to cheat because he wanted to make his parents have a higher *opinion* of him. He realized that he couldn't copy his peers too perfectly, or his teachers would *know* that something was amiss. He detects *fury* in the face of one teacher and *amusement* and *perplexity* in the gestures of another. And he further surmises that even if he confessed his ability to his teachers, his teachers wouldn't *believe* him. It is this kind of mental state attribution, prediction, and explanation that we will explore in this volume.

In the burgeoning literature on the capacity of ordinary people to understand the mind, 'mindreading' has become a fashionable label for this ability. We embrace the fashion for two quite different reasons. First, the term is theoretically neutral in an important way. As we will see in due course, many more traditional terms like 'folk psychology', 'role taking', and 'theory of mind' often carry with them substantive theoretical commitments. For instance, advocates of the influential 'theory theory' account of mindreading sometimes use 'commonsense psychology', 'folk psychology', and 'theory of mind' as labels for a theory-like body of information that serves as the basis for our understanding of the mind, while those who defend the simulation theory sometimes use 'role taking' as a label for a process which, on their account, underlies our ability to attribute mental states. Our use of 'mindreading' is meant to be inclusive, allowing for the possibility that understanding minds depends on either simulation-style processes or information bases, or both (and other processes as well), as we shall in fact argue.

The second reason we have opted for 'mindreading' is that the association with telepathy infuses the term with an aura of mystique, and we think the capacity to understand minds deserves to be regarded with a certain amount of awe. Indeed, our mindreading capacities are in many ways much more impressive and powerful than the telepathic capacities proclaimed by mystics. We engage in mindreading for mundane chores, like trying to figure out what the baby wants, what your peers believe about your work, and what your spouse will do if you arrive home late. Mindreading is also implicated in loftier endeavours like trying to glean Descartes's reasons for thinking that many ideas are innate. So pervasive is the role of mindreading in our lives that Jerry Fodor has remarked that if the ordinary person's understanding of the mind should turn out to be seriously mistaken, it would be 'the greatest intellectual catastrophe in the history of our species' (Fodor 1987: xii).

1.1. The Multifarious Reasons for Studying Mindreading

The preoccupation with mindreading is apparent throughout civilization, from *Gilgamesh* and Herodotus to Dashiell Hammett and David Lodge. But only in the latter half of the twentieth century did mindreading become the object of sustained scientific attention. One of the goals of this book is to harvest some of the fruits of that attention. Before we begin to consider the scientific picture of mindreading, we would do well to consider why the study of mindreading has blossomed into such a thriving area of research. There is, we think, no single reason. Mindreading has captivated researchers from several different fields, and the motivations for studying mindreading vary by discipline.

Behavioural ecology and cognitive ethology

For several decades, evolutionary theorists have maintained that a capacity for mindreading would be enormously fitness enhancing (e.g. Humphries 1976). Animals that are better mindreaders than their competitors will enjoy an advantage in survival and reproduction. This core idea has inspired a large body of work among evolutionary theorists and behavioural scientists. Evolutionary theorists have speculated about different ways that natural selection could lead to improved mindreading capacities. Perhaps the best-known suggestion is that natural selection would favour 'Machiavellian' devices which enable animals to thwart the mindreading efforts of others. This in turn, it is suggested, would lead to an evolutionary arms race, producing increasingly sophisticated mechanisms for mindreading and increasingly sophisticated mechanisms for deception (see e.g. Whiten and Byrne 1997). Although Machiavellianism is the best-known explanation for how selection pressures would favour increasingly sophisticated mindreading capacities, there are other important ways in which selection pressures might favour better mindreading. In some cases, for instance, it might be mutually advantageous to two parties to mindread each other effectively, as when communication is particularly important (e.g. Krebs and Dawkins 1984).

In conjunction with these kinds of broad evolutionary speculations, researchers also hope to evaluate substantive proposals about the evolution of mindreading, and in particular, to chart the evolutionary origins of this capacity in humans. One central goal is to develop and evaluate substantive evolutionary proposals by using the comparative method. In order to use that method, however, it is necessary to have evidence on the presence or absence of the capacity in a variety of species. As a result, there is an enormous amount of interest in determining the distribution of different mindreading abilities in other species. The empirical explorations have been conducted in the wild by behavioural ecologists and cognitive ethologists (e.g. de Waal 1986), and they have been pursued in the lab by experimentalists (e.g. Premack and Woodruff 1978; Povinelli and Eddy 1996; Hare et al. 2000). Unfortunately, the state of the art here remains quite crude—we lack adequate evidence to deploy the comparative method on the human capacity for mindreading in any remotely rigorous fashion. Nonetheless, the project of charting mindreading capacities in other species is clearly of central interest to evolutionary theorists, and it will occupy researchers for decades to come.

Anthropology and cross-cultural psychology

Anthropologists have long maintained that there are striking differences in the thoughts and feelings of people in different cultures. Recent work in cross-cultural psychology is confirming this in fairly dramatic fashion. For instance, Richard Nisbett and his colleagues have uncovered surprising differences in the cognitive processing of East Asians and Westerners (Nisbett et al. 2001). Not surprisingly, then, anthropologists and cross-cultural psychologists who work on mindreading are interested in the extent to which our mindreading practices and strategies are a product of our cultural upbringing. Some anthropologists (e.g. Lutz 1985) and cross-cultural psychologists (e.g. Miller 1984) maintain that it is indeed the case that the ways we interpret each other and the ways we predict and explain others' behaviour are significantly influenced by our cultural heritage.

Developmental science

Mindreading has occupied an especially important role in developmental psychology. Within that discipline, there are quite different motivations for studying mindreading. Perhaps the most widely influential reason for developmental work on mindreading is that the development of mindreading is taken as a paradigm of conceptual change. Experimental work has mapped in impressive detail many of the changes that take place as the child develops an increasingly sophisticated capacity for mindreading, and theorists interested in conceptual change in general often take the development of mindreading to be a model of rich conceptual change (e.g. Gopnik and Meltzoff 1997).

A radically different motivation for studying the development of mindreading derives from the fact that the central concepts implicated in mindreading, for example, *belief, desire, intention,* are remarkably sophisticated concepts referring to unobservable states.[1] Yet these concepts are acquired extremely early, in many cases earlier than more perceptually salient concepts like *yellow.* Because of this, some regard concepts like *belief* as central examples of concepts that must depend on an innate endowment (see e.g. Leslie 2000). Understanding the acquisition of mindreading concepts thus might have broader implications for our understanding of the nature of our innate endowment.

Developmental psychologists also hope to determine whether the ontogeny of mindreading might shed light on other issues in development. For instance, some have suggested that word learning depends on mindreading (Bloom 2000), and others have suggested that the initial understanding of biology grows out of an understanding of minds (Carey 1985).

Psychopathology and clinical psychology

The breakdown of the capacity to understand minds is of theoretical significance to researchers on psychopathologies (e.g. Frith 1992; Baron-Cohen

---

[1] In this volume, we will use italics for terms that denote concepts. Other authors adopt a different convention, using ALLCAPS for terms that refer to concepts.

1995). Some have suggested that the suite of symptoms exhibited in various pathologies might be explained by the hypothesis of underlying deficits in mindreading. For instance, autism has long been associated with a set of diagnostic criteria, and it is not at all clear why the symptoms of autism cluster together. Several theorists have suggested that people with autism suffer a deficit in their capacity for mindreading and that this provides a deep and unifying explanation for the cluster of symptoms associated with autism.

For clinical psychologists, the theoretical concerns of researchers in psychopathology are accompanied by a more practical consideration about mindreading. Clinicians hope to be able to treat or help people who exhibit serious deficiencies in their capacity for understanding minds. As a result, Simon Baron-Cohen, one of the leading theorists in the area of mindreading and psychopathology, has also invested considerable energy in trying to improve the mindreading abilities (and thus, presumably the quality of life) of people with autism (see e.g. Baron-Cohen and Bolton 1993; Howlin et al. 1999).

Philosophy

Although our own interests in mindreading became increasingly multifarious as we dug into this interdisciplinary project, our interest stemmed originally from philosophical concerns. Since the philosophical interest of mindreading may be somewhat less readily apparent, we will explain in some detail why discussion of folk psychology, theory of mind, and mindreading has played such an important role in the philosophy of mind.

To appreciate philosophers' fascination with these themes, it will be useful to begin with a brief reminder about the two most important questions in the philosophy of mind, and the problems engendered by what was for centuries the most influential answer to one of those questions. The questions are the Mind–Body Problem, which asks how mental phenomena are related to physical phenomena, and the Problem of Other Minds, which asks how we can know about the mental states of other people. On Descartes's proposed solution to the Mind–Body Problem, there are two quite different sorts of substances in the universe: physical substance, which is located in space and time, and mental substance, which is located in time but not in space. Mental phenomena, according to Descartes, are events or states occurring in a mental substance, while physical phenomena are events or states occurring in a physical substance. Descartes insisted that there is two-way causal interaction between the mental and the physical, though many philosophers find it puzzling how the two could interact if one is in space and the other isn't. Another problem with the Cartesian view is that it seems to make the Other Minds Problem quite intractable. If, as Descartes believed, I am the only person who can experience my mental states, then there seems to be no way for you to rule out the hypothesis that I am a mindless zombie—a physical body that merely behaves as though it was causally linked to a mind.

In the middle years of the twentieth century the verificationist account of meaning had a major impact on philosophical thought. According to the verificationists, the meaning of an empirical claim is closely linked to the observations that would verify the claim. Influenced by verificationism, philosophical behaviourists argued that the Cartesian account of the mind as the 'ghost in the machine' (to use Ryle's memorable image) was profoundly mistaken (Ryle 1949). If ordinary mental state words like 'belief', 'desire', and 'pain' are to be meaningful, they maintained, these terms cannot refer to unobservable events taking place inside a person (or, worse still, not located in space at all). Rather, the meaning of sentences invoking these terms must be analysed in terms of conditional sentences specifying how someone would behave under various circumstances. So, for example, a philosophical behaviourist might suggest that the meaning of

(1) John believes that snow is white

could be captured by something like the following:

(2) If you ask John, 'Is snow white?' he will respond affirmatively.

Perhaps the most serious difficulty for philosophical behaviourists was that their meaning analyses typically turned out to be either obviously mistaken or circular—invoking one mental term in the analysis of another. So, for example, contrary to (2), even though John believes that snow is white, he may not respond affirmatively unless he is *paying attention, wants* to let you know what he thinks, *believes* that this can be done by responding affirmatively, etc.

While philosophical behaviourists were gradually becoming convinced that there is no way around this circularity problem, a very similar problem was confronting philosophers seeking verificationist accounts of the meaning of scientific terms. Verificationism requires that the meaning of a theoretical term must be specifiable in terms of observables. But when philosophers actually tried to provide such definitions, they always seemed to require additional theoretical terms (Hempel 1964). The reaction to this problem in the philosophy of science was to explore a quite different account of how theoretical terms get their meaning. Rather than being defined exclusively in terms of observables, this new account proposed, a cluster of theoretical terms might get their meaning collectively by being embedded within an empirical theory. The meaning of any given theoretical term lies in its theory-specified interconnections with other terms, *both observational and theoretical.* Perhaps the most influential statement of this view is to be found in the work of David Lewis (1970, 1972). According to Lewis, the meaning of theoretical terms is given by what he calls a 'functional definition'. Theoretical entities are 'defined as the occupants of the causal roles *specified by the theory* . . .; as *the* entities, whatever those may be, that bear certain causal relations *to one another* and to the referents of the O[bservational]-terms' (Lewis 1972: 211; first and last emphasis added).

Building on an idea first suggested by Wilfrid Sellars (1956), Lewis went on to propose that ordinary terms for mental or psychological states could get their meaning in an entirely analogous way. If we 'think of commonsense psychology as a term-introducing scientific theory, though one invented before there was any such institution as professional science,' then the 'functional definition' account of the meaning of theoretical terms in science can be applied straightforwardly to the mental state terms used in commonsense psychology (Lewis 1972: 212). And this, Lewis proposed, is the right way to think about commonsense psychology:

Imagine our ancestors first speaking only of external things, stimuli, and responses . . . until some genius invented the theory of mental states, with its newly introduced T[heoretical] terms, to explain the regularities among stimuli and responses. But that did not happen. Our commonsense psychology was never a newly invented term-introducing scientific theory—not even of prehistoric folk-science. The story that mental terms were introduced as theoretical terms is a myth.

It is, in fact, Sellars' myth . . . And though it is a myth, it may be a good myth or a bad one. It is a good myth if our names of mental states do in fact mean just what they would mean if the myth were true. I adopt the working hypothesis that it is a good myth. (1972: 212–13)

In the three decades since Lewis and others[2] developed this account, it has become the most widely accepted view about the meaning of mental state terms. Since the account maintains that the meanings of mental state terms are given by functional definitions, the view is often known as *functionalism*.[3] We can now see one reason why philosophers of mind have been concerned to understand the exact nature of commonsense (or folk) psychology. According to functionalism, *folk psychology is the theory that gives ordinary mental state terms their meaning.*

A second reason for philosophers' preoccupation with folk psychology can be explained more quickly. The crucial point is that, according to accounts like Lewis's, folk psychology is an *empirical* theory which is supposed to explain 'the regularity between stimuli and responses' to be found in human (and perhaps animal) behaviour. And, of course, if commonsense psychology

---

[2] Though we will focus on Lewis's influential exposition, many other philosophers developed similar views including Putnam (1960), Fodor and Chihara (1965), and Armstrong (1968).

[3] Though beware. In the philosophy of mind, the term 'functionalism' has been used for a variety of views. Some of them bear a clear family resemblance to the one we have just sketched while others do not. For good overviews see Lycan 1994 and Block 1994.

is an empirical theory, it is possible that, like any empirical theory, it might turn out to be *mistaken*. We might discover that the states and processes intervening between stimuli and responses are not well described by the folk theory that fixes the meaning of mental state terms. The possibility that commonsense psychology *might* turn out to be mistaken is granted by just about everyone who takes functionalism seriously. However, for the last several decades a number of prominent philosophers of mind have been arguing that this is more than a *mere* possibility. Rather, they maintain, a growing body of theory and empirical findings in the cognitive and neurosciences strongly suggests that commonsense psychology *is* mistaken, and not just on small points. Rather, as Paul Churchland, an enthusiastic supporter of this view puts it:

FP [folk psychology] suffers explanatory failures on an epic scale, . . . it has been stagnant for at least twenty-five centuries, and . . . its categories appear (so far) to be incommensurable with or orthogonal to the categories of the background physical sciences whose long term claim to explain human behavior seems undeniable. Any theory that meets this description must be allowed a serious candidate for outright elimination. (Churchland 1981: 212)

Churchland does not stop at discarding (or 'eliminating') folk psychological theory. He and other 'eliminativists' have also suggested that, because folk psychology is such a seriously defective theory, we should also conclude that the theoretical terms embedded in folk psychology don't really refer to anything. Beliefs, desires, and other posits of folk psychology, they argue, are entirely comparable to phlogiston, the ether, and other posits of empirical theories that turned out to be seriously mistaken; like phlogiston, the ether, and the rest, *they do not exist*. These are enormously provocative claims. Debating their plausibility has been high on the agenda of philosophers of mind ever since they were first suggested.[4] Since the eliminativists' central thesis is that folk psychology is a massively mistaken theory, philosophers of mind concerned to evaluate that thesis will obviously need a clear and accurate account of what folk psychology is and what it claims.

When functionalists propose that the meaning of mental state terms is determined by folk psychology, and when eliminativists argue that folk psychology is a profoundly mistaken theory, there are various ways in which the notion of folk psychology might be interpreted.[5] We are inclined to think that the most natural interpretation, for both functionalists and eliminativists, is that *folk psychology is a rich body of information about the mind that is utilized by the mental mechanisms responsible for mindreading.* And on this interpretation, constructing a theory about those mechanisms and the

---

[4] For an overview of these debates, see Stich 1996: ch. 1.
[5] See Stich and Ravenscroft 1994.

information they exploit is an integral part of unpacking the functionalist's theory and assessing the eliminativist challenge.

In recent years, another reason has emerged for philosophers to take a keen interest in mindreading and the processes underlying it. Under the banner of 'simulation theory', a number of philosophers and psychologists have argued that the mental mechanisms that make mindreading possible do *not* rely on a rich body of information about the mind. The details of their account will be set out in the chapters to follow. But, as simulation theorists were quick to note, if they are right, then both functionalists and eliminativists have a problem on their hands (Gordon 1986; Goldman 1989). For if functionalists conceive of folk psychology as the body of information that underlies mindreading, and if there is no such body of information, then the functionalist account of the meaning of mental state terms must be mistaken, since there is no folk theory to implicitly define those terms. And if there is no folk theory underlying mindreading, then it *cannot* be the case that folk psychology is a radically mistaken theory as the eliminativists insist.

It was this cluster of philosophical theories and debates that originally prompted us to begin exploring the empirical literature on mindreading. But the philosophical debates will play little role in this book until we return to them briefly in the final chapter. For as our work progressed we came to think that mindreading and the processing underlying it are *at least* as intriguing as the philosophical issues that led us to the topic.

In the remainder of this introductory chapter we will set out some comments on the kind of theory we propose to offer, the sorts of evidence we will be using, and the strategy we have adopted in deciding how much detail— sometimes quite speculative detail—to include in our theory. We will then sketch two important assumptions about the mind that will serve as the backdrop for our account of mindreading.

1.2. Theory, Evidence, and Strategy

In a pair of perceptive and influential essays published about a decade apart, Jerry Fodor (1968) and Daniel Dennett (1978*b*) offered colourful, albeit metaphorical, accounts of the explanatory strategy used in an important family of theories in cognitive science. On Dennett's version, one starts

with a specification of the whole person...—what I call, more neutrally, an intentional system...—or some artificial segment of that person's abilities (e.g. chess-playing [or, we might add, *mindreading*])...and then breaks that largest intentional system into an organization of subsystems, each of which could itself be viewed as an intentional system...and hence as formally a homunculus....Homunculi are *bogeymen* only if they duplicate *entire* the talents they are rung in to explain....If one can get a team or committee of *relatively* ignorant, narrow-minded, blind homunculi to produce the intelligent behavior of the whole, this is progress. (1978*b*: 123)

One way of presenting such a theory is to construct a flow chart in which each of the subsystem homunculi is represented as a box and the lines linking the boxes indicate the sorts of communication that these subsystems have with one another. The theory specifies the function of each component in the flow chart (or 'boxology'),

without saying how it is to be accomplished (one says, in effect: put a little man in there to do the job). If we then look closer at the individual boxes we see that the function of each is accomplished by subdividing it via another flowchart into still smaller, more stupid homunculi. Eventually this nesting of boxes within boxes lands you with homunculi so stupid... that they can be, as one says, 'replaced by a machine'. One *discharges* fancy homunculi from one's scheme by organizing armies of such idiots to do the work. (1978*b*: 123–4)

William Lycan, who has been one of the most avid and insightful advocates of this explanatory strategy, calls theories of this sort *homuncular functionalist* theories (Lycan 1981, 1988).[6]

A few years after Dennett's essay appeared, David Marr (1982) proposed a somewhat similar account, which quickly became quite famous, in which he distinguishes three levels of explanation in theories in cognitive science. Marr's highest level, which he perhaps misleadingly called the *computational level*, presents an analysis of the cognitive capacity to be explained. The analysis gives an explicit account of what the system underlying the capacity does and decomposes the system into a set of simpler subsystems. So Marr's first level of analysis does much the same work as the first level or two of flow charts in a homuncular functionalist theory. At Marr's second level, which he calls the *algorithmic level*, the theory provides formal procedures or algorithms for accomplishing each of the tasks into which the initial target task or capacity has been decomposed. The third, or *physical implementation*, level explains how the algorithms are actually executed by some real physical system—typically some part of the brain. On Marr's view, the three levels of analysis are largely independent of one another.

The account of mindreading we propose in this book can be viewed as a theory at Marr's highest level of analysis or, what amounts to much the same thing, as the first level of a homuncular functionalist theory of mindreading. Our aim is to characterize the complex and variegated skills that constitute our mindreading capacity and to begin the job of explaining how these skills are

---

[6] In his seminal paper on 'Functional Analysis', Robert Cummins (1975) makes a persuasive case that the strategy of explaining complex capacities by decomposing them into simpler ones that are linked together via a flow chart (or a 'program') is not unique to psychology. Much the same strategy is widely exploited in biology and in engineering.

accomplished by positing a cluster of mental mechanisms that interact with one another in the ways that we will specify. These mental mechanisms and the links between them are the 'organization of subsystems'—the first assembly of stupider homunculi—that Dennett describes. Now and again we will offer some speculations on how these subsystems might themselves be decomposed into still simpler subsystems. But more often than not we will simply characterize the function of the subsystems, and their interactions, in as much detail as we can, and leave it to others to figure out how the subsystems carry out their function. Though some of the subsystems we will posit have the capacity to do very sophisticated and difficult tasks, we maintain that none of these tasks is as sophisticated or as difficult as mindreading itself. If we are right about this, then, as Dennett notes, some explanatory progress will have been made.

Most of the competing accounts of mindreading that have appeared in recent years (along with many cognitive theories aimed at explaining other complex cognitive capacities) are best viewed as having the same goals as our theory. They try to explain mindreading (or some other complex cognitive capacity) by positing functionally characterized underlying mechanisms with capacities that are simpler than the capacity they are trying to explain. Thus we will often present both our own theory and competing theories with the help of flow charts akin to those that Dennett describes. We have found these 'boxologies' to be very helpful in setting out our account of the mental mechanisms underlying various mindreading skills and in clarifying and making more explicit what other theorists have in mind. We aren't the only ones who find such depictions useful; indeed, several authors have adopted our depictions of other people's theories and of their own (Goldman 1992a, 1993a; Heal 1998; Gallese and Goldman 1998; Botterill and Carruthers 1999). It is important, however, that the diagrams not be misinterpreted. Positing a 'box' which represents a functionally characterized processing mechanism or a functionally characterized set of mental states does not commit a theorist to the claim that the mechanism or the states are spatially localized in the brain, any more than drawing a box in a flow chart for a computer program commits one to the claim that the operation that the box represents is spatially localized in the computer.

Though it may be helpful to think of our account of mindreading as a theory at Marr's 'computational' level of analysis, there is one important issue on which we differ from Marr. On Marr's view, each level of analysis is largely independent of the level below. On our view, by contrast, findings about the structure and functioning of the brain can, and ultimately will, impose strong constraints on theories of mindreading of the sort we will be offering. For the moment, however, this disagreement with Marr is of little practical importance, since as far as we have been able to discover, there are few findings about the brain that offer much guidance in constructing the sort of cognitive account of mindreading that we will be presenting. Most of the evidence that we will be relying on in constructing and testing our theory derives from experimental studies of the performance of both normal and impaired children and adults on a variety of mindreading tasks. In addition, we will make some use of evidence derived from observational and experimental studies of mindreading skills in non-human species. From time to time we also rely on commonsense observations about mindreading, though we have tried to use only the most obvious and uncontroversial of commonsense claims, since we are impressed by the frequency with which commonsense wisdom about a variety of cognitive capacities has been shown to be mistaken. In principle, our stance regarding evidence is completely eclectic. We would have no reservations at all about using evidence from neuroscience or from history, anthropology, or any of the other social sciences to constrain and test our theory, though we have found relatively little in these domains that bears directly on the questions we will be considering.

As our own theory of mindreading was evolving, we often tried to compare it to other accounts in the literature. But this was no easy task since many of the alternative theories are seriously underdescribed—they tell us far too little about the sorts of mental mechanisms they are presupposing and about how these mechanisms are supposed to explain important aspects of mindreading. In an effort to avoid these problems, we have tried to be much more explicit about the mental architecture that our theory posits, and about various other matters on which competing theories are silent. Though this approach has obvious benefits, there is a downside as well. For at a number of junctures there are several quite different paths that might be followed and, for the moment at least, there is little empirical evidence to indicate which is preferable. At some of these junctures we will pause to consider a variety of options. On other occasions, we will just make our best guess without stopping to explore the alternatives. Inevitably, some of these guesses will turn out to be wrong, and so too will our theory. But that doesn't really worry us, since it is our view that the best way to make progress in this area is to develop explicit, detailed theories that can be refuted and then repaired as evidence accumulates, and not to rest content with sketchier theories which are harder to compare with the growing body of evidence. Being false, as the Logical Positivists often emphasized, is far from the worst defect that a theory can have.

1.3. Two Assumptions about the Mind

In this section we will set out two quite basic assumptions that we will be making about the mind. Both are very familiar and we suspect that both of them are largely shared by most other people working on mindreading, though since more often than not the assumptions are left tacit it is hard to know the extent to which other authors accept the details. We think it is important to be very explicit about these assumptions, because keeping them in mind forces us to be clear about many other details of our theory, details which other writers sometimes leave unspecified. The assumptions will serve as a framework upon which we will build as we develop our theory about the psychological mechanisms underlying mindreading.

We will call the first of our assumptions *the basic architecture assumption.* What it claims is that a well-known commonsense account of the architecture of the cognitive mind is largely correct, though it is far from complete. This account of cognitive architecture, which has been widely adopted both in cognitive science and in philosophy, maintains that in normal humans, and probably in other organisms as well, the mind contains two quite different kinds of representational states, beliefs and desires. These two kinds of states differ functionally because they are caused in different ways and have different patterns of interaction with other components of the mind. Some beliefs are caused fairly directly by perception; others are derived from pre-existing beliefs via processes of deductive and non-deductive inference. Some desires (like the desire to get something to drink or the desire to get something to eat) are caused by systems that monitor various bodily states. Other desires, sometimes called 'instrumental desires' or 'sub-goals', are generated by a process of practical reasoning and planning that has access to beliefs and to pre-existing desires. (We'll have more to say about planning below.) There are also many desires that are generated by a variety of other mental mechanisms whose nature is not well understood. One of us (Stich) is partial to the hypothesis, suggested by evolutionary psychologists, that the mind contains a substantial number of sub-mechanisms, shaped by natural selection, whose job it is to generate desires in response to a variety of cues about the physical, biological, and social environment. But that hypothesis is not an integral part of the account of mindreading we'll be presenting in this book. All we will be assuming here is that the body-monitoring systems and practical reasoning and planning systems are not the only ones capable of generating desires. The practical reasoning system must do more than merely generate sub-goals. It must also determine which structure of goals and sub-goals is to be acted upon at any time. Once made, that decision is passed on to various action-controlling systems whose job it is to sequence and coordinate the behaviours necessary to carry out the decision.

Since the capacity for practical reasoning and planning will play an important role in our account of mindreading, this might be a good place to add a few remarks about how we think this system works. One of the things that the mental mechanisms responsible for reasoning and inference can do is to construct *plans*. As we envision it, plan construction is a process of means-ends reasoning: given a goal or a set of goals, the part of the inference system that is responsible for constructing plans comes up with one or more ways to achieve those goals. It may be the case that the inference system includes a special subsystem for planning; another possibility is that planning is just a special case of problem solving and that the process is subserved by those parts of the inference system that are responsible for solving other sorts of problems. Since we know of no evidence that can resolve the issue, we propose to leave it open. On our account, one of the jobs of the practical reasoning system is to monitor an agent's evolving body of desires and goals and to determine when a call should be made to the Planner to initiate plan construction. Once a plan has been constructed, the practical reasoning system goes back to the desire system and looks for desires that are incompatible with the intermediate steps. If it finds them, it rejects the plan and asks the Planner for another one. If the practical reasoning system does not find any incompatible desires, it accepts the plan and generates new (instrumental) desires for the necessary intermediate steps. Figure 1.1 is a 'boxological' rendition of our basic architecture assumption.

Our second assumption, which we will call *the representational account of cognition*, maintains that beliefs, desires, and other propositional attitudes are relational states. To have a belief or a desire with a particular content is to

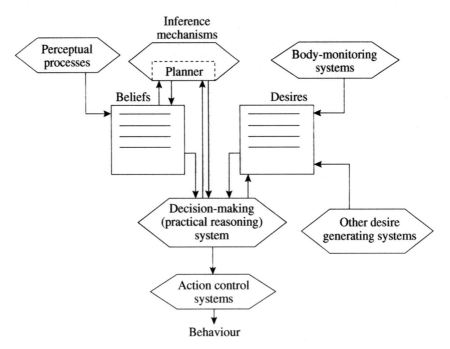

Fig. 1.1   The basic architecture of the cognitive mind

have a representation token with that content stored in the functionally appropriate way in the mind. So, for example, to believe that Socrates was an Athenian is to have a representation token whose content is *Socrates was an Athenian* stored in one's 'Belief Box', and to desire that it will be sunny tomorrow is to have a representation whose content is *It will be sunny tomorrow* stored in one's 'Desire Box'.[7] Many advocates of the representational account of cognition also assume that the representation tokens subserving propositional attitudes are linguistic or quasi-linguistic in form. This additional assumption is no part of our theory, however. If it turns out that some propositional attitudes are subserved by representation tokens that are not plausibly viewed as having a quasi-linguistic structure, that's fine with us.[8] With these background assumptions in place, we are now ready to begin the project of building a theory of mindreading.

[7] We will use italicized sentences to indicate representations or contents. Typically, the context will make clear whether we're referring to a content or to a representation.

[8] For more on the representational account of cognition see Sterelny 1990.

2

A Cognitive Theory of Pretence

2.1. Introduction

Some readers may find it surprising that we are beginning our account with a chapter devoted to pretence. But discussions of pretence have had a prominent place in the recent literature on mindreading, and in developing our own theory of mindreading, thinking about pretence and the cognitive mechanisms that underlie it played a quite pivotal role, because it convinced us that the basic cognitive architecture sketched in Figure 1.1 needed to be supplemented in various ways. Several of the components that have to be added to that basic architecture in order to explain aspects of pretence ultimately came to play a central role in our theory about the cognitive processes that enable us to read other people's minds. Our theory about 'third-person mindreading' will be centre stage in Chapter 3. In this chapter we will be laying the foundations for that theory by explaining and defending a richer account of cognitive architecture than the one set out in Chapter 1. We will also defend a view about the relation between pretence and mindreading that is importantly different from the views of some of the leading figures in the field. While much of what we say in this chapter will have important implications for the theory of mind-reading, our main focus will be on the fascinating phenomena of pretence and pretend play.

In young children, pretend play is so familiar and so natural that it is easy to overlook how remarkable and puzzling it is. The wonder of pretend play hasn't been lost on major figures in developmental psychology (e.g. Piaget 1962; Vygotsky 1967), and there is a large empirical literature on the topic (see Fein 1981 for a review). Until recently, however, the capacity for pretence received surprisingly little attention in the cognitivist tradition. Only in the last fifteen years has there been a sustained attempt to map out the cognitive mechanisms underlying pretend play. During this period there has been an explosion of conceptual and empirical work on pretence (e.g. Currie 1995a, 1997, 1998; German and Leslie 2001; Gordon and Barker 1994; Harris 1991, 1994b, 1995, 2000; Harris and Kavanaugh 1993; Leslie 1987, 1994a; Lillard 1993, 1994; Perner et al. 1994).

Much of the recent discussion of pretend play can be traced to Alan Leslie's attempt to give a cognitive account of pretence (Leslie 1987). As we will see in Section 2.5, Leslie thinks that there are important connections between the child's capacity for pretend play and the child's mindreading capacity. Indeed, on his account, all episodes of pretence involve mindreading. Leslie (1987, 1994a) maintains that pretend play constitutes a strikingly early example of mindreading, since children pretend and seem to understand pretence in others fully two years before they succeed on the standard false belief task, which is the best-known test of mindreading skill.[1] The selective impairments of children with autism, who show deficits both in pretend play and in their ability to solve mindreading problems like the false belief task, provides one important piece of evidence for the connection between mindreading and pretend play (Baron-Cohen 1995).

The capacity for pretence has also been enormously important in the recent literature for reasons that are quite distinct from the connection between pretence and mindreading. A number of writers have argued that the capacity for pretence is implicated in a wide variety of important cognitive capacities including counterfactual reasoning (Goldman 1992a), conditional planning (Goldman 1992a; Harris 1993), empathy (Currie 1995b; Goldman 1992a; Sorensen 1998), and visual imagery (Currie 1995d). It has also been argued that the capacity for pretence underlies imagination more generally (Currie 1995a, 1995b). For instance, our imaginative encounters with fictions have been tied to pretend play or make-believe (Currie 1990, 1995a, 1995b; Walton 1990, 1997), and Currie (1995c) has suggested that these same imaginative mechanisms are also used in moral understanding. Although much of this work has been pursued by writers who advocate one or another version of simulation theory, one needn't be sympathetic with simulation theory to think that the capacity for pretence is crucial for many of these other capacities. Indeed, though we have been frequent critics of simulation theory (Nichols et al. 1995; Nichols et al. 1996; Stich and Nichols 1992, 1995, 1997; this volume Sections 2.5 and 3.4.3), we think it is quite plausible that many of these capacities are intimately connected with the capacity for pretence. But before such proposals can be elaborated and defended, it is essential to have a plausible theory of the mental mechanisms that underlie the capacity for pretence itself.

Our goal in this chapter is to offer such a theory and to compare it with other theories that have been proposed in the recent literature. The theory we

---

[1] We will discuss the false belief task at length in Chapter 3, but for present purposes, a brief description of the task will suffice. In the classic false belief test, Wimmer and Perner (1983) had children watch a puppet show in which the puppet protagonist, Maxi, puts chocolate in a box and goes out to play. While Maxi is out, his puppet mother moves the chocolate to the cupboard. The children are asked where Maxi will look for the chocolate when he returns. Until about the age of 4, children tend to give the incorrect answer that Maxi will look in the cupboard. Only after age 4 do children tend to pass this task and variants of it.

will defend is a highly eclectic one which borrows ideas from a number of other theorists and adds a few of our own. It is our contention that all the other theories of pretence that have been proposed in the recent literature are under-described in important ways, and in particular that all of them tell us far too little about the sort of mental architecture that the theory is presupposing. As a result, as we'll argue in Section 2.5, it is often difficult or impossible to know exactly how these theories would explain one or another example of pretence, or how they would account for various aspects of the capacity to pretend. As noted in the previous chapter, our strategy for dealing with these problems is to make our theory much more explicit about the mental architecture it assumes, and about a variety of other issues on which competing theories are silent.

Here's how we propose to proceed. In the section that follows we will describe a number of examples of pretence, involving both children and adults, drawn from various sources. Then, in Section 2.3, we will draw attention to some of the features of these episodes of pretence—features which, we maintain, a fully adequate theory of pretence must be able to explain. The list of features we assemble will serve as a checklist against which competing theories can be compared. In Section 2.4, we will set out our theory of the cognitive mechanisms that underlie pretence, and explain how the theory can account for the features on the checklist. Finally, in Section 2.5, we will sketch some of the other theories of pretence that have been offered and argue that our theory does a better job at explaining the facts.

2.2. Some Examples of Pretence

Before setting out our theory, it will be useful to offer several examples of the sort of episodes of pretending that we want our theory to explain. A familiar armchair strategy here is simply to make up some examples. But for a variety of reasons, we are not inclined to take that route. We worry that important features of pretence might be neglected if we limit ourselves to examples of our own invention. By looking at a number of real examples of pretence, we hope to get a much better idea of the richness and the range of the phenomena to be explained.

2.2.1. Pretence in children

Much of the literature on pretence has been influenced by two examples from the work of Alan Leslie. We will recount these examples below, because we too think that Leslie's examples are important to understanding pretence. In addition to the examples from Leslie, we will include two more examples of pretend play that have not been discussed in the literature, but are genuine instances of spontaneous pretend play in children.

Pretending that a banana is a telephone

'How is it possible for a child to think about a banana as if it were a telephone...?' With this question Leslie (1987: 412) ignited the recent explosion of interest in pretence in cognitive psychology and simultaneously provided what is perhaps the most widely discussed illustration of pretence in the literature. There are really two different banana/telephone scenarios that often get discussed together. In one scenario, an individual child pretends that the banana is a telephone. For instance, a child might pick up a banana, hold it up to his ear and mouth and say, 'Hi. How are you? [Brief pause.] I'm fine. OK. Bye.' This kind of pretence will no doubt be familiar to parents of young children. Children also engage in pretence with others. For instance, a child and his mother might pretend together that a banana is a telephone. In an episode of this sort the mother may pass the banana to the child, saying, 'It's for you.' From a young age, children will play along in these pretend games, taking the banana and saying 'Hello' into it. These scenarios get treated together by Leslie since he thinks that any child who can pretend that the banana is a telephone can also understand pretence in others. But since it will be important in explaining one of our disagreements with Leslie, we want to maintain a clear distinction between individual pretence and group pretence.[2]

Leslie's tea party

Another widely cited example of pretence also comes from Leslie's work. In a series of experiments, Leslie had children participate in a pretend tea party. Leslie describes the scenario as follows: 'The child is encouraged to "fill" two toy cups with "juice" or "tea" or whatever the child designated the pretend contents of the bottle to be. The experimenter then says, "Watch this!", picks up one of the cups, turns it upside down, shakes it for a second, then replaces it alongside the other cup. The child is then asked to point at the "full cup" and at the "empty cup." (Both cups are, of course, really empty throughout.)' (Leslie 1994a: 223.) When asked to point at the 'empty cup', 2-year-olds pointed to the cup that had been turned upside down.

---

[2] Leslie has never used the banana/telephone scenario in his experimental work though he observed a number of spontaneous examples of the scenario in his own children. (Personal communication.)

Monsters and parents

Our next example of pretend play in children comes from the CHILDES (Children's Language Data Exchange System) database (MacWhinney and Snow 1990). Though this database was initially established to study children's language, it is an invaluable resource for studying a number of features of child psychology (see e.g. Bartsch and Wellman 1995). In the following protocol, Val is 4 years and 7 months, and Abe is 4 years and 9 months (Garvey 1979).

VAL. Pretend we're on the bus ok? (*Val gets on a toy car, then off, gets on, climbs on back.*)

VAL. Enough room for two of us right?

ABE. Right.

VAL. You say hold on to me. (*Abe drives seriously while Val talks. Val puts arms around Abe to keep from falling off.*)

VAL. Pretend we passed one and pretend there's a monster coming ok?...

ABE. No let's don't pretend that.... Cause it's too scary that's why.

VAL. Oh I don't think so....

VAL. Pretend...we can play mother and father.

ABE. OK and this was our car.

VAL. OK. You're going to work. (*Val gets off car as part of game; Abe follows her.*)

VAL. Hey look look. We got this [a lunch box]; we got work tools. (*Val speaks in high enthusiastic voice; Val presents lunch box to Abe who seems to accept it as part of game; Abe takes tools to car; Val goes to stove, opens oven...*)

VAL. We could cook this [shoes] for food. (*Val holds up shoes to show Abe. Val puts shoes in oven, turns knobs, then takes them out and shows Abe.*)

VAL. For food. Do you like chicken?

Dead cat

The final example of childhood pretence that we will mention comes from a set of protocols of spontaneous pretence in children that was assembled by Rosalind Gould (1972). Gould reports that one 3-year-old boy on a jungle gym (climbing frame) said, 'I'm a pussycat. Meow, meow.' He then came down from the jungle gym and lay on the ground, saying, 'I'm dead. I'm a dead pussycat...I got shooted' (Gould 1972: 212).

2.2.2. Pretence in adults

There are a number of limitations to the available examples of pretending in children. However, since we want to develop a theory of pretence that can accommodate adult pretence as well as pretence in children, there is no need to restrict ourselves to examples of pretend episodes in children. Pretend episodes in adults will work just as well. As it happens, there are surprisingly few examples of adult pretence described in the psychological literature. So we set out to collect our own. Our goal wasn't to design an experiment with a clever manipulation, and the kind of data we have doesn't admit of any sort of statistical analysis. Rather, we merely wanted to collect some genuine examples of pretence in adults.

Ten college students participated in our little study. We asked individuals and groups of two to carry out a variety of scenarios, each of which was described on a separate sheet of paper. At the beginning of the session, participants were told to consult the written description and act out each scenario. For the individual pretend scenarios, the descriptions were as follows:

'Pretend that the banana (on the table) is a telephone.'
'Pretend that you're home alone at night and you hear a suspicious noise in the basement.'
'Pretend that you're a train.'
'Pretend that you're a dead cat.'
'Pretend that you're sleeping.'
'Pretend that you're baking a cake.'

For two-person group pretend scenarios, the descriptions were as follows:

'Pretend you are in a fast food restaurant. Decide who will be the cashier and who will be the customer.'
'Pretend you are in a fancy restaurant. Decide who will be the server and who will be the diner.'

Eight students participated in the group pretend scenarios; six participated in the individual pretend scenarios. The order of the scenarios was always the same. Participants were told that they could use whatever props were in the room. The scenarios were carried out in a lab room that had a telephone in it, along with typical office supplies. We supplied a banana for the banana/telephone scenario, and we provided the participants with play money for the fast food restaurant scenario. After participants carried out the scenarios, we had an informal oral interview with them. We asked questions about what the participants remembered from the scenarios, why they behaved the way they did, and about the possible confusion between reality and pretence.[3] In the sections to follow, we

---

[3] For the group pretence participants, the interview was conducted with both participants at the same time. The four students who participated in both individual and group pretence were interviewed about their individual pretence with the other participant in the room. The remaining two individual pretence participants were interviewed alone. All sessions and interviews were videotaped, and the participants knew that the sessions were being videotaped. The videotapes were later reviewed to produce the transcripts.

will draw from the transcripts of the adult pretence episodes where appropriate. But before we conclude this section, we want to include two extended protocols, from which we will draw throughout the chapter.

Fancy restaurant scenario, Episode 1

The participants in this example of pretence were two female college students.

(*B gets pencils and pens for silverware, and a piece of paper for a napkin.*)
A. Hi, how are you doing? (*Hands B a syllabus as the 'menu'.*)
B. Hi. Good. How are you?
A. I'm fine. Can I get you something to drink to start?
B. Yeah, can I just have um, just water to start with. I'm waiting on someone. So. . . . He'll be a second.
A. Would you like to see a wine list or do you wanna wait until your . . .
B. No, that's fine.
A. You sure? OK. You want me to just come back in a few minutes?
B. (*looking at menu*). Yeah. Thank you.
A. OK I'll get that water for you. (*Gets cup from table, pretends to fill cup with water. Brings cup to B.*) Still looking? Do you still want a few more minutes?
B. No, I think I'm ready to order. (*Pretends to be reading from menu.*) I'll have the chicken pasta without any pepper on it. Is there pepper in the sauce?
A. Yeah. I can do it without pepper that's fine. (*Starts to write on pad, 'chicken pasta'.*)
B. I'm allergic to pepper. I'll have the house salad with ranch dressing.
A. Oh, we don't have ranch. We have a vinaigrette.
B. OK, yeah that's fine. And he should be here soon, but go ahead and bring him a house salad too. I'll wait till he gets here. I'll let him order. I don't want to order for him.
A. Do you still want me to bring the salad out?
B. Yeah. That'd be fine.
A. OK. I'll be back in a few minutes.

Fancy restaurant scenario, Episode 2

The participants were two male college students.

D. Pardon me I'd like to give you our specials for this evening. We have a grouper with a side portion of potato. As well as some cranberry juice poured on top as well as a great deal of greenery, I'm not sure what that is. Very pretty.
C. All right, that sounds wonderful. Let's see I had a question about the menu. The lobster tail is that pan seared or is it deep fried? Because I've got bad blood pressure; I gotta watch it.

D. It is deep fried.

C. What about the lamb chops.

D. The lamb chops are exquisite.

C. Give me the lamb chops. Medium rare.

D. And for the woman?

C. I'll order for her. Give her the honey glazed chicken. And as a starter, let's see...(*Pretends to pore over menu.*)

D. I recommend the portabello mushrooms simmered in black oil.

C. I think I'm looking more at the herb crusted goat cheese. Oh, also, we were looking through the wine list. Um, which would you recommend out of these two Merlots?

D. The one from France.

C. The McGuigan brothers?

D. No, that would be the Scottish one. It's a Merlot from Champagne.

C. Oh, I've heard that's great. We'll have that one.

D. Certainly. (*Pretends to leave.*)

D. (*returns*). And the food for the lady, for yourself. (*Pretends to put food on table.*) There's your wine sir. (*Pretends to pour into pretend glass.*) (*C pretends to swirl the wine in glass, sniff, drink.*)

D. (*pretending to pour again*). Go ahead and have some more. It's really good. Can I get you anything else?

C. Can you get me a sharper knife for the lamb chops.

D. Certainly. Anything else?

C. No.

D. All right. (*Leaves.*)

D. (*returns with arms outstretched and pretends to be carrying a large object, pretends to hand large object to C*). Here's your knife sir. It's the biggest we have. I'm sure you'll find it's quite sharp. It is a two-handed serrated blade sword of Japanese descent. Just be careful, we had a gentleman previously chopped...

C. (*pretending to look over the object, incredulous*). Did you take this off the wall?

D. It's the chef's. He's a Japanese man.

C. This is very...pretty.

D. Well, it is specifically for chopping. You requested a sharp knife.

C. Well, thank you. (*Pretends to lay down object on table.*)

D. Can I get you anything else? Some bread?

C. Maybe a little freshly ground pepper?

D. Certainly. (*Leaves.*)

D. (*returns, pretends to put peppercorns on table, pretends to chop them up with the knife*). Let me chop them up here.

C. Uh, ground. Do you have a grinder?

D. Well I really can't. I'll just, I'll just... (*Puts foot up on table, pretends to crush the peppercorns with his heel.*) Excuse me. I know that's a little crass. (*Pretends to put the pepper on C's food.*) Is that enough?

C. I think that's going to be about it.

D. Certainly. For the lady? Would she like some too?

C. Do you think I could talk to your manager?

D. (*pretends to be chopping more peppercorns*). Uh sure. (*Turns, then whips around pretending to be waving the knife.*) Oh, I've cut her head off. I'm sorry. That's a sharp knife. I'll definitely need the manager for this one. Oh, she's bleeding profusely. One moment please.

(*C laughs and indicates that he's finished with the pretence*).

2.3. Some Features of Pretence

In this section we want to draw attention to a number of features that can be found in the examples of pretence we have recounted. Since they can be found in many other cases as well, they are features which a complete theory of pretence might reasonably be expected to explain. The theory that we will offer in the following section won't have satisfying explanations for *all* the features on our list, though as we will argue in Section 2.5, it can handle more of them than any of the other theories that have been proposed.

2.3.1. Getting pretence started: the initial premiss

Typical episodes of pretence begin with an initial premiss or set of premisses, which are the basic assumptions about what is to be pretended. In Leslie's tea party experiments, the assumption is that the child and the experimenter are going to have a tea party. In our fancy restaurant scenario, the assumption is that one of the participants is a diner in a fancy restaurant, and the other is the server. In the example from Gould, the assumption is that the boy is a pussy-cat. To get the pretence going the pretender must either produce the initial premiss (if she initiates the pretence) or (if someone else initiates the pretence) she must figure out what the initial premiss is and decide whether or not she is going to proceed with the pretence. If the pretender decides that she will proceed, her cognitive system must start generating thoughts and actions that would be appropriate if the pretence premiss were true. People don't always agree to accept the premiss of a pretence, of course. In the example from CHILDES, Val proposes that they pretend there is a monster coming, but Abe refuses, because 'it's too scary'.

2.3.2. Inferential elaboration

Inference often plays a crucial role in filling out the details of what is happening in pretence. From the initial premiss along with her own current perceptions, her background knowledge, her memory of what has already happened in the episode, and no doubt from various other sources as well, the pretender is able to draw inferences about what is going on in the pretence. In Leslie's tea party experiment, for example, the child is asked which cup is empty after the experimenter has pretended to fill up both cups and then turned one upside down. To answer correctly, the child must be able to infer that the cup which was turned upside down is empty, and that the other one isn't, although of course in reality both cups are empty and have been throughout the episode. In one episode of our fast food restaurant scenario, the participant who was pretending to be the cashier informed the 'customer' that his order cost $4.85. The customer gave the cashier $20.00 (in play money), and the cashier gave him $15.15 change, saying 'Out of $20; that's $15.15.' In order to provide the correct change, the cashier must perform a simple mathematical inference. An adequate theory of pretence should provide an account of the cognitive processes that underlie these inferential elaborations.

2.3.3. Non-inferential elaboration (embellishment)

In addition to inferential elaboration, children and adults elaborate the pretend scenarios in ways that are not inferential at all. In some instances, this is a matter of filling out the story provided by a scenario. For instance, in the protocol from CHILDES, Val, in playing the mother, pretends to cook chicken, using some shoes as props. However, this elaboration is not logically or causally *entailed* by the pretend scenario. Similarly, in the first fancy restaurant episode we reported, the diner elects to have the chicken pasta for dinner. Some of these elaborations reflect the decisions and choices that the person pretending would actually make. For instance, the diner in the first fancy restaurant episode refused the wine list, and in the post-pretence interview, this participant said that she really would refuse a wine list because she doesn't like to run the risk of being asked for identification to prove that she is old enough to drink. In other cases, the elaborations depart from what the person would actually decide. The same participant claimed (in the pretence) that she was allergic to pepper, but in the post-pretence interview, she said that she just made this up. More dramatically, in the second fancy restaurant episode, the waiter pretended to decapitate one of the diners! This participant assured us in post-pretence interviews that in real life, he would never be so careless with a sword. A theory of pretence needs to be able to accommodate these kinds of elaborations as well as the more sober inferential elaborations.

2.3.4. Production of appropriate pretend behaviour

Perhaps the most obvious fact about pretence is that pretenders actually *do* things—they engage in actions that are appropriate to the pretence. The child in Leslie's famous example takes the banana from his mother, holds it in the way one might hold a telephone, and talks into it. The adults who participated in our study did the same. In the fancy restaurant scenario, when the 'diner' particip- ant ordered a meal, some 'waiters' wiggled one hand in a stylized imitation of writing, while holding the other hand as though it grasped a pad. Other waiters used a real pad and actually wrote down what the diner was ordering. The boy in the dead cat pretence that Gould observed lay on the ground, as a dead cat might, though his accompanying verbal behaviour was not what one would expect from a dead cat, or from a live one. Our adult participants did much the same, though they were quieter. One adult in our study embellished the dead cat pretence by holding her arms up rigidly to imitate the rigidity of the cat's body after rigor mortis has set in. A theory of pretence must explain how the pre- tenders determine what behaviour to engage in during an episode of pretence. How do they know that they should walk around making jerky movements and saying 'Chugga chugga, choo choo' when pretending to be a train, and lie still when pretending to be a dead cat, rather than vice versa? Equally important, an adequate theory of pretence must explain why the pretender does anything at all. What *motivation* does she have for engaging in these often odd behaviours?

2.3.5. Cognitive quarantine: the limited effects of pretence on the later cognitive state of the pretender

Episodes of pretence can last varying lengths of time. When the episode is over, the pretender typically resumes her non-pretend activities, and the events that occurred in the context of the pretence have a quite limited effect on the post-pretence cognitive state of the pretender. Perhaps the most obvious way in which the effects of the pretence are limited is that pretenders do not believe that pretended events, those which occurred only in the context of the pretence, really happened. A child who pretends to talk to Daddy on the banana/telephone does not end up believing that he really talked to Daddy. Moreover, as Leslie emphasizes (1987), even very young children do not come to believe that bananas sometimes *really are* telephones. Nor, of course, do adults.[4] Moreover, even during the course of the pretence itself, what the

---

[4] In our study of adult pretence we asked participants who had pretended that a banana was a tele- phone (1) 'Have you ever seen a real telephone that looked like a banana?' and (2) 'Have you ever seen a telephone that was made out of a real banana?' They all answered 'No' to both questions.

pretender really believes is typically kept quite distinct from what she believes to be the case in the context of the pretence episode. Our adult participants did not really believe that they were in a restaurant, or that they were baking a cake, or that they were dead cats. For example, we asked, 'At any time did it ever seem like you were really in a restaurant? Did you ever get confused and think that you were really in a restaurant?' Our participants uniformly said 'No'. However, the pretender's belief system is not entirely isolated from the contents of the pretence. After an episode of pretence people typically have quite accurate beliefs about what went on in the pretence episode; they remember what they pretended to be the case. Moreover, Gopnik and Slaughter (1991) reported that children find it much easier to recall what was pretended than to recall their own earlier false beliefs. Indeed, children exhibit the capacity to recall what was pretended a year before they can report their own earlier false beliefs. In Gopnik and Slaughter's experiment, all the children (3-and 4-year-olds) performed at ceiling on remembering pretences in the recent past, but most of the younger children (3-year-olds) were unable to attribute to themselves false beliefs that they had recently held. A theory of pretence should be able to explain how the pretender's cognitive system succeeds in keeping what is really believed separate from what is pretended.

While the contents of pretence episodes usually do not affect what the pretender really believes, pretence can often have a significant effect on other mental states. In particular, pretence can apparently have powerful emotional effects. In the CHILDES protocol, Abe seems to expect to be scared if they pretend that there is a monster coming. There is little serious research on emotions in pretend play. However, as we will explain in Section 2.4, we think that our theory of pretence is also a theory of imagination. And there is plenty of research demonstrating that imagination can have a significant effect on emotions. Indeed, a standard way to elicit emotions in the laboratory is by asking the subjects to imagine something that will produce predictable affective responses (Izard 1991: 172). Imagining that something dangerous is happening can lead subjects to feel real fear, or something very like it (see e.g. Vrana et al. 1989). Imagining that one is having a heated conversation with an annoying acquaintance can lead to affect resembling real anger. Most of the research in this area depends on subjects' reporting their affect. However, there is a growing body of work showing physiological effects of imagining. Not surprisingly, there is evidence that imagining erotic encounters can lead to real sexual arousal, as evidenced by both self-report and physiological changes (e.g. Mosher et al. 1989; Smith and Over 1987, 1990). David Buss found that when males imagined their partner having sex with someone else, they showed marked physiological changes, including a significant increase in heart rate (Buss et al. 1992). The link between the imagination and affect raises lots of interesting questions to which neither we nor anyone else has answers. For instance, we don't know whether the imagination always has at least weak links to the emotion system, no matter what the imagination is being used for; and we don't know whether the affective consequences of *imagining that p* always resemble the affective con-sequences of *believing that p*. We believe that developing a detailed account of pretence will help clarify these sorts of issues.

2.4. A Theory about the Cognitive Mechanisms Underlying Pretence

2.4.1. The Possible World Box, the UpDater, and the Script Elaborator: three further hypotheses about cognitive architecture

In the first chapter, we offered a sketch of the basic architecture of the cognit- ive mind that is widely accepted by the researchers working in this area. At the centre of our theory of pretence are three further hypotheses about our cognitive architecture—three new 'boxes' that we propose to add to the account depicted in Figure 1.1. The first of these is what we will call the *Possible World Box* (or the *PWB*). Like the Belief Box and the Desire Box, the Possible World Box contains representation tokens. However, the func- tional role of these tokens—their pattern of interaction with other components of the mind—is quite different from the functional role of either beliefs or desires. Their job is not to represent the world as it is or as we'd like it to be, but rather to represent what the world would be like given some set of assumptions that we may neither believe to be true nor want to be true. The PWB is a workspace in which our cognitive system builds and temporarily stores representations of one or another possible world.[5] We are inclined to think that the mind uses the PWB for a variety of tasks: the PWB interacts with the Planner, enabling it to construct plans to be carried out in a variety of possible situations; it plays an important role in mindreading (a theme we will elaborate in Chapter 3) and in the generation of empathy. Although we think that the PWB is implicated in all these capacities, we suspect that the original evolutionary function of the PWB was to facilitate reasoning about

---

[5] We are using the term 'possible world' more broadly than it is often used in philosophy (e.g. Lewis 1986), because we want to be able to include descriptions of worlds that many would consider *impossible*. For instance, we want to allow that the Possible World Box can con- tain a representation with the content *There is a greatest prime number*. In general, the PWB cannot contain *obvious* contradictions, since these will be eliminated by the inference system, whose role in pretence we will discuss below.

hypothetical situations (see Section 2.5.1 for a discussion of a contrasting view). In our theory the PWB also plays a central role in pretence. It is the workspace in which the representations that specify what is going on in a pretence episode are housed.

Early on in a typical episode of pretence, our theory maintains, one or more initial pretence premisses are placed in the PWB workspace. So, for example, as a first approximation we might suppose that in the banana/telephone scenario the pretence-initiating representation would be one with the content *This* [banana] *is a telephone.* In Leslie's tea party pretence, the episode begins when a representation with the content *We are going to have a tea party* is placed in the PWB. What happens next is that the cognitive system starts to fill the PWB with an increasingly detailed description of what the world would be like if the initiating representation were true. In the banana/telephone case, the PWB presumably comes to contain representations with contents like the following: *People can use this thing* [the banana] *to talk to other people who are far away. In order to talk to people using this thing, you have to put one end near your ear and the other near your mouth. When someone wants to talk to you on this thing, it goes 'ring, ring'*, etc. In Leslie's tea party scenario, at the point in the pretence where *Alan has just turned the green cup upside down* has been added to the PWB, the child's cognitive system has to arrange to get *The green cup is empty* in there too.

How does this happen? How does the pretender's cognitive system manage to fill the PWB with representations that specify what is going on in the pretence episode? One important part of the story, on our theory, is that the inference mechanism, *the very same one that is used in the formation of real beliefs*, can work on representations in the PWB in much the same way that it can work on representations in the Belief Box. In the course of a pretence episode, new representations get added to the PWB by *inferring* them from representations that are already there. But, of course, this process of inference is not going to get very far if the only thing that is in the PWB is the pretence-initiating representation. From *We are going to have a tea party* there are relatively few interesting inferences to be drawn. In order to generate a rich and useful description of what the world would be like if the pretence-initiating representation were true, the system is going to require lots of additional information. Where is this information going to come from? The obvious answer, we think, is that the additional information is going to come from the pretender's Belief Box. So, as a first pass, let us assume that the inference mechanism elaborates a rich description of what the pretend world would be like by taking both the pretence-initiating representations *and* all the representations in the Belief Box as premisses. Or, what amounts to the same thing, let us assume that in addition to the pretence-initiating premiss, the cognitive system puts the entire contents of the Belief Box into the Possible World Box.

There is, however, an obvious problem with this proposal. As we have told the story, when the inference mechanism is elaborating the pretend world description in the PWB it gets to look at what has been placed in the PWB and at *everything* in the Belief Box. This clearly cannot be right, since it will typically be the case that one or more of the representations in the PWB is incompatible with something in the Belief Box. The pretender believes that the cup is empty (not full), that the banana is a banana (not a telephone), that he is a live person (not a dead cat), etc. So if the inference mechanism can look at *everything* in the Belief Box, it is going to generate glaring contradictions within the possible world description that is being built up in the Possible World Box. This would produce inferential chaos in the Possible World Box. Obviously this does not happen, as evidenced by the inferential orderliness displayed in the examples of pretence that we have collected. How can the theory handle this problem?

The answer, we think, is implicit in the fragment of our theory that we have already sketched. To see it, however, we have to step back and think about the operation of the cognitive system while it is carrying out its normal, non-pretence, chores. One of the things that happens all the time is that via perception or via inference or from the report of another person, a cognitive agent learns a new fact or acquires a new belief that is incompatible with what he currently believes or with something entailed by what he currently believes. Nichols believes that his baby is fast asleep in her crib with her Teddy Bear at her side, but suddenly he hears the characteristic thump of Teddy hitting the floor, followed by giggling and cooing in the baby's room. It is a perfectly ordinary event which requires that his cognitive system update a few of his beliefs. Other cases are more dramatic and complicated. One day a long time ago Stich walked into his doctor's office and saw him listening attentively to his radio. 'President Kennedy has been killed,' he said. Suddenly a large number of Stich's beliefs had to be changed. How do our cognitive systems accomplish these tasks? It is notoriously the case that no one has been able to offer anything that even approximates a detailed account of how this process works. To provide such an account it would be necessary to explain how our cognitive systems distinguish those beliefs that need to be modified in the light of a newly acquired belief from those that do not. And to explain how we do that would be to solve the 'frame problem' which has bedevilled cognitive science for decades (see e.g. the essays in Pylyshyn 1987). Though we have no idea how the process of belief updating works, it is obvious that it *does* work and that it generally happens swiftly, reasonably accurately, and largely unconsciously. So there must be a cognitive mechanism (or a cluster of them) that subserves this process. We will call this mechanism the *UpDater*. And since the UpDater is required for the smooth operation of everyday cognition, it looks like we have reason to add another box to our sketch of mental architecture. Some theorists might wish to portray the UpDater as a separate processing mechanism. But we are inclined to think it is best viewed as a subsystem in the inference mechanism, as indicated in Figure 2.1.

We have already assumed that the inference mechanism which is used in the formation of real beliefs can also work on representations in the PWB. Since the UpDater is a subcomponent of the inference mechanism, it too can work on the representations in the PWB. And this looks to be the obvious way of avoiding the explosion of contradictions that might otherwise arise when the pretence premisses and the contents of the pretender's Belief Box are combined in the PWB. The basic idea is that when the pretence is initiated, the UpDater is called into service. It treats the contents of the Possible World Box in much the same way that it would treat the contents of the Belief Box when a new belief is added, though in the PWB it is the pretence premiss that plays the role of the new belief.

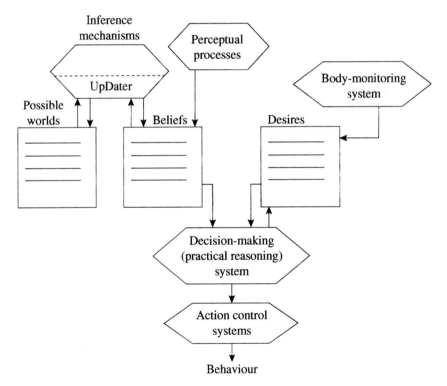

Fig. 2.1 An initial proposal for the cognitive architecture underlying pretence which includes the Possible World Box (PWB) and the UpDater, and indicates that the Inference Mechanisms can work on representations in the PWB in much the same way that it can work on representations in the Belief Box.

The UpDater goes through the representations in the PWB eliminating or changing those that are incompatible with the pretence premisses. Thus these representations are unavailable as premisses when the inference mechanism engages in inferential elaboration on the pretence premisses. Alternatively, one might think of the UpDater as serving as a filter on what is allowed into the Possible World Box. Everything in the pretender's store of beliefs gets thrown into the Possible World Box *unless it has been filtered out (i.e. altered or eliminated) by the UpDater*. Obviously the UpDater will have lots to do during pretence since it is often the case that a large number of beliefs will have to be filtered out very quickly. But we don't think this counts as an objection to our theory. For the task the UpDater confronts in pretence is no more daunting than the tasks it must regularly handle in updating the Belief Box. There too it will often have to make lots of changes and make them very quickly.

One important caveat needs to be added to our claim that the UpDater treats the representations in the PWB in the same way that it treats representations in the Belief Box when a new belief is added. In the latter case, one thing that the UpDater might do is immediately *reject* the new belief because it is too implausible in light of the rest of the agent's beliefs. So, for example, if as the result of a quick glimpse of a man in a crowded railway station, I momentarily form a belief with the content *I just saw John Kennedy* the UpDater will quickly eliminate that belief rather than modifying all the other beliefs that would need to be modified if the belief were true. In pretence, however, we maintain that the initial pretence premiss is temporarily 'clamped'—it *can't* be removed by the UpDater in the initial construction of the description of the possible world of the pretence episode. But the clamping is only temporary since later events in the pretence episode may dictate that the initial pretence premiss is no longer true in that episode. So, for example, if we are pretending that I am asleep and, as part of the pretence, you wake me up, the initial premiss *I am asleep* will be removed from the PWB.

We have suggested that the UpDater and other inference mechanisms treat the pretence representations in much the same way that the mechanisms treat real beliefs, but we have said little about the representational properties and the logical form of pretence representations. One possibility that we find attractive is that the representations in the PWB have the *same logical form* as representations in the Belief Box, and that their representational properties are *determined in the same way*. When both of these are the case, we will say that the representations are *in the same code*.[6] Since mental processing mechanisms like the inference mechanism are usually assumed to be sensitive to the

---

[6] There is much controversy about how the semantic properties of mental representations are determined (see e.g. Stich and Warfield 1994). Our theory takes no stand on this issue apart from assuming that the same account will apply to both Belief Box representations and PWB representations. For clarity of presentation, we frame our discussion in terms of the logical form of

logical form of representations, the inference mechanism will handle pretence representations and belief representations in much the same way. We suspect that there are other mechanisms, for example emotional systems, that take representations from both the Belief Box and the PWB as input. If there are such mechanisms, and if pretence representations and beliefs are in the same code, those mechanisms will process pretence representations in much the same way that they process beliefs.

If we are right that pretence representations are in the same code as beliefs, then the pretence representation *Hamlet is the Prince of Denmark* will have the same logical form as the belief representation *Charles is the Prince of Wales*. The issue of logical form becomes considerably more subtle and complex for pretence involving props, for example pretending that a banana is a telephone. One simple account is that the logical form of such a pretence representation is just *This banana is a telephone*, analogous to the logical form of the belief representation, *This animal is a mammal*. However, some of the responses in our studies speak against this simple account. We asked a number of our participants several questions about their pretence while they were pretending that the banana was a telephone. For example, we asked whether they were pretending that you could sometimes eat a telephone or whether they were pretending that you could sometimes peel a telephone. The participants claimed that they weren't pretending that you could sometimes eat or peel a telephone. This suggests that participants don't include *banana*, with all its attendant properties, as part of the pretence representation. As an alternative to the simple account, we are attracted to the idea that demonstratives often play a crucial role in pretence representations involving props. On this account, in pretending that a banana is a telephone, one has the pretence representation, *This is a telephone*, where '*this*' refers to the banana. We have tried to capture this by putting the referent in brackets, for example, *This [banana] is a telephone*. This 'demonstrative account' can accommodate the responses in our studies. Since the demonstrative ('*this*') need not be tied to any particular features of the prop, there is no reason to expect the pretender to infer that her pretend telephone is edible or peelable. Another advantage to construing such pretence representations as implicating demonstratives is that this fits with the idea that pretence representations have the same logical form as belief representations. It is plausible that there are 'demonstrative thoughts', for example, ***that's** going to explode*, or ***this** is bigger than **that***. Indeed, there is a substantial literature about indexicals and demonstrative

mental representations, which has been the subject of a great deal of research (e.g. Braine 1994; Higginbotham 1995). But if it turns out that some of the mental representations subserving belief and pretence are not quasi-linguistic, the notion of logical form might need to be supplemented by some other notion which plays a role in explaining how such representations are manipulated by the inference mechanism.

thoughts in philosophy and cognitive science (e.g. Leslie et al. 1998; Peacocke 1983; Perry 1993). Perhaps, then, the UpDater and other components of the inference mechanism treat 'demonstrative pretences' in much the same way they treat 'demonstrative thoughts'.

In claiming that the UpDater treats the contents of the PWB in much the same way that it treats the contents of the Belief Box, we want to leave open the possibility that there may be some systematic differences to be found. There is some intriguing evidence suggesting that emotional and motivational factors may affect either the thoroughness with which the UpDater goes about its work in the Belief Box, or the standards it applies in determining whether new evidence is strong enough to lead to the elimination of an old belief, or both. For instance, Ziva Kunda (1987) argues that motivational factors produce self-serving biases in inference. In one of her experiments, Kunda presented subjects with putative evidence on the negative effects of caffeine consumption. She found that heavy caffeine users were much less likely to believe the evidence than low caffeine users (Kunda 1987). It might well be the case that motivational factors play an important role when the UpDater is working on the contents of the Belief Box but that motivational factors play much less of a role when the UpDater is working on the contents of the Possible World Box. It is, we think, a virtue of our strategy of architectural explicitness that it brings empirical issues like this into much sharper focus.

We assume that the contents of a pretender's Belief Box include not only representations whose contents are individual propositions—like the belief that bananas are yellow—but also clusters or packets of representations whose contents constitute 'scripts' or 'paradigms' detailing the way in which certain situations typically unfold (see e.g. Abelson 1981; Schank and Abelson 1977). These scripts often play an important role in guiding and constraining the description of a possible world that gets elaborated in the course of a pretence episode.[7] So, for example, all the students who participated in our fast food restaurant scenario followed the standard pattern of the fast food restaurant script: order first, then pay and get the food, then eat. But while scripts can provide the general structure for many pretence episodes, they leave many aspects of the episode unspecified. Some additional constraints are imposed by the details of what has gone on earlier in the pretence along with the pretender's background knowledge. In one run-through of our fast food scenario, for example, the 'server' decided to pretend that she was working at Wendy's and began her pretence by saying 'Hi. Welcome to Wendy's. Can I take your order?' At this point the 'customer's' background knowledge of the Wendy's menu served

---

[7] In several papers Paul Harris (e.g. 1993, 1994a) has emphasized the importance of scripts and paradigms in pretence and imagination. We are indebted to Harris for prompting us to think more carefully about these matters.

to constrain the sorts of things that she could pretend to be ordering. Hamburgers of various sorts were OK, as were French fries, but hot dogs, tacos, and egg rolls were not. This still leaves many options open, however. Our participant decided to order a small hamburger with ketchup, jumbo fries, and a large sweet tea. In the post-pretence interview she explained that she always had hamburgers with ketchup, though she was aware that there were a variety of other things that she might have ordered instead. So, within the script constraints, there are a variety of choices that the pretender has to make. In the protocols that we collected, sometimes the pretender's choices followed what the pretender would normally do in real life. But on other occasions the pretender deviated from what he would normally do. In one of our (unreported) fancy restaurant episodes, the 'diner' behaved in a boorish manner, but after the pretence he claimed that he would never really act that way in a restaurant. When asked why he chose to be a surly customer, the participant said, 'Because playing is more fun. It's fun to not be yourself.' In addition to the pretender's decisions about what she herself will do, sometimes the pretender must develop the pretence by deciding what happens next in the pretended environment. Does the banana/telephone ring? If so, who is calling? What does the caller want?

Although the pretender's choices often conform to script constraints, the script constraints themselves are only 'soft' constraints, since a really imaginative pretender might order sushi at Wendy's just to make the little exercise more interesting. Indeed, some of our participants violated the script constraints rather dramatically. For example, in the second fancy restaurant scenario we reported, the waiter pretended to crush peppercorns with the heel of his shoe, he gave the diner a sword to cut lamb chops, and he killed one of the patrons with the sword. In these examples, needless to say, the pretender's decision about what to do goes well beyond the restaurant script.

The point of all of this is to emphasize that pretence is full of choices that are not dictated by the pretence premiss, or by the scripts and background knowledge that the pretender brings to the pretence episode. The fact that these choices typically get made quite effortlessly requires an explanation, of course. And we don't have a detailed account of the cognitive mechanisms that underlie this process. There must, however, be *some* mechanism (or, more likely, a cluster of mechanisms) that subserves this process of script elaboration. So we propose to add yet another component to our account of mental architecture, the *Script Elaborator*, which, among other things,[8] fills in those details of a pretence that cannot be inferred from the pretence premiss, the (UpDater-filtered) contents of the Belief Box and the pretender's knowledge of what has happened earlier on in the pretence.

---

[8] As Peter Carruthers has pointed out to us, one of the other things that the Script Elaborator may do is generate some of the initial premisses that get pretence episodes started.

2.4.2. Explaining pretence behaviour: information and motivation

Figure 2.2 is a sketch of the cognitive mechanisms that we now have in place
in our theory. Those mechanisms provide at least the beginnings of an explanation for several of the features of pretence set out in Section 2.3. Since the
representations which describe what is going on in the pretence episode are
stored in the Possible World Box, not in the Belief Box, we have a ready
explanation for the cognitive quarantine that is characteristic of pretence.
People who pretend that there is a burglar in the basement do not end up
believing that there is a burglar in the basement, because they never put a representation with the content *There is a burglar in the basement* in their Belief
Box. Similarly, a child who pretends that a banana is a telephone never has a
representation of *This* [banana] *is a telephone* in his Belief Box, and thus
there is no danger that the child will come to believe that some bananas really
are telephones. Another part of our theory claims that the inference mechanism, which adds, modifies, and removes representations in the Belief Box,
also adds, modifies, and removes representations in the PWB. This, along

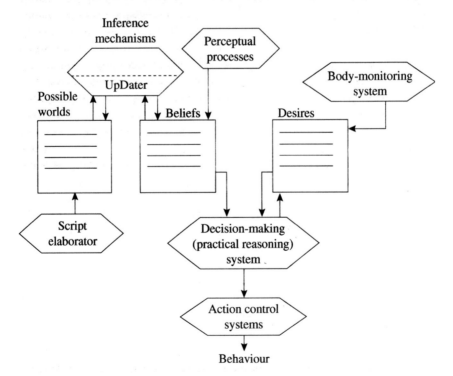

Fig. 2.2   The mental mechanisms posited by our theory of pretence

with our hypothesis that the pretence premiss and most of the contents of the Belief Box are available in the PWB at the start of an inference episode, provides a framework for explaining the sort of inferential elaboration that occurs in pretence. There is, however, one quite crucial aspect of pretence for which our theory has not yet provided any explanation at all. It does not explain why pretenders *do* anything; it offers no explanation of their *behaviour*. Rather, what the theory explains is how a cognitive agent can go about conceiving of or imagining a world which is different from the actual world. So, while it might be offered as a theory of imagination (and, indeed, we maintain that it is a plausible theory of imagination) it is not yet a theory that is able to explain pretence.

Why does a person who is engaging in pretence do the sometimes very peculiar things that pretenders do? Why, for example, does a child or an adult who is pretending to be a train walk around making jerky movements, saying 'Chugga chugga, choo choo'? The answer we would propose comes in two parts, the first of which is really quite simple. Pretenders behave the way they do because they *want to behave in a way that is similar to the way some character or object behaves in the possible world whose description is contained in the Possible World Box*. To pretend that *p* is (at least to a rough first approximation) to behave in a way that is similar to the way one would (or might) behave if *p* were the case. (See Lillard 1994: 213 for a similar treatment.) Thus a person who wants to pretend that *p* wants to behave more or less as he would if *p* were the case. In order to fulfil this desire, of course, the pretender must know (or at least have some beliefs about) how he would behave if *p* were the case. And the obvious source of this information is the possible world description unfolding in the PWB. However, since the PWB is distinct from the Belief Box, we must assume that the contents of the former are accessible to the latter. More specifically (and this is the second part of our answer) we assume that as a possible world description is unfolding in the PWB, the pretender comes to have beliefs of the form:

If it were the case that *p*, then it would (or might) be the case that q_1 & q_2 & ... & q_n

where *p* is the pretence premiss and q_1 & q_2 & ... & q_n are the representations in the PWB. These beliefs, along with the desire to behave in a way that is similar to the way one would behave if *p* were the case, lead to the pretence behaviour in much the same way that Stich's belief that Nichols has just walked around making jerky motions and saying 'Chugga chugga, choo choo' and Stich's desire to behave in a way that is similar to the way in which Nichols behaved will lead Stich to walk around making jerky motions and saying 'Chugga chugga, choo choo'. These conditional beliefs derive from the PWB and play a role in generating pretence behaviour, but they are not beliefs *about* pretence, any more than a belief like *If it were to rain hard tonight, the roof might collapse* is a belief about pretence.[9]

It is worth emphasizing that the pretence-initiating desire—the desire to behave in a way *similar* to the way in which some character or object behaves in the possible world described in the PWB—is typically not a desire to behave in *exactly* the same way. Just how close an approximation the behaviour will be will depend on many factors, including the pretender's other desires and his knowledge about the consequences of various actions. Thus, for example, in our burglar in the basement scenario, one participant picked up the phone that was available and dialed 911, the police emergency number. However, she took precautions to ensure that the call did not really go through. She didn't want her behaviour to be *that* similar to the behaviour elaborated in the PWB; she wanted to be sure that the police didn't really come.

We have suggested that the pretender engages in the pretence action because she *wants* to behave in a way similar to the way that some person or object would behave in a possible world scenario. But there is another motivation question that we have not addressed. We don't explain why people would want to engage in pretend play at all. Our suspicion is that this question, like the question, 'Why do people want to have sex?', may require an evolutionary explanation rather than an explanation in terms of further motivational and cognitive factors.[10]

Obviously, what we have presented in this section is, at best, just the bare bones of a theory of pretence. There are lots of details that we have left unspecified. Despite this, however, we maintain that our theory provides a more promising framework for explaining the facts about pretence than any of the other accounts that have been offered. It is also, in many quite crucial ways, much more *detailed* than other accounts to be found in the literature. In the section that follows, we will defend this view by comparing our theory with the competition.

---

[9] As we will explain in Section 3.1.2, we think the PWB also plays a central role in generating beliefs like these.

[10] Carruthers (1996) offers a story about why people engage in pretend play. He suggests that 'children find rewarding that feature which is common to *all* forms of pretend-play, namely the manipulation of the child's own mental states, through supposing or imagining', and on Carruthers's view, 'you cannot enjoy supposing or imagining without being conscious of your (mental) activity. In general, *enjoying Xing* presupposes *awareness of Xing*,—which is why you cannot enjoy digestion, sleepwalking, or subliminal perception' (1996: 265). We are not particularly sanguine about this account. Even if enjoyment does require awareness, surely producing conscious enjoyment is not the only kind of motivation one might have, and it is not clear why we should assume that the motivation for pretend play is always based on conscious enjoyment. Furthermore, even if Carruthers's story were right, it is at best an account of why people engage in *imagining or fantasizing*; it would not explain pretend *play*, since Carruthers's story says nothing about why children would want to carry out the scenarios they construct in imagination. Nor does Carruthers's account avoid the need for an 'evolutionary' explanation, since he offers no explanation of *why* children find it rewarding to manipulate their own mental states, and it is hard to see how this fact (if it is a fact) could be explained by appeal to other facts about children's motivations or their mental architecture.

2.5. A Comparison with Other Theories

One of our central themes in this section is that theories about the cognitive mechanisms underlying pretence that have been offered by other authors are seriously incomplete. They simply do not tell us how the theory would explain many of the most salient features of pretence, features like those that we have assembled in Section 2.3. A second central theme is that, when one sets out to elaborate and amend these alternative accounts to enable them to explain the facts that they cannot otherwise explain, the most promising proposals tend to make the competing theories look a lot like ours. If, as we would hope, other authors view our suggestions as friendly amendments to their theories, it may well be the case that something like the framework we have presented will emerge as a consensus toward which many theorists are heading from many different directions.

Though there are many suggestions about the cognitive processes underlying pretence to be found in the literature, we think that for the most part, the accounts fall into two distinct clusters. The central idea of one of these clusters is that pretence is subserved by a process of simulation which is quite similar to the 'off-line simulation' process that, according to some theorists, underlies our capacity to predict people's decisions and other mental states. For reasons that will emerge shortly, we will call these '*on*-line simulation' accounts. The central idea of the second cluster is that pretence is subserved by a special sort of representational state, a 'metarepresentation'. We will consider on-line simulation accounts in Section 2.5.1 and metarepresentational accounts in Section 2.5.2. In Section 2.5.3, we will consider one alternative that does not fit easily into either category.

2.5.1. On-line simulation accounts of pretence

'Simulation theory' was originally proposed to explain certain aspects of third-person mindreading, particularly the process that enables us to predict the decisions and behaviour of someone whose beliefs or desires are different from our own.[11] How, for example, might Stich go about predicting what Nichols would do if Nichols were at home alone at night and heard sounds that led him to believe there was a burglar in the basement? On the most prominent version of simulation theory, the 'off-line' simulation account, the prediction process unfolds as follows. First, Stich (or, more accurately, some component of his cognitive system) adds a special sort of belief (often called an

[11] In Chapter 3, we will discuss simulation accounts of third-person mindreading in considerable detail. For present purposes, the brief sketch in this paragraph should suffice.

'imaginary' or 'pretend' belief) to his pre-existing store of beliefs. This 'imaginary' belief would have a content similar or identical to the content of the belief that Nichols would actually have in the situation in question. For purposes of the illustration, we can suppose that the imaginary belief has the content *There is a burglar in the basement.* In many crucial respects, the theory maintains, imaginary beliefs have the same causal powers as real ones. Thus once the imaginary belief is added to Stich's Belief Box, his cognitive system sets about doing many of the things that it would *actually* do if Stich really believed that there was a burglar in the basement. The result, let us assume, is a decision to reach for the phone and dial 911 in order to summon the police. However, one of the ways in which decisions that result from imaginary beliefs differ from decisions that result from real beliefs is that the cognitive agent does not really *act* on them. Rather, the decision that results from the imaginary belief is shunted 'off-line' to a special cognitive mechanism which embeds the content of the decision in a belief about what the 'target' (Nichols) will decide. In this case the belief that is formed is that Nichols will decide to reach for the phone and dial 911. Figure 2.3 is a sketch of this process.

A number of theorists who accept this account of how we go about predicting people's decisions have suggested that, with a few modifications,

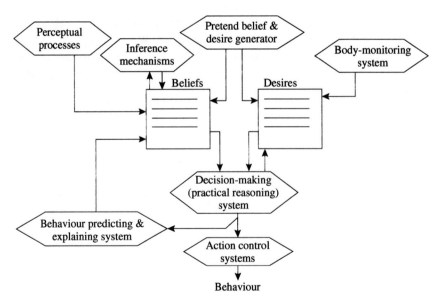

Fig. 2.3   A sketch of the off-line simulation account of behaviour prediction. On this account, the predictor makes a decision based (in part) on 'pretend' beliefs and desires. Rather than being acted upon, the decision leads to a belief that the target will decide to do what the predictor has to do.

it might also serve as an account of the mental processes subserving pretence. The first modification is that in pretence the imaginary belief that is added to the Belief Box is not a belief attributed to some target whose behaviour we want to predict. Rather it will be what we earlier called an 'initial pretence premiss' (or several such premisses) whose content specifies the basic assumption of an impending pretence episode. So, for example, if Stich chose to *pretend* that there was a burglar in the basement, the episode would start with an imaginary belief with the content *There is a burglar in the basement* being placed in his Belief Box. As in the case of decision prediction, once the imaginary belief is added to the Belief Box, the cognitive system sets about doing many of the things that it would *actually* do if the pretender believed that there was a burglar in the basement. And, as before, we will assume that the result of this process, in Stich's case, would be a decision to reach for the phone and dial 911 to summon the police. In the pretence case, however, the decision is not taken 'off-line'. Rather, Stich actually does reach for the phone and dial 911. So pretence, on this account, is very much like off-line prediction of people's decisions, except that the imagination-driven decision is not taken off-line. The pretender actually carries it out. Figure 2.4 is a rendition of this 'on-line simulation' account of pretence.

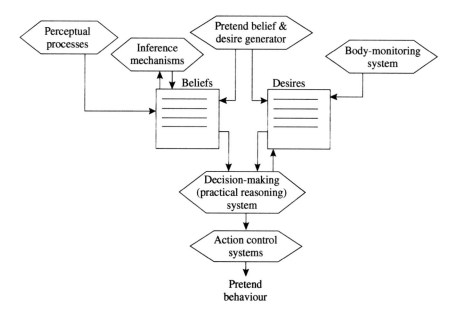

Fig. 2.4 A sketch of the on-line simulation account of pretence. On this account the predictor makes a decision about what to do based (in part) on 'pretend' beliefs and desires and then acts on that decision.

Robert Gordon has been a leader in developing the off-line simulation account of mental state prediction, and though his discussion of pretence is quite brief and sketchy, we are inclined to think the account we have just set out is a plausible interpretation of the theory of pretence proposed by Gordon in collaboration with John Barker. 'In pretence,' they write,

[children] accept an initial premise (or premises)—for example, that certain gobs of mud are pies. By combining the initially stipulated premise with their existing store of beliefs and calling upon their reasoning capacity, they are able to obtain answers to questions not addressed in the initial premise. (Gordon and Barker 1994: 171)

Two paragraphs later, Gordon and Barker sketch an off-line simulation account of decision and behaviour prediction, and explicitly draw the parallel with pretence:

As in pretend play, an initial premise—here, the hypothetical condition—is added to one's store of beliefs, desires, and other inputs to intention-formation and decision making. In one important respect, however, this kind of simulation is unlike children's games of make believe... It stops short of overt action. (1994: 172)

Unfortunately, Gordon and Barker do not say much more about the processes subserving pretence, and thus we cannot be certain that Figure 2.4 really captures what they have in mind. We are, however, much more certain that if this *is* what they have in mind, then the theory confronts some quite fundamental problems. In the following section we pose some problems and suggest some revisions to Gordon and Barker's theory. It is our contention that the most promising proposals for patching the Gordon and Barker theory transform their theory into one that is indistinguishable from ours.

Some problems and repairs for the Gordon and Barker theory of pretence

The first problem is that, as we have interpreted it, the Gordon and Barker theory offers no way of explaining the phenomenon of cognitive quarantine. If, as Gordon and Barker suggest, the pretence-initiating 'hypothetical condition' really is simply '*added* to one's store of beliefs, desires and other inputs to intention formation' then, it would seem, the pretender will actually believe the premiss and anything inferred from it in the course of the pretence. Moreover, when the episode of pretence is over, the pretence premiss and everything inferred from it will still be sitting around in the pretender's Belief Box; Gordon and Barker give us no hint about how they propose to get them out.

To handle the problem, perhaps the most obvious proposal is that, though pretence premisses get added to the Belief Box, they must come specially marked in some way, and this marking ensures that (1) they aren't treated as real beliefs except in the context of an episode of pretence, (2) they don't get left behind after the pretence is over, and (3) neither do any of the representations that are inferred from pretence premises during the course of the pretence. But, of course, to say that the pretence premises and everything inferred from them have a special marker when thrown into the Belief Box, and that this special marker has important consequences for how the pretence-subserving representations are treated, is tantamount to saying that these pretence-subserving representations are functionally different from the other representations in the Belief Box. And since the 'box' metaphor is just a way of distinguishing representations that have systematically different functional or computational properties, to say that pretence-subserving representations are functionally distinct from other representations in the Belief Box is equivalent to saying that they are in a box of their own. So the obvious way for Gordon and Barker to handle the problem of cognitive quarantine is to posit a Pretence Box which is similar to the Possible World Box posited in our theory. The Pretence Box is a functionally distinct component of the mind, a workplace in which pretence-subserving representations are stored and elaborated.

A second problem with the Gordon and Barker theory is that it offers no explanation for the fact that when pretence assumptions are added to the pretender's store of beliefs, and the inference mechanism does its work, the result is not simply a chaotic stream of contradictions. When Stich pretends that there is a burglar in the basement he simultaneously believes that there is no one in the basement. (If he didn't believe that he'd stop pretending in a big hurry. There would be more important things to do.) So it would appear that on Gordon and Barker's account Stich has two representations in his Belief Box, one with the content *There is a burglar in the basement* and one with the content *There is no one in the basement*. Something must be said to explain why these patently incompatible beliefs don't lead to an inferential meltdown.

Since there are independent reasons (set out in Section 2.4.1) to posit an UpDater mechanism whose job it is to make appropriate changes in the Belief Box when new representations are added, an amendment to the Gordon and Barker theory can stipulate that the UpDater filters and modifies the contents of the Belief Box for compatibility with the pretence premiss before they are allowed in to the Pretence Box. With these extensions to Gordon and Barker's account, the revised theory is growing to look a lot like ours.

A third problem confronting the sort of theory sketched in Figure 2.4 is that in many cases it provides no plausible account of the pretender's motivation to perform the actions he performs in the course of the pretence. The problem does not arise in the burglar example, since if Stich really did believe there was a burglar in the basement, he would certainly want to summon the police. But consider another case: the child making mud pies. Here, according to Gordon and Barker, the pretence premiss is that certain gobs (lumps) of mud are pies. From this, let us suppose, the pretender infers that the gobs of mud can be eaten. But why does he actually pick them up and (pretend to) eat them? There are, after all, lots of occasions on which a child sees a *real* pie, but does not try to eat it because he is simply not hungry. And it is clearly possible for a child (or an adult) to engage in the mud pie pretence even though he is not at all hungry. Suppose this is the case in the example at hand. What explains the pretender's behaviour? Why does the imaginary belief that the gobs of mud are pies lead to (pretend) eating? The theory that we have attributed to Gordon and Barker offers no answer.

There is some textual evidence that Gordon and Barker and others who urge accounts similar to theirs would deal with this problem by positing that, in some instances of pretence, imaginary desires are added to the Desire Box in much the same way that imaginary beliefs are added to the Belief Box. So, for example, in the mud pie pretence, the theory would propose that an imaginary desire with the content *I eat some pie* gets added to the real desires in the pretender's Desire Box. However, for two quite different reasons, we are inclined to think that this is not the best way to deal with the problem. The first reason is that if this imaginary desire has causal powers similar to the causal powers of the real desire with the same content, then the desire would produce the wrong behaviour. An (imaginary) desire to eat some pie along with an (imaginary) belief that the gob of mud is a pie would presumably lead the pretender to actually eat the mud pies. But pretence behaviour of this sort is rarely seen in children and almost never seen in adults. The second reason is that there are cases in which the imaginary desire account looks to be quite hopeless. Though it is conceivable that an adult who is pretending to be a dead cat has added an imaginary representation with the content *I am a dead cat* to her Belief or Pretence Box, there is no plausible candidate for the imaginary desire which might interact with this belief to produce the sort of behaviour that we described in Section 2.2. Dead cats don't have desires.

A much better way to patch the Gordon and Barker theory, we maintain, is to drop the idea of imaginary desires altogether and to explain a pretender's motivation the way we did in Section 2.4.2. What is in the Pretence Box is not a pretend belief that might be attributed to a dead cat. Rather, the Pretence Box has a representation with the content *This* [my body] *is a dead cat*, along with some additional representations about what the dead cat looks like. And what leads the pretender to do what she does is not some bizarre desire that might be attributed to a dead cat, but simply a quite real desire to 'behave' in a way that is similar to the way a dead cat described in the Pretence Box would behave. In the mud pie case, what is in the Pretence Box might be a set of representations describing what the world would be like if the mud gobs were pies and someone was eating them. The motivating desire is not an imaginary desire to eat a pie, but a real desire to behave in a way that is similar to the way that the imagined person behaves. But, of course, the pretender also has a competing desire not to eat mud, so she does not want to behave in exactly the way that a person fitting the description would behave, since the pretender knows that if she did she would get a mouth full of mud. Similarly, in the burglar in the basement pretence, the motivating desire is to behave in a way similar to the way that someone might behave if there was a burglar in the basement, but since the pretender also desires *not* to summon the police, she does not behave exactly that way. On the theory we are attributing to Gordon and Barker, these differences between real and pretend behaviour are unexplained.[12]

As they set it out, Gordon and Barker's account clearly has many short-comings. They might, of course, accept the various additions and revisions we have proposed. If, as we would hope, they take our suggestions on board as friendly (albeit occasionally quite fundamental) amendments, the resulting account is all but indistinguishable from the theory that we have proposed.

Other simulation-based accounts of pretence

A number of other authors who are sympathetic to off-line simulation accounts of mental state prediction have developed accounts of pretence and imagination that are presented as simulation based in some broad sense. In their 1993 monograph, Harris and Kavanaugh offer a 'flagging' account of pretence according to which pretend episodes depend on 'flagging' objects with make-believe stipulations (Harris and Kavanaugh 1993: 60). More recently, Harris revised the flagging theory to say that in pretend play, we 'adopt a make-believe stance', by which he means that 'the representation of the episode is prefaced by an attitudinal marker equivalent to the statement: "In this episode, imagine that..." ' (1995: 177). Though Harris does not tell us where these sorts of representation are located we don't think it is too much of a stretch to read him as positing something rather like the Pretence Box that we urged on Gordon and Barker. This interpretation is supported by his claim that in normal development children acquire 'an increasing capacity for the internal creation of a complex script' which is detached from 'the external context' (Harris 1993: 234). Since the representations in the child's Belief Box are closely tied to the external context, this 'complex script' must be elaborated in some functionally distinct component of the mind. Harris (1991) has also stressed the importance of using one's own beliefs as 'default settings' in imagination and pretence, and the role of stored prototypes in the elaboration of a pretence script. We have taken both of these ideas on board

---

[12] Gordon and Barker do note that 'One does not carry out the decision, say to call the police, even in overt pretend play' (1994: 172). However, they don't explain how this fits with their claim that in games of make-believe, the pretend decisions result in overt action.

in our own theory. So we see Harris's account of pretence as broadly compatible with our own, though he is silent on a number of crucial issues including the avoidance of contradictions in pretence 'scripts', the motivation for pretence behaviour, and the systematic differences between pretence and non-pretence behaviour.

Gregory Currie's account of pretence is much sketchier than Harris's and much harder to interpret. According to Currie, 'It is natural to think that childhood games of pretence in which the actors play at being pirates or bears are driven by the actors mentally taking on these roles and imagining being pirates or bears. In doing these things, the children simulate, to the best of their ability and within the compass of their relevant knowledge, the experience of being pirates or bears' (Currie 1996: 251). Unfortunately, Currie tells us little about the mental mechanisms that subserve this sort of simulation and how they are related to the mental mechanisms involved in non-pretence cognition. In another passage in which he discusses 'a *simulationist* theory of pretending' he refers the reader to Goldman's work on mental simulation, and Goldman has explicitly endorsed a model similar to Figure 2.3 as a plausible boxological rendition of his account of simulation (Goldman 1992a, 1993a). Currie also refers the reader to Gordon's work. So there is some reason to suppose that Currie might be interpreted as endorsing an account of pretence along the lines depicted in Figure 2.4. However, Currie also insists that pretending is a propositional attitude which is distinct from both believing and desiring, and that pretend beliefs have functional roles that are systematically different from real ones (Currie 1998). So there is also some reason to suppose that Currie's account of pretence would include a separate Pretence Box. Indeed, the following passage suggests that Currie's account may also include two Pretence Boxes, one for pretend beliefs and one for pretend desires: 'If mental simulation is how we understand the minds of others, there must be states that stand to desire as imaginings stand to beliefs; for us adequately to simulate the mental states of others, we must simulate their desires as well as their beliefs. So as well as pretend or imaginary beliefs—what I have been calling imaginings—we need pretend or imaginary desires' (Currie 1995a: 150). This, then, seems to be a point on which our theory and Currie's diverge. For the reasons set out in our discussion of Gordon and Barker, we think that positing pretend desires raises more problems than it solves, and that our theory offers a more plausible account of the motivation of pretence behaviour.

There is one aspect of Currie's theory that we think deserves special mention: his account of the evolutionary origin and biological function of pretence. According to Currie, the function of the mechanisms subserving imagination and pretence is to 'test-run' possible courses of action. 'Strategy testing', he writes, 'is, on my hypothesis, the proper function of the imagination: the function appeal to which explains why we have the faculty of imagination (Millikan, 1984). Daydreaming and fantasy, along with imaginative involvement with fictions, are made possible by a system that already exists for other purposes: the running of simulations' (Currie 1995*b*: 158). Currie describes simulation as follows:

[R]unning a test in the simulator should be a bit like having the experiences we would have if we really were acting out the strategy. Not quite like it, of course. That would be difficult, and dangerous too, because it would amount to the conditions of an hallucination. A compromise would be to reproduce the kinds of affective states we would have if the test were real. In the real case affective states are mediated by our beliefs and desires; we feel the sensations of fear not because the tiger is about to attack us but because we believe it is and desire it not to. So what the simulator does is to retain the connections between inner representation and bodily sensation that would be there if the representation was functioning as a belief; what is not retained is the belief-like connection to behaviour. (1995*b*: 157)

Currie's hypothesis that strategy testing is the proper function of the imagination has been adopted by some researchers of quite different theoretical persuasion (e.g. Carruthers 1996: 266). On our view, however, this hypothesis is overly restrictive. Currie's proposal entails that the function of the pretence mechanisms is limited to considering possible courses of action or strategies that might be adopted. But one might also use the imagination and pretence mechanisms described in our theory to work on problems that are not strategies for action. For instance, one might use the mechanisms to figure out what will happen to one's domicile if there is a great deal of rainfall. Thus, on our view, it is plausible that the 'proper function' of the pretence mechanisms is more broadly for hypothetical and counterfactual reasoning.

2.5.2. Metarepresentational accounts of pretence

The second cluster of theories of pretence that we will consider are those in which a special kind of metarepresentation plays a central role. The most influential of these is the theory developed in a series of publications by Alan Leslie and his collaborators (Leslie 1987, 1994*a*; Leslie and Thaiss 1992; Leslie and Roth 1993). As we see it, Leslie's theory can be divided into two quite distinct parts. One of these parts is comfortably compatible with the theory we have proposed in Section 2.4 though the other is not.

A central concern of Leslie's theory is the avoidance of what he calls 'representational abuse'. Pretence emerges quite early in children, at a time when their knowledge of the world and their understanding of terms and concepts is still quite fragmentary. But when children pretend that a banana is a telephone or that an empty cup is full of tea, it is plausible to suppose they are relying on mental representations that 'distort reality'—they represent states of affairs that are simply not the case. 'Why', Leslie asks, 'does pretending not undermine their representational system and bring it crashing down?' (1987: 412) Why, for example, doesn't the child end up believing that some bananas are telephones or that cups can be full when they clearly look to be empty? The phenomenon that Leslie is concerned with here is, of course, just a special case of the one that we noted in Section 2.3.5. In both children and adults, episodes of pretence have only a quite limited impact on the post-pretence cognitive states of the pretender, and these effects are very different from what they would be if the pretender really believed the contents of the pretence. So a theory of pretence must explain how the representations that underlie episodes of pretence are 'marked off, or "quarantined," from the primary representations' (1987: 415) whose job it is to provide a 'literal and "sober"' account of the world (1987: 414). The infant must 'have some way of marking information from pretend contexts to distinguish it from information from serious contexts' (1987: 416). As Leslie notes, one strategy for explaining how children manage to avoid representational abuse would be to posit a separate code or representational format for pretence-subserving representations. But this would make it significantly more difficult to explain the fact that pretenders can use their general knowledge and background beliefs to draw inferences within an episode of pretence since the pretence-subserving representations and the background beliefs would be stored in two different codes. What Leslie proposes instead is that the representations that subserve pretence are 'marked' in a special way to indicate that their functional role is different from the functional role of unmarked (or 'primary') representations. To use the terminology that Leslie employs, these marked representations are *decoupled* copies of the primary representations which do not have the 'normal input-output relations' (1987: 417) that unmarked primary representations have.

The notational device that Leslie uses to mark pretence-subserving representations is to enclose them in quotation marks, and since quotation marks are standardly used to form names of the representational expressions that they enclose, Leslie initially called these marked representations *metarepresentations*. This, however, proved to be an unfortunate choice of terminology which provoked a great deal of misunderstanding and criticism, much of it turning on the question of whether the young children, to whom Leslie attributed these marked representations, actually had the *concept* of *representation*, and therefore could think of a representation *as* a representation. If they couldn't, critics urged, then the marked representations were not really *meta*representations at all (Perner 1988, 1991, 1993).[13] Leslie's response to these objections was to

[13] For instance, Perner writes, 'In our use of the term "metarepresentation" we should adhere to Pylyshyn's (1978, p. 593) implicit definition as *representing the representational relation*

insist that he intended 'metarepresentation' as a technical term for representations that played the role specified in his theory, and that the theory did not claim that people who had these representations conceived of them as representations of representations. To avoid further confusion, he abandoned the term 'metarepresentation' in favour of the more obviously technical term 'M-representation'.

Once these terminological confusions are laid to rest, it should be clear that the part of Leslie's theory that we have sketched so far is very similar to part of the theory that we have been defending. For, as we noted in 2.5.1, to claim that a class of representations is specially marked, and that the marking has important consequences for how the representations are treated by the cognitive system, is another way of saying that marked representations and unmarked representations are functionally different. Since the 'box' metaphor is just a notational device for distinguishing representations that have systematically different functional or computational properties, Leslie's hypothesis that representational abuse is avoided because the representations subserving pretence are 'quarantined' or 'marked off' (1987: 415) is equivalent to claiming, as we do in our theory, that pretence-subserving representations are in a box of their own.[14] Another point of similarity between Leslie's theory and ours is that it does not posit a separate code or system of representation for the cognitive processes underlying pretence. The representations in the Possible World Box (in our theory), or within the quotation marks (in Leslie's theory) are tokens of the same types as the representations in the Belief Box (to use our preferred jargon) or in the pretender's primary representations (to use Leslie's). Also, in both theories the pretender's real beliefs (or 'general knowledge' (1987: 419)) can be used as premises in elaborating an episode of pretence, and the inference mechanism that is responsible for these elaborations is the same one that is used in reasoning using only real beliefs. Leslie does not address the problem of avoiding contradictions between general knowledge and pretence assumptions, nor does he offer an account of the motivation for the behaviour produced in pretence. So there are mechanisms and processes posited in our theory without any analogues in Leslie's account. Nonetheless, the part of Leslie's theory that we have set out so far can plausibly be viewed as simply a notational variant of part of our theory. Actually,

---

itself, because his definition is unambiguous, and he was one of the first to use this term in cognitive science' (Perner 1993: 114–15).

[14] As we discuss below, Leslie actually disavows the Pretence Box hypothesis. However, the existence of a Pretence Box is entirely compatible with the part of Leslie's theory that we have described thus far. Leslie's rejection of a Pretence Box depends, rather, on the second part of his theory, according to which pretence representations have a distinctive content and are stored in the Belief Box. So, on Leslie's account, unlike ours, pretence representations are quarantined from other representations both by their function and by their content.

though, the point should be made the other way round: part of our theory is a notational variant of part of his—and this is no accident since Leslie's work has been an important influence on our own.

A second central theme in Leslie's theory, and one that does not fit comfortably with ours, is the claim that 'pretend play ... [is] a primitive manifestation of the ability to conceptualize mental states' (1987: 424) and thus that 'pretence is an early manifestation of what has been called *theory of mind*' (1987: 416). Because he thinks that pretence involves some under-standing or conceptualizing of mental states, and also because he sees a close parallel between the 'semantic properties of mental state expressions' (like 'believe', 'expect' and 'want') and the 'basic form[s] of pretence' Leslie thinks that 'mental state expressions can provide a model with which to characterize the representations underlying pretend play' (1987: 416). In developing this idea, Leslie proposes 'a second extension to the primary code' to work in conjunction with the quotation marks whose job it is to quarantine the pretence-subserving representations. Here is how Leslie elaborates this idea:

Language has its mental state terms that denote relationships between agents and opaque propositions. In fact, the verb *pretend* is just such a term. I can add to my model formal elements that play a corresponding role in underlying mental representa-tion. The second extension to primary code will be an item, PRETEND, representing an informational relation. This relation will hold between whatever primary representa-tions of agents (e.g. mother) the infant has and decoupled expressions. Pretend metarepresentations might thus have the general form: **Agent–Informational Relation–'expression.' Agent** ranges over, for example, persons and self, whereas **'expression'** can be filled by any decoupled representation. (1987: 417)

As an illustration, Leslie proposes that one of the mental representations underlying the tea party pretence might have the form: I PRETEND **'this empty cup contains tea'** (1987: 420). Since Leslie claims that all pretence repr-esentations include the PRETEND concept, the pretence box is not needed to distinguish pretence representations from other mental states. And, indeed, Leslie explicitly rejects the pretence box. Ironically, the clearest place this comes out is in a paper he co-authored with us (Nichols et al. 1996).

According to Leslie, in terms of boxology, there is no such thing as the 'pretend box', and thus no such thing as simply 'having a pretend'. Instead, pretending is a special case of placing a representation in the 'belief box', where the representation says in effect, 'someone is pretending such and such'. (Nichols et al. 1996: 56)

On our view, this second component of Leslie's theory—the hypothesis that pretence-subserving mental representations always include both a specifica-tion of an agent and a representation of the 'informational relation' in which the agent stands to the decoupled representations that indicates what is going on in the pretence—is unnecessary and unwarranted. The theory of pretence doesn't need it to explain the evidence and would be better off without it. In defending our view it will be useful to begin by comparing Leslie's two-part theory with the theory that we set out in Section 2.4.

Let's start with some facts that are not in dispute. As we noted in Section 2.4, adults and older children typically have beliefs about what they are pretending (and about what others are pretending, when they are engaged in collaborative pretence), and they can report these beliefs when asked, using sentences like 'I am pretending that this empty cup contains tea'. On our theory, there are two quite distinct mental representations implicated in these first-person reports. First, there is a pretence-subserving representation in the PWB whose content is (roughly): *This* [empty] *cup contains tea.* Second, since adults and older children can monitor their own pretence and form true beliefs about what they are pretending, there is a representation in the Belief Box whose content is (roughly) *I am pretending that this* [empty] *cup contains tea.* Though the former representation is an important part of the causal process that leads to the formation of the latter, it is only this latter representation that is directly responsible for a subject's verbal report about what she is pretending. The former representation, by contrast, is the one that is directly implicated in the production of pretence behaviour, the drawing of inferences about what is happening in the pretence, etc. Note that this pretence behaviour can include *verbal behaviour*, e.g. 'Should I pour some tea?' In principle, of course, the pretence could proceed without the subject having any beliefs with contents like *I am pretending that this* [empty] *cup contains tea.* Indeed, on our theory, the pretence could proceed perfectly well even if the subject did not have the concept of *pretence* and thus could have no beliefs at all with contents of the form: *I am pretending that p.*

There is, on our theory, a close parallel between beliefs and reports about pretence, on the one hand, and beliefs and reports about desires, on the other.[15] Just as adults and older children have beliefs about what they are pretending and can report those beliefs, so too they typically have beliefs about their desires, particularly those desires that are currently guiding their behaviour. On our theory, there are typically two quite distinct mental representations implicated in the causal process leading a subject to make a report like 'I want to drink some water'. First, there is the representation that subserves the desire itself. This representation, which is located in the subject's Desire Box has the content: *I drink some water.* Second, there is a representation in the subject's Belief Box whose content is *I want to drink some water.* As in the case of pretence, the first of these representations is an important part of

---

[15] Currie (1998) has explored this parallel in some detail, and our development of the point has been significantly influenced by Currie's discussion.

the causal process that leads to the formation of the second. But only the second representation, the one in the Belief Box, is directly involved in producing the subject's verbal report. By contrast, it is the representation in the Desire Box (in conjunction with various beliefs about the environment) that leads the subject to reach for the glass of water in front of her and raise it to her lips. And, just as in the case of pretence, the process that leads to drinking could proceed perfectly well even if the subject did not have the concept of *wanting* and thus could have no beliefs at all of the form: *I want that p*. So, on our theory, it is entirely possible that young children, or non-human primates, have lots of beliefs and desires though they are entirely incapable of conceptualizing mental states.

On Leslie's theory of pretence, the parallel that we have drawn between desiring and pretending breaks down. For Leslie, all episodes of pretence are subserved by representations of the form: I PRETEND 'p'. Thus, while Leslie would agree that an agent can have desires and act on them without having the concept of *desire*, his theory entails that an agent *cannot* engage in pretence without having the concept of *pretence*. (He also seems to think that an agent cannot engage in pretence without believing that she is pretending.) As we see it, however, there is no more reason to suppose that young children who pretend have the concept of *pretence* (Leslie's PRETEND) than there is to suppose that young children who have desires have the concept of *desire*. We attribute this latter concept to older children and adults not because they *act* on their desires but rather because they *talk* about desires and indicate in various ways that they are reasoning about them. Since young children can pretend without talking about pretending or indicating that they are reasoning about pretending, the claim that they have the PRETEND concept seems unwarranted. (See Harris and Kavanaugh 1993: 75 for a similar argument.)[16]

Why does Leslie think that pretence is 'a primitive manifestation of the ability to conceptualize mental states' (1987: 424) and that a representation involving the PRETEND concept underlies all episodes of pretence? As best we can tell, he has three arguments for this view. One focuses on the fact that individual and group pretence emerge at the same time; a second focuses on the parallels between pretence and mental state expressions; the third turns on the fact that autistic children are poor at mindreading tasks and do not exhibit normal pretend play. We are not convinced by any of these arguments, and in the remainder of this section we propose to say why.

The first argument we want to consider is aimed quite explicitly at theories like ours on which pretending does not require the concept of *pretence* (just

---

[16] This is not to say that the young child has no understanding of pretence at all. Rather, we think that the young child has what we will call a 'behavioural' understanding of pretence, a notion explained below.

as desiring does not require the concept of *desire*). If this were true, Leslie maintains, it would be entirely possible for a child to engage in solitary pretence without being able to engage in pretence with another person or understanding what the other person was doing when she pretends; but, Leslie's argument continues, as a matter of empirical fact this simply does not happen (personal communication; Leslie 1987: 415–16; Nichols et al. 1996; 56). Children begin to pretend by themselves and to engage in joint pretence at exactly the same time. Theories like ours, Leslie argues, have no explanation for this important empirical fact, while his theory has an obvious explanation. If engaging in pretence and understanding pretence in others both depend on representations that include the PRETEND concept, then neither will be possible until that concept becomes available.

We see a pair of problems with this argument, one of which is primarily conceptual, while the other is largely empirical. We will start with the concept-ual point. What is it to *understand* what another person is doing when she pretends that *p*? There are, it seems, two quite different accounts that might be offered. On a 'behavioural' account, what one understands is that the other person is *behaving in a way that would be appropriate if p were the case*. On a 'mentalistic' account, what one understands is that the other person is behav-ing in a way that would be appropriate if *p* were the case *because she is in a particular mental state, viz. pretending that p (or, perhaps, wanting to behave in that way)*. This account is 'mentalistic' insofar as it invokes the idea that the behaviour is produced by underlying mental states of a certain kind (see also Harris 1994*b*: 251). Now, as Leslie notes, if a child has no understanding at all of pretence, then pretence behaviour will often seem utterly bizarre and puzzling (1987: 416). (Why on earth would Momma be talking to a banana?!) But by the age of 2 or even earlier children obviously see nothing puzzling about pretence behaviour. Quite the opposite; when Momma pretends that the banana is a telephone, they plunge right in and join the pretence. But, and this is the crucial point, in order to do this the child needs no more than a *behavi-oural* understanding of pretence. In order to engage in the banana/telephone pretence, the child must understand that Momma is behaving in a way that would be appropriate if the banana were a telephone. But, as several researchers have noted, the child need not have a *mentalistic* understanding of pretence (Harris 1994*b*: 250–1; Jarrold et al. 1994: 457; Lillard 1996: 1718). Indeed, a child with a behavioural understanding of pretence could engage in a quite elaborate two-person pretence *without understanding that the other person has any mental states at all*. So, from the fact that a child engages in group pretence it does not follow that the child is exhibiting 'a primitive manifestation of the ability to conceptualize mental states'. Participation in two-person pretence does not support Leslie's claim that the pretender has mental representations of the form: **Agent PRETEND 'expression'**.

Let us now turn to the empirical issue. Leslie claims that an understanding of pretence in others emerges at the same time as the ability to engage in pretence oneself. Is this true? In light of the distinction between *behavioural* and *mentalistic* ways of understanding pretence, it should be clear that the claim is ambiguous. It could mean that pretence behaviour appears at the same time as a *behavioural* understanding of pretence, or that pretence behaviour emerges at the same time as a *mentalistic* understanding. With the former claim, we have no quarrel. Though, as we have just argued, it lends no support to the second part of Leslie's theory. If, on the other hand, what Leslie claims is that pretence behaviour and a mentalistic understanding of pretence emerge at the same time, then it is far from clear that this claim is supported by the facts. As we have seen, the mere fact that children engage in two-person pretence is not enough to establish that they have a mentalistic understanding. Moreover, several investigators have maintained that a mentalistic understanding of pretence emerges gradually and is not fully in place until some years after the child begins to engage in pretence behaviour (e.g. Jarrold et al. 1994; Lillard 1993, 1996; Lillard and Flavell 1992; Rosen et al. 1997). If this is correct, then the empirical claim in Leslie's first argument is not merely unsupported; it is false.

Leslie's second argument for the 'second extension' part of his theory turns on what he takes to be the close parallel between the semantic properties of mental state expressions like *believe, expect,* and *want* and the 'basic forms' of pretence. The parallels that Leslie has in mind are the following: (*a*) Mental state expressions create referentially opaque contexts. Even if the sentences 'Mrs. Thatcher is the Prime Minister' and 'Sarah-Jane believes that the Prime Minister lives at No. 10 Downing Street' are both true, it does not follow that the sentence 'Sarah-Jane believes that Mrs. Thatcher lives at No. 10 Downing Street' is true. This, Leslie maintains, is parallel to the fact that 'object substitution' takes place in pretence. When a child pretends that a stick is a horse, it does not follow that one can freely substitute 'stick' for 'horse' in attributing psychological states to the child. So, even though sticks are inanimate, a child can pretend that a stick is a horse without pretending or believing that a horse can be inanimate. (*b*) 'Propositions involving mental state terms do not logically imply the truth (or falsehood) of propositions embedded in them.' (1987: 416). Thus, for example, the sentence 'John believes that the cat is white' does not entail that 'The cat is white' is true (or that it is false). This, Leslie suggests, is parallel to the fact that a person can pretend that a cup is empty whether or not the cup actually is empty. (*c*) 'Assertions involving mental state terms do not logically entail the existence of things mentioned in the embedded proposition' (1987: 416). So the sentence 'Jacqueline believes the king of France is bald' can be true even though the king of France does not exist. The parallel here, according to Leslie, is that a person can pretend that something exists when it does not.

Though there are various quibbles that one might reasonably raise with the parallels Leslie notes, we are prepared to grant that they are real enough. However, it is our contention that Leslie has failed to see the real explanation of these parallels and that the conclusion that he wants to draw from them is implausible. As we see it, the explanation for the parallels that Leslie notes is that pretending, believing, wanting, and expecting are all *propositional attitudes*, and that 'pretend', 'believe', 'want', and 'expect' are all propositional attitude *terms*. All the facts about pretence mentioned in the previous paragraph have exact parallels for believing, wanting, and expecting. One can, for example, want it to rain tomorrow (or believe that it will) whether or not it rains tomorrow. And one can want to meet Santa Claus (or expect to) whether or not Santa Claus exists. Similarly, all the facts that Leslie notes about mental state terms like 'want', and 'believe' have exact parallels for 'pretend'. So the deep parallels are not those between pretending and the *terms* for propositional attitudes, but between pretending and propositional attitudes themselves, and between the term 'pretend' and other propositional attitude terms. Once this is seen, it makes Leslie's proposal to add 'PRETEND' to the mental representations subserving pretence look very odd indeed. For if it is plausible to suppose that the mental representation subserving the pretence that a certain cup contains tea has the form I PRETEND 'this empty cup contains tea', then, given the parallels we have noted, the mental representation subserving the belief that this cup contains tea should be I BELIEVE this cup contains tea, and the mental representation subserving the desire that it rain tomorrow should be I DESIRE that it rain tomorrow. And if this were the case, then it would be impossible to believe *anything* without having the concept of *belief*, and impossible to desire *anything* without having the concept of *desire*. So any organism that had any beliefs and desires at all would have to have these concepts and thus at least the beginnings of a 'theory of mind'. The way to avoid this package of unwelcome conclusions is clear enough. We should buy into the first half of Leslie's theory (which, it will be recalled, is a notational variant of part of our theory) and reject the second half.

There is one further argument that figures prominently in Leslie's defence of his theory of pretence. The argument turns on the interesting and important fact, discovered by Leslie and others (Baron-Cohen et al. 1985; Leslie and Roth 1993) that autistic children typically exhibit a pair of quite striking deficits: the first is that their ability to engage in pretend play is severely impaired when compared with other children of the same mental age. The second is that their performance on false-belief understanding tasks and other standard tasks that are taken to indicate an understanding of mental states is also severely impaired when compared with other children of the same mental age. This suggests that the processes underlying pretence and the processes underlying our ability to understand mental states share some common mechanism. Leslie's hypothesis is that the impairment is in the decoupling mechanism. This, it will be recalled, is the mechanism that marks mental representations with quotation marks to indicate that they do not have the same functional role that these representations would have if they were subserving belief. In our version of the theory, what Leslie calls 'decoupling' is accomplished by putting the representations in the Possible World Box. In order for it to be the case that a defect in the decoupling mechanism (or the system that puts representations into the PWB) leads to an impairment in mindreading skills, it must be the case that decoupling (or putting representations in the PWB) plays a central role in understanding and reasoning about mental states. This is an intriguing and important hypothesis which Leslie develops and which we will discuss in Chapter 3. What is important, for present purposes, is that if the hypothesis is right (and we think it is) it offers no support at all for what we have been calling the second half of Leslie's theory of pretence. If the decoupler (or the system that puts representations into the PWB) is impaired then we would expect to find deficits in the ability to pretend, no matter what account one favours about the exact form of the representations that subserve pretence. And if the decoupler (or the system that puts representations into the PWB) also plays a central role in reasoning about the mind and solving mindreading tasks, then we should also expect deficits in this area no matter what account one proposes about the exact form of the representations subserving reasoning about the mind. So the facts about autism are simply irrelevant to the second half of Leslie's theory, which claims that the representations subserving pretence have the form I PRETEND 'p'.

One final concern we have with Leslie's account of pretence is that it offers us no explanation of why pretenders *do* anything. The central idea of Leslie's theory is that pretence is subserved by representations like I PRETEND 'this empty cup contains tea' and Momma PRETENDS 'this banana is a telephone' which are stored in the pretender's Belief Box. But representations in the Belief Box do not motivate behaviour; that is the job of desires, not beliefs. Leslie might, of course, adopt something like our account, on which pretenders behave the way they do because they want to behave in a way that is similar to the way one would behave if *p* (where *p* is the pretence premiss). But it is far from clear how our account of pretence motivation can be integrated with what Leslie tells us about the mental representations subserving pretence, since those representations do not include beliefs about how one would behave if the pretence premiss were true.

Where does all of this leave us? As we see it, the case for the second part of Leslie's theory—the part that maintains that all episodes of pretence are subserved by representations of the form: I PRETEND 'p'—is beset by difficulties on every side. The empirical evidence that would be needed to support the claim is not there; the analogy between pretence and propositional attitude verbs is not a good one; the argument from autism is of no help; and it offers no account of the motivation for pretence behaviour. All of these difficulties can be avoided if we drop the second part of Leslie's theory and stick with the first part. And that part, it will be recalled, is fully compatible with the theory we developed in Section 2.4.

2.5.3. Perner's account

Josef Perner, another leading developmental psychologist, has offered an account of pretence that is, in certain respects, rather similar to Leslie's. Perner's account, like Leslie's, is motivated by the fact that in order to avoid confusion, pretend representations need to be 'quarantined' from representations of reality. However, in contrast with Leslie, Perner maintains that this problem can be solved without claiming that young children have any understanding of mental states. Rather, Perner suggests, 'Pretend representations are not representations of the world as it is but of the world as it might be' (1991: 59). Perner elaborates this suggestion by exploiting an analogy with temporal contexts. He writes:

The same need for quarantining exists when information about different times is to be stored. It won't do to mix 'I am 2 years old' with 'I am 3 years old.' To avoid confusion about one's age, one must mark one of these representations as 'past' or the other as 'future.' Analogously, my suggestion for pretense is to mark off the pretend scenario as 'nonreal' or 'hypothetical.' So, although the need for quarantine is clear, it is not clear why quarantining requires metarepresentation. The need for quarantine is served adequately by multiple models representing different situations. (1991, 60–1; see also 1991: 54–6; 1993: 117–18)

Though Perner's proposal can be interpreted in a variety of ways, we think the best interpretation is that, on Perner's view, pretence representations are distinguished from beliefs in two ways: (1) they have different functional roles, and (2) they have systematically different meanings or contents. We are encouraged in this reading of Perner by evidence of two quite different sorts. The first is a passage in Perner (1991) in which he maintains that the markers that quarantine pretence from belief 'modify whether the model represents a *real* or a *hypothetical* situation' and that they also 'direct "internal" use [i.e. functional role] and thereby allow differentiation between *real* and *hypothetical*' (1991: 35). The second is that Perner himself has indicated that this is the proper interpretation of his view. 'I am . . . happy to be put in with Alan Leslie as claiming that the MRCs [the "metarepresentational comments" "real" and "hypothetical"] make both a difference in function and content. . . . My quarrel with [Leslie] concerned only the kind of context marker one uses. I opted for a weaker marker that differentiates only real from hypothetical. . . . Leslie had opted for the stronger marker "pretend".'[17]

[17] Josef Perner (personal communication). We are grateful to Perner for pointing out the passage in Perner 1991 and for allowing us to quote from his written comments on an earlier draft of this chapter.

The problem we have with this view is that it is not at all clear what the difference in content is supposed to be between belief representations and pretence representations. In Perner (1991), it seems that the difference in content is that they 'represent two different situations: the real situation and a hypothetical situation' (p. 54). However, since it is possible both to pretend and to believe that the cup is empty, it is difficult to see how these represent different situations. On the contrary, there seems to be no reason to think that a pretend representation cannot have exactly the same content as a belief, in much the same way that a desire can have exactly the same content as a belief. Using a marker to indicate that pretence representations have different functional roles from beliefs is, as we noted earlier, the equivalent of positing a separate box for pretence representations, and that suffices to quarantine pretences from beliefs. Positing an additional difference at the level of content does no additional work. As a result, pending a further explication of the difference in content between pretence representations and belief representations, we see no reason to adopt Perner's view that there is a systematic difference in the contents of the representations underlying pretence and belief.

2.6. Conclusion

Despite the length of this chapter, we claim only to have provided a bare sketch of a theory of pretence. Nonetheless, our account is considerably more explicit than the other accounts in the literature. Before moving on, we would like to recapitulate the main features of our theory. At the core of our theory is the idea that pretence representations are contained in a separate workspace, a Possible World Box which is part of the basic architecture of the human mind. The evolutionary function of the PWB, we have suggested, is to enable hypothetical reasoning. Pretence representations, on our theory, are not distinguished from beliefs in terms of the content of the representations. Here we differ sharply from both Leslie and Perner. In pretence episodes the set of representations being built up in the PWB is inferentially elaborated and updated by the same inference and UpDating mechanisms that operate over real beliefs. The importance of the UpDating mechanism in avoiding inferential chaos is another central theme in our theory which sets it apart from other accounts in the literature. In addition to inferential elaboration, pretenders also elaborate the pretence in non-inferential ways, exploiting what we have called the Script Elaborator. One of the virtues of the architectural explicitness of our theory is that it makes clear the need for a Script Elaborator (a point on which other theorists have said relatively little) and it underscores how little we know about how this component of the mind works. All of this mental architecture is, we think, essential to both imagination and pretence, but it does not explain why pretenders *do* anything—why they actually enact the pretend scenarios. That is a problem about which a number of leading theorists, including Leslie and Perner, have said very little. On our theory, the motivation for pretend play derives from a real desire to act in a way that fits the description being constructed in the PWB. This, we have argued, is a much more satisfactory account than the proposal, hinted at by Gordon and Barker and other simulation theorists, that pretence behaviour is motivated by 'pretend desires'. Finally, while our account does not claim that pretence requires mindreading or theory of mind capacities—another important disagreement with Leslie—the account does leave open the possibility that pretence and mindreading capacities use some of the same mechanisms—the PWB is an obvious candidate—and thus that breakdowns would be correlated.

While there are obviously many points on which we disagree with other theorists and a number of hitherto neglected issues that our account addresses, it is also the case that our theory is a highly eclectic one which borrows many ideas from other theorists. Our central goal in this chapter has been to show how ideas taken from competing and incompatible theories, along with some new ideas of our own, can be woven together into a theory of pretence which is more explicit, more comprehensive, and better able to explain the facts than any other available theory. We would, of course, be delighted if other theorists who began from very different starting points were to agree that the eclectic synthesis we have proposed is (near enough) the account toward which they too have been heading.

3

Pieces of Mind:
A Theory of Third-Person Mindreading

In this chapter we will present our account of the mechanisms underlying third-person mindreading—the attribution of mental states to others. In the first section, we will tell an extremely speculative story about the evolutionary origins of the capacity for third-person mindreading. In the second section, we will set out some basic facts about mindreading and some central empirical findings that we think need to be accommodated by any adequate theory. In the third section, we give a detailed rendering of our theory of the mental mechanisms underlying mindreading, and we explain how our theory is supposed to account for the facts set out in Section 3.2. In the fourth section, following the pattern we adopted in the previous chapter, we will consider other theories of mindreading, and we will argue that each of them fails to explain some of the important facts. Now, then, on to telling our story.

3.1. The Evolutionary Origins of Mindreading: A Just So Story

We are about to tell you a Just So Story about the evolution of the cognitive mechanisms that enable us to read other people's minds. Why tell a Just So Story? There are several reasons. First, it is a very useful expository device. Sketching how the mechanisms underlying adult mindreading might have been gradually assembled by marshalling pre-existing mechanisms and adding new ones enables us to make a first pass at explaining what the various mechanisms we are positing do and how they work together. Those who think that evolutionary Just So Stories are utterly useless as attempts to understand the actual origins of the trait or mechanism in question can view our story as *only* an expository device which, like Wittgenstein's ladder, can be kicked away after we have climbed it. But we are inclined to think that Just So Stories like ours are theoretically useful as well. If there is nothing in the story that conflicts with the known biological and psychological facts or with what little is known about the actual origins of the mechanisms in question, then the story provides an account of how the mechanisms we posit might *possibly* have evolved. It provides what some have called a 'how possible' explanation (e.g. Brandon 1990). And why would one want such a 'how possible' explanation? Well, at the very least it forestalls the objection that the sorts of mechanisms we are positing to explain mindreading make no biological sense since they could not possibly have been produced by natural selection. Finally, while we are certainly not prepared to claim that we have got all the historical details right and that the mechanisms subserving mindreading really did emerge in just the way that we set out in our story, we think that the general outlines of the story we have to tell are not merely *possible* but that they are at least to some degree *plausible*—that there is some reasonable albeit modest probability that important parts of the story we tell are *true*.

Our Just So Story begins in The Beginning, of course. Once upon a time, a long, long time ago, the distant ancestors of modern humans had nothing much like the contemporary capacity to read minds. What they did have, however, were all the components of the mind that are sketched in our discussion of the basic architecture assumption in Chapter 1; they also, of course, had an UpDater, of the sort explained in Section 2.4.1. So the minds of these distant ancestors had beliefs, desires, an inference mechanism, a practical reasoning mechanism, a Planner, and all the other bits and pieces sketched in Figure 3.1, though they had no inkling *that* they had minds like this nor did they have any

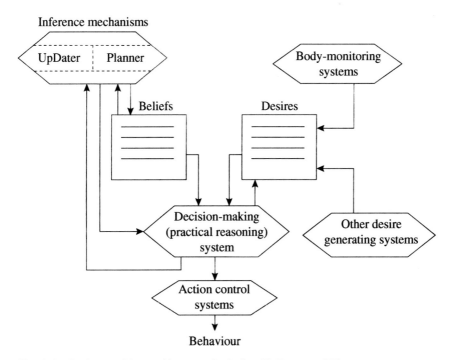

Fig. 3.1   Basic cognitive architecture, including UpDater and Planner

idea that their conspecifics or other organisms did. But then two quite unrela-
ted things happened. We have no serious idea about which happened first,
though if we had to make a guess, we would say that they happened in the
order that we will describe them.

3.1.1. The emergence of the Goal and Strategy strategy

Back in The Beginning, our very non-human forebears surely must have had
some capacity to anticipate or predict the behaviour of other organisms—both
conspecifics and members of other species. For a capacity to anticipate what
other organisms were likely to do would have been a great boon to creatures
with intermittent desires to eat and mate and enduring desires to avoid being
eaten. But back in The Beginning, we are supposing, this capacity was relatively crude and clunky. Perhaps it did no more than link stereotypical cues
with behaviour patterns: if a predator has his gaze fixed on me and is running
toward me, then probably he is going to attack. If a rival bares his teeth at me,
he is more likely to fight. Note, however, that this capacity to anticipate
behaviour patterns is not the same as the capacity to recognize goals. A crea-
ture might be able to exploit correlations between cues and subsequent behaviours without appealing to or even understanding the notion of goal.

Then one glorious day (well, it probably took longer than a day) a new idea
emerged—but it was more than an idea, really. It was a *theory*. The central
theoretical notion in the theory was the concept of a *goal*. Goals are things
that organisms have (or states that they are in—the difference here was no
doubt too subtle for our ancestors to appreciate). Each goal is linked to an
action or a state of affairs—actions like catching and killing that gazelle, for
example, and states of affairs like being out of the rain—which, if it occurred,
would satisfy the goal. Early on in the evolutionary process, we suspect, there
were only a small number of goals that could be attributed to other organisms;
the idea that many different states of affairs could be goals emerged only
gradually. Initially goals were attributed on the basis of single cues, but gradually creatures came to recognize that goals are indicated by multiple cues.
When an organism has a goal, the theory maintains, it will exhibit one of a
number of very different ('goal directed') patterns of behaviour.[1] Which patterns? Well, those that would be effective at bringing about the goal. So how
should you go about predicting what an organism (the target) will do if he has
the goal to do A? The answer, according to this theory, is that you should
figure out (as best you can) the best way for the target to do A, and then

---

[1] This variability is one of the main advances of goal-based prediction over the behaviour
prediction strategy that was available in The Beginning. That earlier strategy simply matched
cues with specific behaviour patterns.

Box 3.1

(i) Cues → behaviour pattern
(ii) Cue → goal → how to achieve goal in circumstances → behaviour
(iii) Multi-Cue → goal → how to achieve goal in circumstances → behaviour

Three ways to predict behaviour. In (i) the predictor expects stereotypical cues to be followed by specific patterns of behaviour. In (ii) the predictor attributes a goal on the basis of a single cue, tries to figures out what behaviour would best achieve that goal, and then predicts that the target will engage in that behaviour. In (iii) the predictor uses multiple cues to attribute a goal, and then proceeds as in (ii).

predict that that is what he'll do (see Box 3.1). Of course, it is not likely that these creatures did a very good job at figuring out the best way for the target to achieve a goal. But no matter. This strategy would still provide a powerful means of predicting the behaviour of conspecifics and of many other creatures as well. All of this is vastly over-intellectualized, however. What is really needed at this stage are just three things:

1. A strategy or set of strategies for attributing goals to other organisms.
2. The capacity to try to figure out the best way to achieve the goal in the target's situation.
3. The inclination to believe that that is what the target will do.

We will call this the *Goal and Strategy strategy* for predicting behaviour since it proceeds by attributing goals and trying to determine the best strategy for achieving them.

3.1.2. The evolution of the Possible World Box

What would happen if I tried to cross the river after a heavy rain? What would happen if my mate gave some of those berries to the children? What would happen if this tree fell down? Or if it rains hard tonight? Important questions, these. Organisms that could answer them accurately would be likely to have more descendants than organisms that couldn't. But how can such questions be answered? Well, as we noted in our discussion of pretence, one very promising strategy is to have a special workspace, a Possible World Box, in which one can work out the answer. To figure out what would happen if one were to do A, one adds a representation with the content, *I do A* to the PWB and 'clamps' it. Whatever else happens, that representation stays until the PWB is cleared and set to work on some other chore. Next, all the representations in the Belief Box are added to the PWB and the collection is UpDated just as it would be if *I do A* had been added to the Belief Box. (Well, not *just* as it would be. The one thing that can't happen is that *I do A* is removed. It's clamped.) The resulting world description that is elaborated in the PWB is the one that I use when I want to know what would happen if I did A.

So that, on our account, is how hypothetical reasoning works. But in The Beginning, there was no PWB. Its emergence (and the emergence of its links to other mechanisms like the Inference Mechanism and the UpDater) is the second Big Event in our story. After that Big Event, the minds of our fore-bears were no longer quite so sparse and Humean. Instead, they looked like Figure 2.2 (Q. 36).

Could our ancestors pretend, even way back then? Probably not. Pretence requires the capacity to insert and clamp representations in the PWB more or less at will; it also requires the desire to act in the way that some character or object described in the PWB does. All this, we think, came much later. Pretence might well be a luxury that was made possible by the evolution of a mechanism for hypothetical reasoning.

3.1.3. Getting it together: the emergence of the Goal-PWB strategy

It is a platitude that Mother Nature is a tinkerer, and one of her favourite tricks is to co-opt old mechanisms for new purposes. The literature in evolutionary biology is rife with examples in which a mechanism that was selected for one function ends up being used for another. For instance, Gould and Vrba report that the wings of the black heron serve two important functions. The heron uses its wings in flight, but it also uses them as a fishing aid. It fishes in shallow water, and it uses its wings to shade the water; this facilitates the bird's ability to see the fish (Gould and Vrba 1982: 8–9). The black heron inherited its wings from its ancestors, for whom the evolutionary function of the wings was flying. However, in the black heron, the wings have taken on an additional role as fishing aids. Clearly, since this can enhance the bird's feeding, it might now be an important selective feature. Gould and Vrba introduce the notion of exaptation, which captures such cases. Exaptations are properties or 'characters' that are 'evolved for other usages . . . and later "coopted" for their current role' (Gould and Vrba 1982: 6). Or, as Vrba puts it, 'An exaptation is a character that is currently useful (and subject to selection) in a particular role, but that was not shaped by step-by-step selection for that role' (Vrba 1989: 130). Gould and Vrba argue that exaptations form an extremely important category in evolutionary biology. We think that the notion of exaptation proves useful in thinking about the evolution of psychological mechanisms as well.

At the current point in our story about the evolution of mindreading, what Mother Nature has to work with are the mechanisms underlying the Goal and Strategy strategy and a PWB in which to elaborate descriptions of worlds that are different from the world described in the agent's Belief Box. Now, the Goal and Strategy strategy is very useful, of course. But if one has a PWB around, then with a bit of tinkering it can be improved on. For sometimes the predictor can see things that the target cannot. And with the knowledge that this affords, the predictor can figure out a way of achieving the target's goal that is better than any the target can figure out. If there is a hungry lion dead ahead of you and your goal is not to be eaten, you might think that the best strategy would be to run down the path to your right. But if there is another hungry lion along that path that I can see and you can't, I'm likely to come up with a better way of achieving your goal than you would. That's not such a good thing, however, if what I'm trying to do is predict your behaviour. To predict effectively, I need to determine what the best strategy would be in the world as you believe it to be, not in the world as I believe it to be. How am I to do that? Well, if I have a PWB (and I do) and if I can come up with a few strategies for adding clamped representations to the PWB which reflect what you would believe about the world, given your perceptual situation, then I could use the apparatus for hypothetical reasoning which is already in place to construct a description of the world that is closer to the description in your Belief Box. And if I can use that PWB description in figuring out the best strategy for accomplishing your goals, then my prediction of your behaviour will be more accurate.

So the third stage in our Just So Story is the hypothesis that this is what happens. The PWB, initially used just for hypothetical reasoning, becomes an exaptation; it gets recruited as a mechanism for behaviour prediction. We predict the behaviour of others by (1) using available strategies to figure out their goals and (2) figuring out the best way to accomplish these goals using the world description in the PWB—a description that is different from the one in our Belief Box. We will call this the *Goal-PWB strategy* for predicting behaviour.

3.1.4. Fine tuning: getting the PWB to be a better model of the target's Belief Box

Once the Goal-PWB strategy has emerged, all the basic architecture is in place. To get from there to modern mindreading all that is required is to make the system *smarter* by coming up with better ways to attribute goals and putting representations into the PWB that more accurately reflect the target's beliefs. How can the PWB model of the target be improved? We think that there are several different ways. We will group them into two classes, one for putting new representations into the PWB and one for taking representations out.

New strategies for adding representations to the PWB

As we have told the story so far, the predictor only uses information about the target's perceptual situation (along with inference and UpDating) to build up his PWB model of the target's beliefs. But there are lots of other ways to determine the target's 'discrepant' beliefs, that is beliefs which differ from one's own beliefs. Sometimes I can figure out what you believe from what you're doing, if I know your goals. If your goal is to find your keys, and you are ransacking your closet, you probably believe that's where your keys are. Often I can determine your beliefs from what you say or from what other people say about you.[2] Gradually, our Just So Story maintains, our ancestors acquired increasingly sophisticated strategies for figuring out the target's discrepant beliefs and adding to the PWB clamped representations with the same content as the target's discrepant beliefs; when such representations are added to the PWB, the Goal-PWB strategy produces predictions of the behaviour of others that are more sensitive to the differences between oneself and others. Thus gradually the PWB came to be a better and better model of the target's actual beliefs. And, of course, Mother Nature thought this was a Good Thing, since the closer the match between the target's Belief Box and the predictor's PWB, the better the predictions.

New strategies for keeping one's own beliefs out of the PWB

As we have told the story so far, the mindreading system simply dumps all of the predictor's beliefs into the PWB, and relies on the UpDater to remove those that are incompatible with the clamped representations already there. This process of attributing one's own beliefs to the target is what we call *default belief attribution*. But one quite sophisticated way to make mindreading smarter is to realize that not all of our own beliefs can be simply dumped into the PWB in this way. Default attribution has its limits. In predicting the behaviour of almost anyone, I am on safe ground in supposing that he believes that water quenches thirst, that fire burns, and that night follows day. But if I am trying to predict the behaviour of a tribesman from a tropical rain forest, I had best not default attribute my belief that water freezes when it is very cold. If my target is a Communist, then I'd best not default attribute my beliefs about free markets. And if my target is the new neighbour down the street, it is best to keep my religious beliefs out of the PWB when trying to

---

[2] Some of the basic mechanisms of mindreading (e.g. some mechanisms for detecting goals) are probably present in some non-linguistic creatures. However, the emergence of language was no doubt a great boon to the evolution of mindreading. Language provides a huge resource for discovering the mental states of others (cf. Pinker 1994 and Baron-Cohen 1995). Language also provides a resource for providing misleading information about the mind. As a result, it might be an extremely powerful engine for honing mindreading skills.

predict his behaviour. All of these restrictions on default attribution are, in our story, quite late additions to the process, and the exact pattern of default attribution restrictions almost certainly varies from culture to culture and from person to person.

3.1.5. Some further issues

Talking about other people's beliefs

The Just So Story that we have told has focused on the prediction of behaviour. And that is no accident. For as far as Mother Nature is concerned, that is how mindreading first earned its keep. But obviously we modern humans do more than just predict behaviour. We also talk about other people's goals, desires, and beliefs. Indeed, this seems to be one of our favourite topics of conversation. When did this start? And how is it possible? To the first of these questions we have a ready answer: We haven't a clue. (All Just So stories should include a bit of mystery.) On the second question we have a bit more to say. To talk about mental states, our forebears had to have *concepts* for mental states and *terms* to express them. Though most of the processes of behaviour prediction that we have described require little or no conscious access, to talk about mental states mindreaders must have beliefs about mental states which are verbally expressible.[3]

What is the relation between goals and desires?

As we have just noted, one salient feature of mindreading is that people talk about goals, desires, and beliefs. And we have previously discussed mechanisms for attributing goals and beliefs. However, so far we haven't said anything about *desires*. There is no consensus in the literature on the distinction between goals and desires, so we propose to adopt explicitly a policy on usage. Goals, on our approach, are just a proper subset of desires. Roughly, goals are desires for which one can formulate plans that one can act on now or soon. So, it is my goal, now, to get a drink of water. Desires that are *not* goals include desires for things that one cannot act on soon—for example, the desire to live somewhere with a more congenial climate after retirement—and for things one cannot do anything about at all—like the desire that there be Divine Justice in the universe. *Preferences*, as we will use the notion, are dispositions to have desires of varying strengths. If I prefer chocolate ice cream to vanilla then, other things being equal, when given a choice my desire to eat

---

[3] For more detail on all this, see Section 3.3.

chocolate will be stronger than my desire to eat vanilla.[4] Obviously the ability to attribute desires and preferences will significantly augment a mindreader's ability to predict and explain behaviour. For once one has the ability to attribute desires and preferences, one is better equipped to predict what a person will do when presented with novel situations.

When do people have the concepts of belief, desire, mind, etc.?

On our account a concept, which we have been calling *goal*, was used in Belief Box representations quite early in the evolution of mindreading. Somewhat later, concepts that we have been calling *desire* and *belief* appear in Belief Box representations. But can these really, early on, be taken to be the concepts of *goal*, *desire* and *belief*, properly so called? When our distant ancestors first had the capacities to deploy the Goal and Strategy strategy, did they really have the concept of *goal*?

Our answer here is a familiar one: Yes, all these critters had something like the modern concept. But since important components that are part of the modern process of mindreading were not yet in place, their concepts and ours had rather different 'causal powers' or 'conceptual roles'. So at what point do their concepts count as really being the concept of *goal*, *desire*, *belief*, etc.? On our view, there is no principled way of answering this question, and it is not a question we propose to take seriously.[5]

In this section, we have been rather freewheeling in our speculations about the origin of the mechanisms underlying mindreading. In Section 3.3 we will offer a much more detailed account of those mechanisms and will appeal to the growing body of empirical evidence to support our theory. Before getting to that, however, we will devote the next section to assembling a catalogue of facts about mindreading that we think any adequate theory of mindreading must explain.

3.2. Some Features of Mindreading

The empirical and theoretical literature on mindreading that has developed over the last two decades is enormous. However, we don't think that any of the accounts of third-person mindreading to be found in the literature provide an explanation of what we take to be the basic facts about the phenomenon. In this section we will set out some uncontroversial observations about

---

[4] Of course, there are much finer distinctions to draw between different kinds of desires and preferences (see e.g. Marks 1986; Schueler 1995). But the rough distinction we deploy should be adequate for our purposes.

[5] For arguments in support of this stance, see Stich 1983: chs. 4 and 5.

mindreading and assemble a list of central empirical findings. These will constitute a checklist that we will use in evaluating both our own theory and competing accounts.

3.2.1. Mindreading in adults

It is a commonplace by now that one of the remarkable features of the 'folk psychological' capacity to read minds is that it is so successful. Fodor, for instance, likes to emphasize that folk psychology is vastly better at predicting behaviour than any scientific alternative (1987). Dennett, although his views differ in many ways from Fodor's, is similarly enthusiastic about the success of folk psychology:

How good is folk psychology?...If we concentrate on its strengths we find first that there are large areas in which it is extraordinarily reliable in its predictive power. Every time we venture out on a highway, for example, we stake our lives on the reliability of our general expectations about the perceptual beliefs, normal desires, and decision proclivities of the other motorists. Second, we find that it is a theory of great generative power and efficiency. For instance, watching a film with a highly original and unstereotypical plot, we see the hero smile at the villain and we all swiftly and effortlessly arrive at the same complex theoretical diagnosis: 'Aha!' we conclude (but perhaps not consciously), 'he wants her to think he doesn't know she intends to defraud his brother'. (Dennett 1987: 49)

We think Fodor and Dennett are quite right to remark on the success of folk psychology, but in order to characterize the cognitive processes underlying mindreading, we need a sharper picture of where folk psychology is successful and where it isn't.

Successes

There are two familiar yet remarkable mindreading capacities that we want to call attention to. First, people are very good at attributing beliefs to others, even in cases where they have no apparent evidence. For example, on the first day of class we are confident that our new students believe that Prince Charles has a belly button. But it is hard to imagine what evidence we could have for this since we have never asked them (or anyone else!) whether they believed that the Prince has a belly button. Moreover, there are indefinitely many other beliefs that we readily attribute to people without any evidence. Our ability to do this is one of the more striking features of mindreading. The second capacity that merits special mention is that adults are quite good at predicting the inferences of targets, even their obviously *non-demonstrative* inferences. Suppose, for example, that Fred comes to believe that the President of the

United States has resigned, after hearing a brief report on the radio. Who does Fred think will become President? We quickly generate the prediction that Fred will conclude that the Vice-President will become President. However, we know perfectly well, and so, we presume, does Fred, that there are lots of ways in which this inference could be mistaken. The Vice-President could be assassinated; the Vice-President might resign before being sworn in as President; a scandal might lead to the removal of the Vice-President; there might be a coup. It is easy to generate stories on which the Vice-President would not become the new President. Yet we predict Fred's non-demonstrative inference without hesitation. And in most cases like this, our predictions are correct. An adequate theory of mindreading needs to accommodate these facts.

Failures

To build a plausible theory about the cognitive mechanisms underlying third-person mindreading, it is equally vital to accommodate the rather striking *failures* of mindreading. Experimental studies have found that mindreading goes wrong in quite a number of ways, and we will discuss some of those results later in this chapter. But there are two domains in which the failures of the mindreading system are particularly noteworthy: we are very bad at predicting perceptual illusions and we are also quite bad at predicting a class of counter-intuitive decisions that have loomed large in social psychology.

As we will see later, people are actually quite good at predicting other peoples' perceptual states and perceptual judgements under a range of conditions (see Section 3.3.3). For example people (even very little people) are quite capable of determining whether a person can see an object that is positioned behind or next to an occluder. Sometimes, however, the perceptual system produces percepts and judgements that are quite surprising, as indicated by the vast and varied catalogue of perceptual illusions (see e.g. Gregory 1997). And in these cases we often do a very poor job of predicting both other people's perceptual judgements and our own. To take one example from the recent literature on visual cognition, consider Figure 3.2. The two pictures displayed are identical except for the fact that in the lower picture the large plane engine is missing. Suppose you were shown one of these pictures on a computer monitor followed by a very brief delay (e.g. 100 milliseconds), then the other picture, then a brief delay, then the first picture, and so on. How long do you think it would take to detect the difference between the two pictures? Recent research on 'change blindness' indicates that it takes very long indeed (for reviews see Simons and Levin 1997; Simons 2000). In 'flicker' experiments with alternating pictures like those in Figure 3.2, the average length of time it takes for subjects to notice the change is typically over 5 seconds, and some subjects take considerably longer (e.g. Resnick et al. 1997). The

Fig 3.2

phenomenology of subjects in these experiments is also noteworthy. Once they see the difference between the pictures, they are astounded that they didn't notice it right away. If this is the first you have heard about the change blindness experiments, we expect you will find these results surprising.[6] And that, of course, is our point. The difficulty of the task is not something that our mindreading capacity enables us to predict. Indeed, part of what makes perceptual illusions so fascinating and so much fun is that the illusions are often utterly unexpected.

Like the perceptual system, the decision-making system sometimes does things that are completely surprising to common sense. The continuing saga of these surprises comes largely from work in social psychology (for reviews, see Nisbett and Ross 1980; Kahneman et al. 1982; Ross and Nisbett 1991). As with perception, there are many cases in which we are quite good at predicting what decisions people will make. For example, normal adults are quite good at predicting a target's decision when they know that the target has just found out that his most pressing desire can be easily and quickly satisfied by performing some common action. However, there is a wide range of conditions in which people decide to do things that seem quite bizarre and often deeply disturbing. To take one classic example, Milgram (1963) had a 'teacher' subject flip switches that were supposed to deliver shocks to another subject, the 'learner' (actually an accomplice). For each mistake the learner made, the teacher was instructed to deliver progressively stronger shocks including one labelled 'Danger: Severe Shock' and culminating in a switch labelled '450-volt, XXX'. If the teacher subject expressed reservations to the experimental assistant, he was calmly told to continue the experiment. The result of the experiment was astonishing. Several different variations were carried out, and in many of these experiments, a clear majority of the subjects gave all the shocks. Just as in the case of perceptual illusions, people often find these results hard to believe. Indeed, the Milgram findings are so counter-intuitive that in a verbal re-enactment of the experiment, people still did not predict the results. Nisbett and Ross give the following description of Bierbrauer's (1973) re-enactment:

In Bierbrauer's study, observers were exposed to a verbatim reenactment of one subject's obedience to the point of delivering the maximum shock to the supposed victim, and then were asked to predict how other subjects would behave. Bierbrauer's observers consistently and dramatically underestimated the degree to which subjects generally would yield to the situational forces that they had viewed at first hand. The

---

[6] At the time this volume went to press, impressive demonstrations of change blindness were available on the web at http://www.usd.edu/psyc301/ChangeBlindness.htm and http://nivea.psycho.univ-paris5.fr/Mudsplash/Nature_Supp_Inf/Movies/Movie_List.html. Though URLs change frequently, additional demonstrations can be located easily by doing a search for 'change blindness demonstration' on any standard search engine.

observers did so, moreover, even in a set of conditions in which *they themselves* played the role of a subject in a vivid reenactment of Milgram's experiment. (Nisbett and Ross 1980: 121)

An adequate account of the mental processes underlying mindreading needs to accommodate the fact that in fairly large areas of perception and decision making, mindreading is often strikingly unsuccessful.

3.2.2. Mindreading: evidence from developmental psychology and psychopathology

The most extensive evidence on mindreading has been collected, over the last two decades, by researchers in developmental psychology and psychopathology. Much of this research is focused on characterizing the mechanisms underlying the performance of children and individuals with autism in various experiments that probe their mindreading abilities. Though it would take an entire book to review all the significant findings in this area, we think that there are some core results that deserve a prominent place on the checklist we'll use for evaluating competing theories. In this section we will offer a brief survey of these central findings.

After 3: A leap in mindreading ability in normal children, but not in children with autism

Between ages 3 and 5, children gain an increasing facility in tasks that require predicting the behaviour of others whose beliefs are different from their own. The most famous results come from work on the false belief task, first used by Wimmer and Perner (1983). As we noted in Chapter 2, in their version of the experiment, children watched a puppet show in which the puppet protagonist, Maxi, puts a piece of chocolate in a box and then goes out to play. While Maxi is out, his puppet mother moves the chocolate to the cupboard. When Maxi returns, the children are asked where Maxi will look for the chocolate. Numerous studies have now found that 3-year-old children typically fail tasks like this (predicting that Maxi will look in the cupboard), while 4-year-olds typically pass them (e.g. Baron-Cohen et al. 1985; Perner et al. 1987; Wellman et al. 2001).

In a series of studies published in 1985, Baron-Cohen, Leslie, and Frith found that in the false belief task most autistic children responded like 3-year-olds. The autistic subjects in Baron-Cohen et al.'s study, who had a mean chronological age of about 12 and mean verbal and non-verbal mental ages of $9:3$ ($= 9$ years, 3 months) and $5:5$ respectively, failed the false belief task (Baron-Cohen et al. 1985). By contrast, a control group of Down's syndrome subjects matched for mental age performed well on the false belief task. Since this landmark paper, the study of children with autism has played a central role in work on mind-reading. As with the young child's failure on the false belief task, Baron-Cohen et al.'s finding has been replicated many times and is also found using different versions of the task (e.g. Baron-Cohen et al. 1986; Perner et al. 1989). One widely accepted interpretation of these data is that autistic individuals have a deficit in their mindreading ability, more specifically a deficit that impairs their capacity to attribute false beliefs (Leslie and Thaiss 1992; Baron-Cohen 1995).

Although these findings on the false belief task are by far the best-known results on mindreading, it is, as many developmentalists point out (e.g. Gopnik and Wellman 1994; Bloom and German 2000), a mistake to put too much emphasis on the standard false belief task. For one thing, there are several ways to elicit better performance from young children on false belief tasks.[7] And there are a number of other belief tasks that are solved by children much earlier than they can pass the standard false belief task. For instance, at around the age of 3, children pass the 'discrepant belief' task, in which the child is shown that there are bananas in two locations (the cupboard and the refrigerator) and told that the target thinks that there are bananas in only one location (the cupboard); 3-year-old children correctly predict that the target will look for the bananas in the cupboard (Wellman and Bartsch 1988: 258). Children also show an understanding of ignorance earlier than they can pass the standard false belief task (Hogrefe et al. 1986).

Thus, the data present an exceedingly complicated picture of the young child's developing fluency with the attribution of belief. But rather than focus on the minutiae of development, we want to emphasize some more general claims that are supported by a broad range of findings. What the data suggest is that before the age of 3, children display at best a limited understanding of belief, and after the age of 3, normal children gradually come to have a more and more sophisticated understanding of belief. Some of the most telling evidence here comes from the analysis of children's spontaneous speech. Bartsch and Wellman analysed a large body of children's spontaneous speech, and found that around the age of 3 children started talking about beliefs. Indeed, according to Bartsch and Wellman, the children they studied even attributed *false* beliefs typically shortly after the third birthday. By contrast, before the age of 3, the children basically did not talk about beliefs at all (Bartsch and Wellman 1995). What both the protocol data and the experimental data indicate is that

---

[7] For example, in a slight modification on the standard false belief task, Siegal and Beattie (1991) found that 3-year-olds did much better if they were asked, 'Where will Sally look *first* for her marble?'. Three-year-olds also have a much easier time using false beliefs to *explain* behaviour rather than predict it (Bartsch and Wellman 1989). This and other work suggests that it is misleading to characterize 3-year-olds as lacking the conceptual resources to attribute false beliefs (see also Clements and Perner 1994; Surian and Leslie 1999).

between the ages of 3 and 5, children develop better and better ways of detecting beliefs and using belief attributions to predict behaviour. In these years there is a profound leap in the mindreading abilities of normal children. An adequate theory of mindreading needs to provide some account of the ability that older children have that younger children and children with autism lack.

Desire without belief

One of the most striking and widely discussed findings in the literature over the last decade is that children seem to exhibit an understanding of desire and emotion much earlier than they exhibit an understanding of belief (e.g. Wellman 1990; Gopnik and Wellman 1994; Bartsch and Wellman 1995; Harris 1996). The empirical work indicates that before the age of 3, children attribute desires, predict emotional responses on the basis of desire attributions, and predict and explain behaviour in terms of desire. Empirical work also shows that young children attribute emotions on the basis of facial expressions (e.g. Gross and Ballif 1991). The early understanding of desire and emotion is further supported by the protocol data assembled and analysed by Bartsch and Wellman (1995) and Wellman and colleagues (1995). Wellman et al. report that children under 3 frequently attributed a variety of emotions to others and often cited the causes of emotions. Bartsch and Wellman found that all the children in the sample were making genuine reference to desire by the age of $2\frac{1}{2}$. By contrast, the children's genuine references to belief typically didn't occur until around age 3. In the sample Bartsch and Wellman studied, the average lag between genuine reference to desire and genuine reference to belief was 7 months. This probably underestimates the lag, since, as Bartsch and Wellman note, many of the children were already talking about desires in their first transcripts (1995: 96). Indeed, several of the children made genuine references to desire before their second birthday.

Interestingly, despite their difficulties with mindreading, there is no compelling evidence that autistic children have deep deficiencies in their understanding of desire. Tan and Harris (1991) found that autistic children seemed able to report on unsatisfied desires. In one of their experiments, they gave children a choice of one of three pieces of candy. The chosen candy was set aside, and the child was told that he would get it at the end of the session. Later, the child was given a different piece of candy. Autistic children were just as likely as normal and mentally handicapped children to correct the experimenter, by saying, for example, 'That's not the one I wanted' (Tan and Harris 1991: 170).[8] In addition, Baron-Cohen found that autistic children understand that people

---

[8] These studies were done on autistic children with a mean verbal mental age (VMA) of 6:3. It will be important to see whether autistic children with lower VMA will also pass such tasks.

are happy when their desires are fulfilled and sad when their desires are not ful-filled (Baron-Cohen 1991*b*). Baron-Cohen also found that people with autism did as well as the mentally handicapped subjects at recalling their own past desires that had recently changed (Baron-Cohen 1991*a*). Finally, Tager-Flusberg's study of language use in autistic children shows that they use the term 'want' appropriately and with some frequency (Tager-Flusberg 1993).[9] And, more anecdotally, Baron-Cohen notes that autistic children 'say things like "She wants the ice cream"...identifying desires' (Baron-Cohen 1995: 63).

Predicting behaviour without attributing belief

Although children under the age of 3 have difficulty with belief attribution, they engage in a good deal of behaviour prediction. Wellman found that 2-year-old children are quite capable of predicting behaviour on the basis of desire attributions. For instance, in one experiment, 2-year-olds were told that Sam (represented by a cardboard cutout) wants to find his rabbit and that the rab-bit might be hiding in one of two locations. Then Sam walks toward one loca-tion where he finds either the rabbit, a dog, or nothing. The children were asked, 'Will he look in the [other hiding location] or will he go to school?' (Wellman 1990: 214.) Most of the children who saw Sam find nothing in the first location predicted that Sam would look in the other location, and most of the children who saw Sam find the rabbit in the first location said that Sam would go to school (Wellman 1990: 222). An adequate theory of mindreading must explain how behaviour prediction can occur without relying on belief attribution, since children under the age of 3 are largely incapable of belief attribution.

The pretence-mindreading link in autism

Autistic children typically do not exhibit the profound leap in mindreading abilities found in normal children after the age of 3. As we have seen, aut-istic children have considerable difficulty with false belief tasks. Furthermore, in her studies of spontaneous speech in autistic children, Tager-Flusberg found that, in marked contrast to Down's syndrome children, autistic children basically did not talk about belief at all (Tager-Flusberg 1993: 150). It is a

---

[9] Tager-Flusberg's spontaneous language-use data are particularly impressive, since they provide a kind of internal control for verbal mental age. Tager-Flusberg uses mean length of utterance (MLU) to control for language ability. (MLU is a common measure of language level that is calculated as a function of the average number of morphemes produced per utterance; see, e.g. Brown 1973). She then compares the frequency of desire attributions in autistic chil-dren with Down's syndrome children who are at the same MLU level. What she finds is fairly striking. Autistic children and Down's children exhibit similar patterns at MLU stages I, II, III, and IV, but at MLU stage V, autistic children (but not children with Down's syndrome) show a dramatic increase in reference to desires (Tager-Flusberg 1993: 150).

striking fact about autism that in addition to their difficulties with mindreading, the capacity for pretend play also seems to be compromised in autistic children (Wing and Gould 1979). Many of the symptoms of autism, such as social difficulties, can plausibly be explained in terms of their mindreading difficulties, but an adequate theory of mindreading should also explain the link between the deficits in pretence and mindreading found in autism.

3.2.3. A checklist of facts that theories of mindreading should explain

In this section we have set out some uncontroversial observations about mindreading and recounted a number of crucial empirical findings that an adequate theory needs to accommodate. Here is a brief summary that will serve as our checklist for evaluating alternative theories:

- Normal adults readily attribute large numbers of beliefs to other people, even when they have no apparent evidence. Moreover, most of these attributions are correct.
- Normal adults are also very good at predicting the inferences of other people.
- Though adults are good at attributing some perceptual states, their ability is limited; they are quite bad at attributing perceptual states that result from perceptual illusions.
- Though adults are good at predicting some decisions, their ability to predict decisions is restricted; in a wide range of contexts, adults are quite bad at predicting the decisions that people will make.
- For normal children, though not for children with autism, there is a significant leap in mindreading abilities after the third birthday.
- Desire attribution precedes belief attribution in young children.
- Autistic children apparently have some capacity for desire attribution despite their difficulties with belief attribution.
- Children can predict behaviour effectively before they exhibit understanding of belief.
- Both pretend play and mindreading are deficient in autistic children.

3.3. A Theory about the Cognitive Mechanisms Underlying Mindreading

Now that we have set out some of the central features of mindreading, we are ready to flesh out our proposal about the mechanisms that subserve mindreading. At the core of our Just So Story was the idea that in human evolutionary history, there were two mindreading systems, staggered phylogenetically. The older of these systems predicts behaviour by attributing goals and determining the best strategy for achieving them. The more recent system builds on the phylogenetically older system, but the newer system also exploits representations of the target's 'discrepant' beliefs by building a model of the target's beliefs in the Possible World Box. We now want to make the related claim that *ontogenetically*, there are two mindreading systems. By itself, this claim is hardly controversial; virtually everyone who has addressed the issue in the last decade would agree that there are *at least* two systems (e.g. Wellman 1990; Baron-Cohen 1995; Leslie 1995; Gopnik and Meltzoff 1997). The hard work comes in being more explicit about the mechanisms underlying these mindreading systems and in clarifying the relation between them.

3.3.1. The early mindreading system: The Desire and Plan system

Although most recent theorists maintain that there is an early mindreading system and a later mindreading system, these theorists have not been as clear as one would like about the components of those systems nor about how the systems go about generating predictions about a target's behaviour. We propose that the early system depends on three rather different sorts of mechanisms.[10]

The Desire Detection Mechanisms

First, there is a cluster of mechanisms for attributing desires to others. We will call them the Desire Detection Mechanisms. One of the oldest of these, and as we will see below also apparently one of the first to appear as the child develops, uses a variety of cues for determining a target's goals from his nonverbal behaviour. It is this mechanism that enables us to observe the behaviour of a cheetah chasing a gazelle and form the belief that the cheetah wants to catch the gazelle. We suspect that some of the strategies used to infer goals from behaviour are innate, but they are enriched and supplemented as children (and adults) learn more about the behavioural cues that are associated

---

[10] Some recent authors have speculated that there might be another type of mechanism—a specialized mechanism for detecting animacy or agency (see e.g. Baron-Cohen 1995). Such a mechanism might serve as a trigger that leads to a bit of behaviour being processed by the mechanisms that generate mental state attributions. The evidence here remains equivocal, but if it turns out that there is such a mechanism, it would be comfortably compatible with the rest of our theory. We discuss this idea further in Section 3.3.5.

with various sorts of goals. So, for example, it might be the case that if target 1 moves rapidly, changing direction frequently, and target 2 follows, the goal-from-behaviour system is innately disposed to generate the belief that target 2 wants to catch target 1. Later on, a child may come to recognize stalking behaviour and to form the belief that target 2 wants to catch target 1 when she sees target 2 lurking behind some bushes, staring at target 1 and slowly following him. With growing sophistication people also get better at assessing the *strengths* of a target's desires.

Another strategy for attributing desires on the basis of behaviour that deserves special mention exploits targets' facial expressions to determine what they want. As we will see below, there is evidence that this strategy is up and running quite early on in development. We would not be at all surprised if it turned out that the mechanism subserving this sort of desire attribution is innate and perhaps part of a larger innate mechanism that also subserves the attribution of emotions on the basis of facial expressions (Ekman 1992).

A quite different strategy for attributing goals and desires is to base those attributions on what the target says. The young child might form the belief that a target wants A whenever the target *says* 'I want A,' though with growing sophistication, the child may withhold the desire attribution if the target's facial expression, gestures, or tone of voice indicate that the target is joking, teasing, or being ironic.[11] Later, as we learn about the many reasons why targets may wish to mislead us about their desires, we develop much more complex strategies for going from a target's assertions about his desires to our own beliefs about his desires.

Yet another strategy for attributing desires relies on what *other people* say about the target's desires. Here again, we suspect that early on children generally accept third person claims quite uncritically, though as they get older they learn to recognize facial expressions and body language that indicate when third person desire attributions are not to be taken at face value. Still later, they develop an increasing appreciation of the many ways in which people may attempt to mislead us about what other people want, and they modify desire attributions accordingly.

The final strategy we will mention for attributing desires to others is to generalize from one's own case and assume that others have some of the same standing desires that we do. So, for example, a child who has tasted jalapeño peppers and who desires not to taste them again might well attribute this desire to everyone. As the child learns more about desires she will realize that

[11] Alan Leslie (personal communication) has suggested that even very young children may be sensitive to the sorts of facial expressions, gestures, and tones of voice which indicate that a target does not really want what he says he wants, and that this sensitivity may play an important role in young children's recognition of pretence.

people who have never tasted jalapeños may not share her desire to avoid them. And later still she may learn, to her amazement, that some people who *have* tasted jalapeños have no desire to avoid them. The extent to which children and adults attribute their own standing desires to others is an intriguing question on which much empirical work remains to be done.

We don't claim that this brief list provides a complete catalogue of the desire attribution strategies that people exploit. Quite the opposite, we expect that as children mature they discover all sorts of strategies for attributing desires to others and for assessing the strengths of desires. Though as we will argue in Section 3.4.3, even adult mindreaders make some startling mistakes in predicting other people's desires and their own, and these mistakes play a central role in explaining the failures of decision prediction noted in our checklist. Of course, we do not claim that the more sophisticated versions of the strategies we have discussed are part of the early mindreading system. What we do claim is that the earliest stages of each of the strategies we've mentioned are available quite early in development and that they constitute one crucial element of early mindreading.

The Planner

A second component of the early mindreading system is a mechanism for determining how to go about achieving a goal. As we noted earlier, there is ample reason to think that our pre-human ancestors already had something to do this job, a Planner.[12] For quite apart from any considerations about mindreading, there must have been a mechanism that enabled creatures to select courses of action that stood a reasonable chance of achieving their goals. Indeed, we have suggested that mechanisms subserving this sort of planning probably exist quite far down the phylogenetic chain.[13] Thus they must exist in creatures who have no capacity for mindreading of any sort. We think that this Planning mechanism was a convenient 'pre-adaptation' that came to play a crucial role in mindreading. When the Desire Detection system has generated a belief about the target's desires, the Planner is called upon to figure out how those desires can best be satisfied. The result is a plan of action which is passed on to the third component of the early mindreading system, which we will discuss in a moment. Sometimes, of course, the Planner will not be able to generate a unique best plan for satisfying the specified desires. If Stich knows that Nichols is in New Jersey and wants to meet him in New York at

___

[12] See Section 1.3.

[13] For some interesting speculations on the evolutionary origins of planning and means-ends reasoning, see Papineau 2000. Though Papineau thinks that planning may be a relatively recent evolutionary innovation, he argues (2000: 194) that it must have been in place before the emergence of mindreading.

noon, his Planner may be quite unable to determine whether it would be best to take the train, take the bus, or drive. In other cases, the Planner may be able to come up with no plan at all.

On our view, the Planner is essential to the early mindreading system. But it is important to note that in early mindreading, the Planning mechanism typically finds the best way to achieve the goal *by the attributer's lights*. So, for instance, in early mindreading, the attributer may be unaware that some targets are significantly stronger than the attributer and some are significantly weaker. The absence of this sort of information will affect the Planner's choice of strategies, and sometimes lead to a mistaken prediction about what the target will do. Also, much more importantly, in the early mindreading system, the Planner is not sensitive to the fact that the target might have different beliefs from the attributer. This too, of course, will sometimes lead to mistaken predictions. Problems of the former sort will gradually disappear as the attributer learns more about the target and her situation. But problems of the latter sort are, we think, much harder to eliminate. Children cannot handle these sorts of cases until the later mindreading system is in place.

The Mindreading Coordinator

Neither the Desire Detection Mechanisms nor the Planner are in the business of generating predictions about a target's behaviour. That task, on our account, is allocated to the third component of the early mindreading system whose job it is to coordinate the process. The Coordinator works as follows: when a prediction about the future behaviour of a target is required, the Coordinator's first job is to assemble information about the target's goals or desires. Some Desire Detection strategies may operate automatically and more or less continuously. Others perhaps need to be turned on by the Coordinator, or to have their attention focused on the target.[14] After this is done, the Coordinator collects whatever information it can find in the Belief Box about the target's desires and sends a call to the Planner. The Planner's charge is to come up with the best plan for satisfying those desires for an agent in the target's situation. When the Planner reports back with a plan of action, the Coordinator then generates a belief that the target will try to act in accordance with that plan. And it is that belief that is used to predict the target's behaviour. When the Planner fails to produce a *unique* plan, the Coordinator may simply generate the belief that the target will satisfy her desires *in some way or other*. It is less clear what the Coordinator will do when the Planner can come up with no plan at all. Sometimes, no doubt, the prediction will be that the target will do nothing—or at least nothing that is

---

[14] For more on this see Section 3.3.5.

related to the specified goals. On other occasions, the Coordinator may predict that the target *will* satisfy the desire, though say nothing about how this will be done. We suspect that skill in handling these sorts of cases requires a fair amount of learning, and that the learning process may well continue through adolescence and into adulthood. Figure 3.3 is a sketch of the mechanisms that comprise the early mindreading system.

We think that the Coordinator also plays a rather different role in mindreading—it generates beliefs about instrumental desires. When the Planner presents the Coordinator with a plan that includes various intermediate steps along the way to the goal, a mindreader will typically come to believe that the target desires to accomplish each of these intermediary steps. The Coordinator is the mechanism that generates those beliefs and does so in a way that keeps track of their instrumental status. The Coordinator is also responsible for removing the belief that the target desires some instrumental goal when the mindreader comes to believe that the target no longer desires the final goal. Though this is the primary route via which mindreaders form beliefs about instrumental goals, we strongly suspect that, sometimes at least, beliefs about instrumental goals are formed without accessing the Planner. If a mindreader knows that a target wants to do A, and that the target believes that the best way to accomplish A is to do B, then the mindreader will

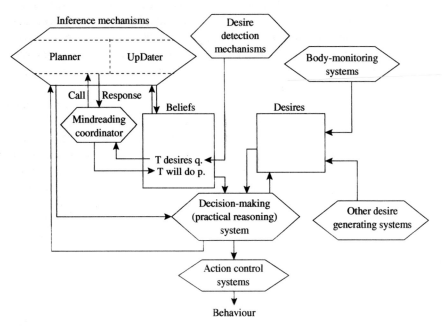

Fig. 3.3   The early mindreading system: The Desire and Plan system

typically come to believe that the target also wants to do B. Since this second route to beliefs about instrumental desires requires that the mindreader have some sophisticated beliefs about the target's beliefs, we don't think this route is available to children who are still in the Desire and Plan stage. We know of ` no evidence indicating whether or not the other route to beliefs about instrumental desires, via the Planner, is functional in early mindreading.

Some empirical evidence for (very) early mindreading

We will postpone a detailed discussion of the empirical evidence concerning early mindreading until Section 3.4, where we will compare our theory with other accounts that have been proposed. However, we think this would be a good place to mention several studies suggesting that some of the early mindreading system is up and running *very* early on in development. Repacholi and Gopnik (1997) found that 18-month-old children use the facial expressions of a target as evidence of the target's desires. In this study, the experimenter tasted one food item (either broccoli or Goldfish crackers) and made an expression of disgust; she also tasted the other food and made an expression of happiness. The toddler was then told to offer some food to the experimenter. Although the 14-month-olds consistently offered the food they themselves preferred (typically the crackers), the 18-month-olds tended to offer the food toward which the target exhibited a positive facial expression, regardless of the toddler's own preference. Using quite a different methodology, Meltzoff found that when 18-month-old children observe a person carrying out an incomplete action, like pulling on the ends of a dumbbell but failing to dislodge them, the toddler infers the goal of the action and imitates it by pulling the dumbbell apart (Meltzoff 1995).

Goal attribution in infants has also been studied using the preferential looking time methodology. This methodology exploits the infants' inclination to look longer at events when something unexpected happens. In an experiment by Gergely, Csibra, and their colleagues, 12-month-old infants are habituated to computer-generated stimuli in which a small ball moves in a parabolic trajectory over a block that looks like a barrier and then makes contact with a big ball (Gergely et al. 1995). After habituation, babies are shown one of two conditions in which the barrier is absent. In one condition the small ball shows the same trajectory as in habituation trials (so it looks like the ball is leaping even though the barrier is absent); in the other condition the small ball moves in a straight line. They found that the babies' looking times in the former condition were longer than those in the latter condition, despite the fact that the motion in the latter condition is novel, and that babies generally look longer at novel events. These results have been interpreted as showing that young babies attribute goals (Baron-Cohen 1995; Gergely et al. 1995; Premack and Premack 1997). But if this interpretation is right, the results show more than merely that the babies attribute goals—they show that babies attribute goals and that they predict that the target will try to achieve the goal in the most direct way possible. Our account provides an explanation of this capacity that appeals to relatively simple mechanisms.[15]

A glance at the checklist

Before going on to the later mindreading system, let's pause for a moment to consider which of the features of mindreading assembled in our checklist in Section 3.2 can be explained by the account we have offered of the cognitive processes underlying early mindreading. One of the items on the checklist is that children can predict behaviour effectively before they exhibit any understanding of belief. On our theory, this is just what would be expected, since the early mindreading system does not require any understanding of belief or even of perception. The Planner must, of course, make use of the attributer's beliefs about the world, but on our account of early mindreading none of those beliefs are about the beliefs or perceptual states of the target. Another fact on the checklist is that desire attribution precedes belief attribution. Here again, our theory offers a ready explanation: the initial stages of the Desire Detection strategies that we described are in place quite early on in development, while the belief attribution strategies that we will discuss in the next section emerge significantly later. Moreover, since on our account the initial stages of the Desire Detection strategies are independent of later mindreading, our theory can accommodate the fact that Desire Detection seems to be selectively spared in autism. As we will explain below, on our theory, autism is an impairment of the later mindreading system, and we think that the early mindreading system is intact.

3.3.2. The later mindreading system: the PWB and Desire system

There is a more flexible and sophisticated mindreading system that emerges ontogenetically in humans sometime after the Desire and Plan system. We

---

[15] Gergely and colleagues (1995) propose that the infant uses a theory of 'rational action'. In support of this, they cite Dennett (1987), who has long insisted that we use a 'Theory of Rationality' to interpret and predict people and that without this assumption, it is impossible to attribute mental states and predict action. It is not clear to what extent Gergely and colleagues are really committed to Dennett's account; they may have in mind something closer to the model that we have proposed. But we think that it is quite clear that Dennett's account has serious problems (see Section 3.4.4).

call it the *PWB and Desire* system, since if we are right the crucial advance over the earlier system is that the PWB is recruited to assist with mindreading. The PWB, on our view, is on-line quite early, as evidenced by the early emergence of pretence in the second year. By the age of $2\frac{1}{2}$ years, children can both pretend and engage in hypothetical reasoning, and we have argued that both of these capacities exploit the PWB. However, $2\frac{1}{2}$-year-olds do not use the PWB to build models of the beliefs of targets. We maintain that sometime after the third birthday, the child gradually starts to use the PWB to assist in mindreading, and this is the beginning of the great leap in mindreading abilities. We think it is currently quite unclear whether this system is distinctively human or whether it might also be present in higher primates. At any rate, there is no clear evidence that the system is present in non-humans (e.g. Call and Tomasello 1999). We will explore this issue further in Section 3.3.6.

As we saw in Chapter 2, in typical instances of pretence and hypothetical reasoning, all one's beliefs are deposited into the PWB. Similarly, when the PWB gets co-opted for mindreading, all of the mindreader's own beliefs are included in the model of the target's beliefs that is being built in the PWB. This is the process that we have been calling *default belief attribution*, and on our view it plays a central role in mindreading.[16] In our account of pretence and hypothetical reasoning, we argued that the inference mechanism, *the very same one that is used in the formation of real beliefs*, can work on representations in the PWB in much the same way that it works on representations in the Belief Box. We also maintained that when a representation in the PWB is 'clamped', the UpDater works to remove representations from the PWB that are incompatible with the clamped representations. Of course, when the PWB is co-opted for mindreading, these features follow along as well. Thus, if we have determined that the target believes p, though we don't, p gets clamped in the PWB, and although we initially default attribute all of our beliefs to the target, the UpDater will quickly remove from the PWB representations that are obviously incompatible with p.

We are now in a position to explain why adults are so good at two aspects of mindreading that were included on our checklist. Adults can effectively attribute beliefs in the apparent absence of evidence because they rely on the default strategy of attributing their own beliefs to others. Inference prediction is successful because, like hypothetical reasoning, it relies on the very same inference mechanisms that are used for drawing inferences with real beliefs.

---

[16] There are a number of interesting further questions about default attribution, including: to what extent do people use default attribution for mental states other than belief? Also, it is obvious that adults do not default attribute *all* of their own beliefs to all mindreading targets. So there must be strategies for restricting which of one's own beliefs are added to the PWB when it is being used for mindreading, and we suspect that some of these strategies are in place fairly early. In Section 3.3.3 we'll propose one principle that limits default attribution.

So, to return to the example of the presidential resignation (discussed in Section 3.2.1), on our theory, the same inference and UpDating mechanisms are used in the following cases:

(1) I believe that the President resigned and infer that the Vice-President will take over.
(2) I engage in hypothetical reasoning from the assumption that the President resigns, to infer that the Vice-President would take over.
(3) I predict that a target who believes that the President resigned will infer that the Vice-President will take over.

In the latter two cases, the representation *the President resigned* is clamped in the PWB, and the normal UpDating and inference mechanisms produce the new representation in the PWB, *the Vice President will take over*. We think that the account we have sketched is by far the most plausible one that has been offered to explain people's success at inference prediction. Indeed, the only clear alternative that has been proposed is that we have a tacit theory detailing how other people draw inferences, and to our knowledge, no one has ever actually defended this kind of radical 'theory theory' about inference prediction (see Stich and Nichols 1997; Nichols and Stich 1998).

Although the capacity to predict each other's beliefs and inferences is of considerable interest, where folk psychology really earns its keep is in predicting *action*. Accordingly, the effectiveness of the PWB and Desire system is best seen in the context of action prediction. In the PWB and Desire system, the Desire Detection Mechanisms still determine the desires of targets, and the Mindreading Coordinator still generates predictions based on desires and plans. But in the PWB and Desire system, the Planner does not determine the optimal strategy *by the predictor's own lights*. Rather, in this later mindreading system the Planner uses the model built up in the PWB instead of the predictor's own beliefs in figuring out how the target's desires should be satisfied. So, for instance, even if I believe that the chocolate is actually in the cupboard, I can predict the behaviour of a chocolate-seeking target who believes that the chocolate is in the box. I do this by building a model of the target's beliefs in the PWB including a representation with the content *the chocolate is in the box*. My Planner then uses that model in determining the plan for getting the chocolate. The output of this process is then used by the Coordinator to generate a prediction about the target's behaviour. In predicting behaviour when one knows about the false beliefs of a target, the Planner can typically rely on the inferences that would be drawn from those false beliefs. The sophisticated inference predictions made possible by the PWB system help to build up a more accurate and flexible model of the target.

The PWB and Desire system that we have described in this section is depicted in Figure 3.4. Note that all of the mechanisms that play a role in our

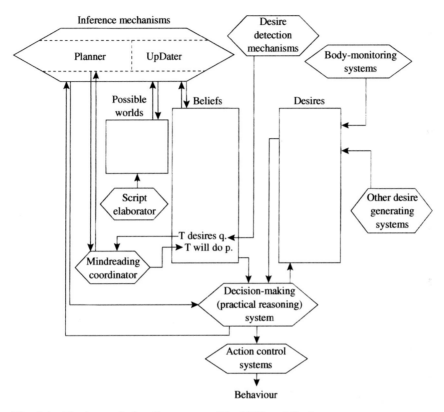

Fig. 3.4 The later mindreading system: The PWB and Desire system

account of the PWB and Desire system are independently motivated (at least if we're right about the Desire and Plan system). The Desire Detection Mechanism, the Planner, and the Mindreading Coordinator are the same mechanisms that are utilized in the early mindreading system, and the PWB system is the system that underlies hypothetical reasoning and pretence (see Chapter 2).

3.3.3. Discrepant belief attribution mechanisms

At this point, we have explained how mindreading makes use of the PWB, and we have suggested that in mindreading the PWB gets much of its content through default belief attribution. But, of course, if the PWB relies *only* on default attribution, the system is not taking advantage of the distinctive and powerful possibilities of the PWB. Indeed, a mindreading system that used default belief attribution exclusively to fill up the PWB in predicting behaviour would make the same predictions as the early mindreading system. So, we have not yet provided an account that can explain one of the central features outlined in Section 3.2. The account doesn't explain why this system is better at predicting behaviour than the system used by 2-year-olds. The power of the later mindreading system only emerges when there are *overrides* to default belief attribution. We think that there are a number of different ways in which default attribution can be overridden. In this section, we will provide a brief description of some of them.

A number of the pathways that lead to an override of default belief attribution also involve the formation of a belief about the target's perceptual states. As we will see, these pathways can be quite complicated. To account for the capacity to form beliefs about a target's perceptual states, we posit the existence of an innate Perception Detection Mechanism (PDM), or perhaps a cluster of such mechanisms, which uses information about a target and her environment to produce beliefs about the target's perceptions—beliefs like *target sees the food, target can't see R*, and *target can't see what is around the corner*. Obviously, a mechanism that can pull this off must also be able to draw on a fair amount of information about the links between environmental situations and perceptual states. The Perception Detection Mechanism starts to emerge quite early, as indicated by young children's success on 'level-1' perspective-taking tasks in which the subject has to determine whether another person can see an object or not. For instance, a child might be shown that a piece of cardboard has a picture of a rabbit on one side and a picture of a turtle on the other. The child is then shown the turtle side and asked whether the person on the other side of the cardboard sees the picture of the rabbit or the picture of the turtle. Lempers and colleagues (Lempers et al. 1977) found that $2\frac{1}{2}$-year-old children passed these perspective-taking tasks (see also Flavell 1978). Autistic subjects are also capable of this and even more complicated perception attribution (Tan and Harris 1991). However, on our view, the Perception Detection Mechanism is quite limited even in normal adults. In particular, the mechanism does not provide predictions or explanations for perceptual illusions. The strengths and limits of the PDM explain the fact, noted on our checklist, that people are quite good at some perception attribution tasks and quite bad at others.

We turn now to a consideration of some of the pathways involving perception attribution that lead to the attribution of discrepant beliefs and from there to the elaboration of a PWB model of a target's beliefs. The simplest of these uses a negative perception attribution like *target did not see the chocolate being put in the box* as the basis of a negative belief (or knowledge) attribution like *target does not believe (or know) that the chocolate was put in the box*. Surprisingly, though both young children and autistic children can make successful negative perception attributions, autistic children typically do *not* go on to make the corresponding negative belief attributions. Autistic children will correctly assert that a target did not see the chocolate being put in the box, but they will also assert that a target who didn't see the chocolate being put in the box thinks that the chocolate *is* in the box (Perner et al. 1989; Baron-Cohen and Goodhart 1994). By contrast, by the time normal children are $3\frac{1}{2}$, they are fairly adept with this transition from *didn't see* to *doesn't believe (think/know)* (Pratt and Bryant 1990).[17]

This step alone will not allow children to solve standard versions of the false belief task. To see why, let's first consider the relocation or 'Maxi' task in which the child sees the chocolate moved from one location to another and is asked where Maxi, who did not see the transfer, thinks the chocolate is. Once the child has mastered the transition from *didn't see* to *doesn't believe* she will know that Maxi does not believe the chocolate is in the new location. But this, by itself, does not enable the child to say where Maxi *does* believe the chocolate to be. How does the child solve this problem? On our account, when a child who is old enough to handle false belief tasks first encounters Maxi she builds a model of Maxi's beliefs in her PWB by default attributing all of her own beliefs to Maxi. This will include the belief that the chocolate is in location 1, since at the beginning of the experiment that's where it is, and both the child and Maxi have seen it placed there. Then Maxi leaves and the chocolate is transferred to location 2. The child forms the belief that the chocolate is in location 2. Ordinarily, a newly acquired belief would be added to the model in the PWB and default attributed to Maxi as well. (So, for example, if while Maxi is playing outdoors it begins to rain heavily, the child will believe that it is raining and she will attribute this belief to Maxi.) However, in the relocation experiment the child believes that Maxi did not see the transfer and does not believe the chocolate is in location 2. One of the principles governing default attribution, we maintain, is that a belief of the form *T does not believe that p* will *block* the transfer of *p* to the PWB model of T's beliefs.[18] So the child does not transfer the belief that the chocolate is in location 2 to the PWB model, and the child's prediction is based on the pre-existing PWB model which includes the belief that the chocolate is in location 1.

---

[17] Older children and adults clearly treat the *didn't see* → *doesn't know* inference as *defeasible*. They are aware that there are lots of ways in which people can come to know or believe that *p* without having seen that *p*. There is a bit of evidence that in some contexts, children mistakenly rely too rigidly on the *didn't see* → *doesn't know* principle (e.g. Wimmer et al. 1988). But we think it very likely that verbal assertions of belief suffice to override the inference even in quite young children. If the child knows that Johnny didn't see the bunny in the box, but Johnny correctly asserts, 'there's a bunny in the box', the young mindreader will probably attribute to Johnny the belief that there's a bunny in the box.

[18] If *p* has already been added to the PWB, a related principle removes *p* when the mindreader comes to have a belief of the form *T does not believe that p*. For example, this might happen if, after adding *p* to the PWB by default attribution, the mindreader comes to believe *T did not see p*, and this leads her to believe *T does not believe that p*.

Another standard false belief task, the 'deceptive container' task poses a rather more complex problem for the young mindreader. In this task, the child is initially shown a closed candy container. (The best-known version was done with 'Smarties', a candy popular in the UK.) After the child is shown the Smarties box, she is shown that the box contains pencils rather than candy. Then the box is closed again and the child is asked what another child (who has not seen the contents of the box) will think is in the box. Children pass this task after the fourth birthday, about the same time as they pass other standard false belief tasks. How do they do it? On our theory, when the child is asked about the target, she builds a PWB model of the target's beliefs, and most of her own beliefs are default attributed to the target. However, the child has a perceptual belief, *target did not see that there are pencils in the box*, which produces the belief that *target does not believe that there are pencils in the box*. And this belief blocks the default attribution of *there are pencils in the box*. So far, the case is quite parallel to the Maxi case. But how does the child go on to attribute the right belief to the target, the belief that there is candy in the box? In the Maxi case, we assumed that the child already *had* a PWB model of the target which contained the right belief. All that was necessary was to prevent the newly acquired belief about the new location of the chocolate from being default attributed. In the Smarties case, by contrast, the target was not on the scene until after the child acquired the belief that there are pencils in the box. So there was no pre-existing PWB model that contained the right answer. Perner et al. (1987) have suggested that in cases like this children will attribute to targets beliefs about the way the world *usually* is: Smarties boxes usually contain Smarties, so that is what the target will think is in the box. Another possibility is that the child will recall her own belief prior to seeing the pencils, and attribute this belief to the target. Whatever the right answer is, it is clear that by the time children can solve these problems they must have quite a substantial store of information about the ways in which targets go about forming, retaining, and changing discrepant beliefs.[19]

Thus far we have been focusing on the role of *negative* perception attributions (*target did not see p*) in the construction of PWB models. But perception attributions can also play a positive role. Suppose, for example, that you have been shown that there is a frog in a box, and because you know that the target has not seen what is in the box, you believe that the target does not believe there is a frog in the box. If the target is now allowed to look in the box, your Perception Detection Mechanism will form the belief that *the target sees that there is a frog in the box*. This, in turn, will lead to the belief that *the*

---

[19] Our focus here is on explaining what is involved in *successful* false belief attribution. We offer no detailed story about why young children fail the false belief task. On our account, there are two broad kinds of explanation available for systematic failures on the false belief task: either the child is not using the PWB for mindreading, or the child's discrepant belief attribution mechanisms are not up to the task.

target believes there is a frog in the box, which will be added to your PWB model of the target (Pratt and Bryant 1990).[20]

Another way in which we can determine a target's discrepant belief is to seek an explanation for the target's behaviour when we already know something about the target's desires. Suppose, for example, that as you are standing in the back yard, you hear the neighbour's dog barking excitedly on the other side of the house. Then a cat appears, dashes across the yard, and scurries under the fence into next yard. Seconds later the dog, obviously in hot pursuit, enters the yard, looks around apparently puzzled, and then begins barking up the tree in the centre of the yard. The natural hypothesis, here, is that the dog believes that the cat is in the tree. Some theorists urge that in constructing explanations like this we are exploiting a commonsense psychological theory that is acquired in much the same way that scientific theories are acquired (e.g. Gopnik and Wellman 1994; Gopnik and Meltzoff 1997). Others maintain that belief attributions and explanations of this sort are subserved by a special purpose modular mechanism (Leslie 1994b; Roth and Leslie 1998). (These authors also offer competing accounts of perception-based belief attributions of the sort mentioned in the previous paragraph.) We will offer some arguments about the relative merits of these proposals in Section 3.4. But on any plausible account, the mechanisms subserving this sort of explanation-based discrepant belief attribution will need to call on a quite rich body of knowledge about mental states and the way they interact. Moreover, the ability to generate discrepant belief explanations of this sort is in place quite early in development. In one study, children were shown a drawing of a girl and told, 'Here's Jane. Jane is looking for her kitten. The kitten is hiding under a chair, but Jane is looking for her kitten under the piano. Why do you think Jane is doing that?' (Bartsch and Wellman 1989: 949.) From the age of 3, children will correctly note that Jane is behaving this way because she thinks that the kitten is under the piano. This is noteworthy since children succeed on this task earlier than they succeed at the standard false belief task. It is also worth noting that in these cases the children may well be coming up with discrepant belief attributions without first attributing any perceptual states to the target (for a similar finding, see Roth and Leslie 1998: experiment 2).

Language provides an additional (and vast) resource for determining the beliefs of others. One of the unsung heroes of belief attribution is the humble verbal assertion. It is obvious that as adults, one of the most direct ways we find out about the beliefs of others is by their sincere assertions. What is

---

[20] Things aren't always this simple, however. If we know that the target firmly believes not-*p*, then even if we know that he perceives *p*, we might not conclude that he believes that *p*. For instance, he might think that the appearance is deceptive. As children get older, they gain an increasingly sophisticated understanding of conditions under which a target's perceiving that *p* does not lead the target to believe that *p*. As a result, our claims about how perception attribution leads to belief attribution should be taken with a healthy dose of *ceteris paribus*.

striking is that young children rely on this strategy too. In an experiment by Roth and Leslie (1991: 326), a speaker asserted something that was clearly false, and the 3-year-olds in this experiment attributed the false belief to the speaker even though the child did not share the belief.

Language also provides a quite different avenue for belief attribution. Certainly for adults, many of our belief attributions are based on third-person reports. For example, much belief attribution gets passed along as gossip. (Mary doesn't know that her husband is cheating on her. Bill thinks he's going to get the promotion.) This third-person reporting works for young children as well. Indeed, many of the studies exploring mindreading abilities in children exploit the fact that the subject will accept a belief attribution that is uttered by a third person. For example, in the 'discrepant belief task' described in Section 3.2.2, the child is told that the target thinks that the bananas are in the cupboard (Wellman and Bartsch 1988), and the child effectively uses this information to predict the target's behaviour.

In this section we have recounted several quite different ways in which mindreaders arrive at belief attributions that differ from the attributions that they would make by default. No doubt there are many more ways in which people can learn to override default attributions. But, at this juncture, the crucial point is that we can use these strategies to modify the model of the target that we build up in the PWB. Now that we have a fuller sketch of the PWB-Desire mindreading system, we can more adequately address the fact, included on our checklist, that older children are better at predicting behaviour than younger children. Older children have a range of strategies for attributing discrepant beliefs, and these serve as the basis for adjusting the default PWB model of the target's beliefs. As a result, the older child can make much more accurate predictions of the target's inferences, decisions, and plans.

3.3.4. From belief attribution to a PWB model (and back)

On our theory there are several ways in which representations can get into the model of a target that mindreaders construct in their PWB. First, a large number of representations become part of the model simply by default attribution. Second, the UpDating process generates new representations in the PWB, and removes representations that are already there. Third, representations are added to the PWB model via the various belief attribution strategies discussed in Section 3.3.3. These belief attribution strategies, we think, typically work by first generating a belief about the target's belief (or lack of belief) in the mindreader's Belief Box.[21] The mindreader then uses this belief to make the

---

[21] Another, more radical, proposal is that one or more of the discrepant belief attribution processes sketched in Section 3.3.3 circumvent the mindreader's Belief Box and generate the

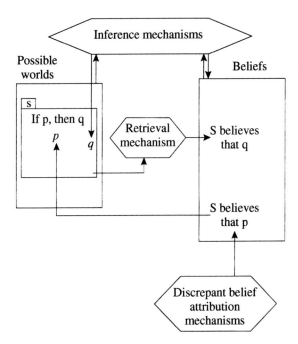

Fig. 3.5 Discrepant belief attribution

appropriate change in the PWB model. If it is a belief with the content *target believes that p*, a token of *p* is added to the PWB. If it is a belief with the content *target does not believe that p*, and the PWB model already contains a token of *p*, it is removed, while if the PWB does *not* contain a token of *p*, but the mindreader's Belief Box does (because the mindreader believes that *p*), default attribution of *p* is blocked. Of course, sometimes in order to reap the benefits of having an evolving model of the target's beliefs in the PWB, the mindreader also needs to be able to *retrieve* the contents of the PWB in the appropriate fashion. When, for example, the mindreader reports that the target has some belief that was added to the PWB model by the UpDater, the report is subserved by a belief about the target's belief. So there must also be a mechanism that takes the appropriate part of the output of the PWB model-building process and embeds it in an appropriate 'meta-belief'. Thus, for example, if *Reno is east of Los Angeles* is in the PWB, this mechanism would, when necessary, generate a token of *Target believes that Reno is east of Los Angeles*, in the mindreader's Belief Box. Figure 3.5. depicts the mechanisms underlying this process.

appropriate representations directly in the PWB. Though we favour the idea that mindreaders first come to have 'meta-beliefs' about the target's beliefs, we admit that persuasive evidence for this choice is not thick on the ground.

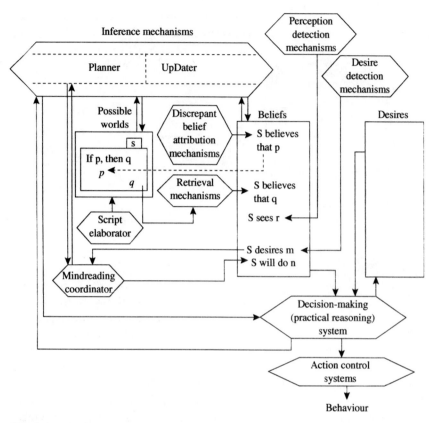

Fig. 3.6   The full third-person mindreading system

Putting all the pieces together renders the teemingly complex Figure 3.6, which is the composite account of the cognitive architecture subserving mind-reading that we have discussed so far.

3.3.5. Turning on the mindreading system

One question that we have not yet addressed is how the mindreading system gets turned on. We are not even tempted to attribute mental states to most of the things we interact with in our everyday life, though we do attribute mental states (or at least generate tentative mentalistic interpretations which we may not really believe) to a remarkable variety of things including people, many animals, and images of actors and cartoon characters on a movie screen. What is it that determines which of the items we encounter get interpreted as having mental lives and which do not?

There are two different sorts of questions that need to be addressed about the mechanism (or mechanisms) that determine what gets interpreted mentalistically. One is a question about mental architecture. Is there a separate component of the system (or perhaps several components) whose job it is to detect objects that are candidates for mentalistic interpretation? Or do various parts of the mindreading system, like the Desire Detection Mechanisms, the Perception Detection Mechanisms, and perhaps some of the mechanisms that subserve various strategies of discrepant belief detection, each have their own built-in triggering subsystem which enables that part of the system to recognize likely candidates for having mental states?

The second question focuses on the features of the environment that trigger mindreading. There has been some fascinating experimental work exploring the sorts of stimuli that will engage the mindreading system. In a classic study, Heider and Simmel (1944) showed adult subjects a film of moving geometric objects (a large triangle, a small triangle, and a circle), and nearly all of the subjects described the film in anthropomorphic and mentalistic ways. As discussed earlier, Gergely, Csibra, and colleagues obtained results indicating that even infants attribute goals to computer generated geometric stimuli (Gergely et al. 1995; Csibra et al. 1999). Dasser et al. (1989) found similar results on somewhat older children. Baron-Cohen suggests that these results indicate that there is an 'Intentionality Detector', which 'will interpret almost anything with self-propelled motion... as a query agent with goals and desires' (1995: 34).

While these studies suggest that geometric objects can trigger intentional attributions, more naturalistic experiments on everyday objects have indicated that infants tend to attribute goals to people but not to mechanical objects. Woodward (1998) had 6- to 9-month-old infants watch an experimenter reach into a display with a ball and a clown. The experimenter grasped one of the objects and held it until the infant habituated. In the experimental trials, the locations of the objects were switched, and the experimenter again reached in and grasped one of the objects. Infants looked longer when the experimenter reached to the same place to get a different object than when the experimenter reached to a different place for the same object. Woodward also ran a control condition with a mechanical claw in place of a human hand, and in this condition there was no effect. Woodward interprets these findings as follows: 'Taken together, these findings indicate that by the time they are 6 months of age, infants have a store of knowledge that leads them to selectively encode the goal-related properties of reaching events, and, moreover, that this knowledge does not extend to similar events involving inanimate objects' (Woodward 1998: 28).

Using a radically different methodology, Meltzoff also found that infants attributed goals to people but not to a mechanical device. We mentioned this experiment earlier (in Section 3.3.1), but it is worth spending a bit more time on the details at this point. In Meltzoff's experiment, 18-month-old infants observed an adult 'failing' to carry out a goal. For instance, in one of the tasks, an adult tried to pull apart a small dumbbell. The infants were then allowed to manipulate the dumbbell themselves. Some of the infants were exposed to an adult successfully pulling it apart, others were exposed to an adult merely manipulating the dumbbell, and, in the target group, the adult picked up the dumbbell 'by the wooden cubes... It appeared that the experimenter was trying to pull the ends outward. However... one of his hands slipped off the end of the object' (Meltzoff 1995: 840). Meltzoff found that infants in this condition were just as likely to pull the dumbbell apart as infants in the 'success' condition. In a follow-up experiment, Meltzoff devised a mechanical device that mimicked the human action of trying to pull the dumbbell apart; the device even had a spring so that the 'hand' closed after being removed from the dumbbell. Strikingly, infants did not carry out the 'failed intention' in the mechanical condition. According to Meltzoff, the results from this experiment 'demonstrate that physical movements performed by a machine are not ascribed the same meaning as when performed by a person. Therefore, even a weak reading of the data suggests that infants are thinking in terms of goals that are connected to people and not to things' (1995: 848). Meltzoff claims that the experiments show that '18-month-old children already situate people within a psychological framework. They have adopted a key element of a folk psychology: People (but not inanimate objects) are understood within a framework that includes goals and intentions' (1995: 840).

The infants' apparent failure to attribute goals to objects that aren't people might lead one to think that in order for the mindreading system to be turned on, the object must be recognizably human. However, Johnson (2000) showed that infants would follow the 'gaze' of a very non-human-looking fuzzy brown object if the object interacted contingently with the infants (by beeping and flashing lights when the infant babbled or moved). If the fuzzy brown object did not exhibit such contingent interactions, the infants would not follow its 'gaze'. One possible interpretation of these findings is that they indicate that infants have an innate 'Agency Detection' mechanism that is triggered by contingent interaction. Such a mechanism could well serve as a trigger for the rest of the mindreading system, as that system develops. But, of course, even if there is an Agency Detection mechanism that is sensitive to contingent interaction and that triggers mindreading in adults, there is no reason to suppose that this is the *only* mechanism that triggers mindreading. Indeed, the work of Heider and Simmel and Dasser et al. clearly shows that mindreading can be triggered without contingent interaction with the mindreader.

On our view there is currently not enough evidence available to decide among a number of possible answers to the questions we have been considering. If there is a free-standing Agency Detector that comes to trigger the mindreading system, then there must also be a variety of other ways in which mindreading can be triggered. These other mechanisms might be separate from the rest of the mindreading system, as we have been supposing the Agency Detector is, or they might be subsystems built into the Desire Detection Mechanisms and other components of the mindreading system. A great deal more research is needed before we know what sorts of environmental factors these mechanisms are sensitive to, and the extent to which these factors are innate or acquired.

3.3.6. Some speculations on the development of the mindreading system: ontogeny & evolutionary precursors

To complete our picture of the role that PWB models play in mindreading, we would like to offer some speculations about how the process emerges both ontogenetically and phylogenetically. To begin, recall that if you assume that the target shares all of your beliefs, then the PWB is quite irrelevant to your predictions. It is only when you think that the target's beliefs diverge from your own that the PWB becomes an important tool. Hence, the attribution of ignorance or of false beliefs is a crucial precursor to exploiting the PWB in mindreading. As we have seen, the capacity to attribute false beliefs emerges somewhat earlier than is suggested by the traditional false belief tasks. Bartsch and Wellman's analysis of spontaneous discourse indicates that young children attribute false beliefs by about the age of 3. And the work by Roth and Leslie suggests that one of the earliest sources of evidence for false belief attribution is *verbal assertion*. There is good reason to think, then, that in these circumstances, the young child comes to have a representation in her Belief Box that attributes a false belief to the target.

But while the protocol evidence analysed by Bartsch and Wellman and the experimental work of Roth and Leslie both indicate that children as young as 3 have the capacity for attributing false beliefs, it is not at all clear that these children exploit false belief attributions in PWB models of the target. Bartsch and Wellman (1995) point out that it is a striking feature of 3-year-olds that they typically don't exploit their capacity for false or discrepant belief attribution in predicting behaviour. Though the vast collection of protocols that they examined contain many examples of young children making false belief attributions, children of this age do not go on to use this information to predict what the target will do. Bartsch and Wellman (1995) label this the 'desire-belief psychology' phase in the development of mindreading, noting that the children 'recognize the existence of beliefs, at least at times, yet reason about and explain action primarily in terms of desires' (1995: 149–50). On our account, the lag between attributing false beliefs and *using* false beliefs to predict behaviour can be explained in several different ways. One possibility is that the young child has no trouble using belief attributions to build up a model of the target in the PWB, but still lacks the capacity to disengage the Planner from the Belief Box and let it use the PWB in formulating a plan about the best way for the target to accomplish his goal. Another possibility, that we think is more likely, is that although the 3-year-old child has beliefs about false beliefs, she is not yet able to use those beliefs to form a model of the target in the PWB. And, we suggest, it is only after the child gains the capacity to use the PWB for mindreading that the explosion in mindreading abilities emerges.[22]

The picture of mindreading that we have elaborated, not entirely coincidentally, fits nicely with our Just So Story. In that Story, the mechanisms exploited in mindreading emerged at different points in our evolutionary history. Correspondingly, in our cognitive account of mindreading in humans, mindreading implicates several separate mechanisms, which might well have emerged at different points in human evolution. But is there any reason to believe that the mechanisms subserving mindreading did in fact emerge independently and in something like the order proposed in our Story? It would be particularly nice to be able to say that there is evidence showing that the mechanisms we posit are 'phylogenetically dissociated' as it were. That is, it would be nice to have evidence showing, for instance, that some non-human primates have the Goal and Plan system, but not the PWB-Desire system. Unfortunately, research on mindreading in non-human primates is nowhere near being able to tell us whether there are such dissociations. However, there is a smattering of evidence that might shed some light on the issue.

The investigation of primate behaviour in naturalistic settings provides one sort of evidence that apes might use information about goals to predict the behaviour of others. There are, for instance, impressive cases of collaborative

---

[22] It is important to note that there are empirical studies that could decide between these two options. If the 3-year-old child is building a model in the PWB, then she should be UpDating when discrepant beliefs are added. So if she believes *Target believes that p*, and *p* is straightforwardly incompatible with *q*, which the child believes, then she should think that *Target does not believe that q*. And if *p* plus some of the child's background beliefs obviously entail *r*, where *r* is some proposition that the child does *not* believe, then the child should think *Target believes that r*. If, on the other hand, the 3-year-old just has *Target believes that p* in her Belief Box and *can't* put *p* into the PWB and UpDate, then she should *not* think *Target does not believe that q* or *Target believes that r*. Though we know of no studies that examine this issue directly, both Wimmer et al. (1988) and Ruffman (1996) have found that younger children have difficulty attributing beliefs that targets acquire via inference, and this suggests that the PWB is not yet being utilized to build models of targets' beliefs.

hunting in which different chimpanzees occupy positions in different trees and on the ground to trap a monkey (see e.g. Boesch and Boesch 1989). Although the issue is fraught with controversy, in these kinds of cases one interpretation is that the chimpanzees are aware that they all have the goal of catching the monkey, since they are apparently coordinating their efforts at achieving that goal. Convincing experimental data that a mindreading system is present in non-humans is somewhat thin on the ground. The best-known results come from Premack and Woodruff (1978) who had a chimpanzee, Sarah, observe videotapes of a human attempting to do something. The video was stopped before the human achieved the goal, and Sarah then was required to choose from a set of photographs depicting various outcomes. In the first trial, in 18 out of 20 cases, Sarah chose the photograph in which the human achieved the goal. According to Premack and Woodruff, these results indicate that Sarah had the ability to attribute goals, and many subsequent researchers seem to agree (Baron-Cohen 1995; Leslie 1995). But there is also a good deal of controversy over the study (see the discussion in Tomasello and Call 1997). One major problem is that the study had only one subject, and she was extensively trained. More recent studies on the chimpanzee's ability to attribute goals have been quite mixed. Call and Tomasello found that chimpanzees and orangutans did seem to discriminate between intentional and accidental behaviours (Call and Tomasello 1998). In their experiment, the experimenter placed a marker on one of three boxes. The box with the marker contained food and the animals were trained to select the box with the marker on it. In the test phase, the experimenter placed markers on two of the boxes, one 'intentionally' and the other 'accidentally'. After 'accidentally' dropping the marker on the box, the experimenter made a facial expression of disapproval. Call and Tomasello found that the apes tended to select the box on which the marker was intentionally placed. This suggests that the apes appreciated the distinction between intentional and accidental action. However, as Call and Tomasello note, it is possible that the apes simply avoided the box that was paired with the negative emotion, since the accidental action was always followed by a facial expression of disapproval (Call and Tomasello 1998: 204). Povinelli et al. (1998) failed to find evidence that chimpanzees discriminated between intentional and accidental behaviours. In one experiment, for example, chimpanzees watched one experimenter accidentally spill juice that was to be given to the animal while handing it to a trainer, and they watched another experimenter intentionally throw a cup of juice to the floor. The apes were then allowed to 'choose' one of these experimenters to receive a reward, and they showed little tendency to prefer one experimenter over the other. Furthermore, recent studies by Povinelli show that chimpanzees are remarkably oblivious to visual perceptual access. For instance, they are just as likely to beg from an experimenter with a bucket over her head as from an experimenter with a bucket next to her head. As a result, some have suggested that mindreading is exclusively a human specialization (e.g. Povinelli and Eddy 1996).

Although there is a recent wave of pessimism about mindreading capacities in non-human primates, it is worth remembering that most of the studies that encourage this pessimism show that chimpanzees fail tasks that are passed by children aged 3–6. And, as we have seen, children's mindreading capacities emerge much earlier than the age of 3. So, it may well be that, although chimpanzees lack the mindreading capacities of 3-year-old children, they have some of the earlier developing abilities. Further, one might worry that the traditional training methods used in these experiments do not provide sufficiently sensitive tests of capacities in non-human primates. Jerry Fodor once remarked that the better our scientific instruments get, the smarter human infants turn out to be. We wouldn't be surprised if something similar held for mindreading capacities in non-human primates. Indeed, as we have already seen, experiments exploiting looking time methods have revealed that primitive mindreading capacities emerge strikingly early in infancy (e.g. Gergely et al. 1995; Woodward 1998). There is good reason to expect that these more sensitive methods will also reveal mindreading capacities in non-human primates.

In addition to the promise of work in the looking time tradition, there is new experimental evidence that directly undermines Povinelli's suggestion that chimpanzees lack an understanding of perceptual access. In some recent work, Hare and colleagues found that chimpanzees were extremely sensitive to the perceptual access of another chimpanzee (Hare et al. 2000). The methodological advance was to put two chimpanzees in a competitive food acquisition context. In this context, subdominant apes were much more likely to attempt to get food that dominant chimps couldn't see. Like looking time studies, these studies have the virtue that they require no training and they are ecologically plausible. And these new techniques are beginning to reveal that some non-human primates might be fairly good mindreaders after all.

3.4. Our Theory Meets the Alternatives

In this section we will compare our theory to other accounts of third-person mindreading that have been proposed in the literature. Though the points we will make are many and varied, they can be organized into a few basic themes. As we have noted with some frequency, our theory is *very eclectic*. In attempting to account for the complexities of mindreading, we have borrowed ideas from many sources, added a few of our own, and woven them together in what we believe are new and interesting ways. Other theorists, by contrast, have been much more *monolithic* in their approach; they have focused on one sort of mechanism or process and tried to use it to explain most or all mind-reading phenomena. A priori, this is not an unreasonable approach. If you've got a hot new idea (or even a hot idea that is not so new) it makes good sense to push it hard and see how much explanatory work you can wring from it. Some years ago, when we first started working on mindreading, this was the strategy we were inclined to adopt. Gradually, however, we became convinced that the monolithic approach is just not tenable. Mother Nature is a tinkerer, and in designing a skill as complex and as important as mindreading, she has used lots of different tricks. Trying to explain everything about mindreading using a single sort of mechanism or process, we found, is a bit like trying to fit a round peg into an irregular trapezoidal hole. But if that's right, why haven't other theorists recognized the problems with monolithic approaches? One reason, we believe, is that most theorists have had much too narrow a view of the *range of phenomena* that needed to be explained. Having adopted a monolithic theory, they have focused on the sorts of mindreading skills that their theory can explain and, by and large, ignored those that their theory cannot explain. Thus, one theme that will run through our critique of competing theories is that there are lots of facts about mindreading that our theory can explain which one or another group of theorists have not even *tried* to explain.

Another reason why advocates of monolithic theories have failed to note the shortcomings of their approach is that, all too often, they offer only a hint or a brief sketch of how their preferred mechanism or process can account for a given phenomenon; they do not pause to develop the explanation in detail. By contrast, in setting out our theory and comparing it to other accounts, we have tried to fill in many more details. When one adopts this approach, one often sees that the sort of mechanism or process advocated by a more monolithic theorist couldn't possibly explain the phenomena that need explaining unless it is supplemented with further mechanisms or processes that are quite different from those that the monolithic theorist favours. This *need for more stuff* is another major theme that runs through our critiques. It will often be the case that when a monolithic account is supplemented with the sorts of further mechanisms required to produce a reasonably explicit and detailed explanation of the phenomena at hand, the resulting theory comes to look a lot like ours. That's no coincidence, of course, since one of the main strategies we used in building our theory was to start with a proposal made by another theorist and to ask ourselves what would be required to turn that proposal into a detailed and explicit explanation.

Sometimes that strategy led us to posit a richer and more heterogeneous account than other theorists had proposed—an account that might well be viewed as a friendly amendment, if only other theorists were not so doggedly

monolithic! But on other occasions the strategy had a rather different outcome. As we tried to make other theorists' explanatory sketches more explicit
and detailed it became increasingly clear that there was no plausible way in
which their sketches could be *supplemented*. They were barking up the wrong
tree, and some quite different approach was called for. So a third theme running through our critiques is that some competing theorists have just started
in the wrong place; there is no plausible way to use their preferred approach
as even a *part* of a fuller explanation of the phenomena that they thought they
could explain.

   In this section we will be considering the views of many authors. For the
most part, however, they can be grouped into a small number of categories. The
most important distinction is between those who think mindreading is an
information-rich process and those who think it is an *information-poor* process.[23]
In explaining mindreading skills, those in the first group posit a rich set of mental
representations containing substantial amounts of information (or, sometimes,
*mis*information) about mental states and their interactions with environmental
stimuli, with behaviour, and with each other. Among developmental psychologists, perhaps the most widely held view is an information-rich account which
maintains that the rich store of information subserving mindreading takes the
form of a *theory* that has much the same structure as a scientific theory and is
learned in much the same way that scientific theories are learned (e.g. Gopnik
and Wellman 1994; Gopnik and Meltzoff 1997). The researchers who take this
approach call their view the '*theory theory*'; however the term 'theory theory'
has also been used more broadly as a label for *all* information-rich accounts
(e.g. Goldman 1989; Stich and Nichols 1992, 1995; Nichols et al. 1996). In this
volume, we will use the term 'theory theory' in this broader sense. As a result,
to avoid terminological confusion, we will call the account promoted by
Gopnik and colleagues the 'scientific-theory theory' (STT). In Section 3.4.1,
we will explain why we think our theory is superior to the STT.

   Another important group of theorists have defended a quite different
account of the information exploited in mindreading. According to these
theorists, the information is *not* learned or stored in the way that a scientific
theory is. Indeed, on their view, a substantial part of the rich body of information required for mindreading is not learned at all. Rather it is contained in one
or more *innate modules* which gradually come on-line as development proceeds (Leslie 1994*b*; Scholl and Leslie 1999; Baron-Cohen 1995). The
information contained in a module may be stored as a cluster of special purpose
algorithms or as a set of mentally represented propositions to which only the
appropriate mindreading modules have access (or in both ways). We will call

---

[23] Much the same distinction was first introduced by Goldman (1992*b*), who used the terms
'knowledge-rich' and 'knowledge-poor'.

these accounts *modularity* theories. We will have more to say about modules, and about the problems facing modularity accounts, in Section 3.4.2.

Until the mid-1980s, information-rich theories of mindreading were the only games in town, and they still dominate the field. In 1986, however, a family of information-poor theories began to emerge, and in the intervening years they have attracted a significant group of supporters. The central idea of these information-poor theories is that predictions about other people's mental states and their behaviour can be made without a rich body of internally represented information about human psychology, since people can use their own mental processes to *simulate* the mental processes of a target (Goldman 1989; Gordon 1986; Harris 1991; Heal 1986). As we saw in Chapter 2, the prototype of simulation theories maintains that we predict other people's decisions and actions by taking our own decision-making system 'off-line' and supplying it with 'pretend' beliefs and desires which have the same content as the beliefs and desires that we attribute to the target. We then let our decision-making system make a decision, and we predict that this is the decision that the target will make. A decision prediction system that worked in this way would be 'information poor' because it has no need of a separate set of mental representations containing information about how the decision-making system works. Rather, it would use the mindreader's own decision-making system as a model for the target's decision-making system. We will discuss information-poor simulation theories in Section 3.4.3.

There is one account of mindreading that has attracted a great deal of attention in the philosophical literature which cannot be readily classified as either an information-rich theory or an information-poor theory. This theory, whose principal advocate is Daniel Dennett, maintains that we attribute mental states to people (and to non-humans as well) and predict their behaviour, by assuming that they are *rational* and making the attributions and predictions that would be appropriate for a rational agent in the target's environment (Dennett 1978a, 1987; Gergely et al. 1995). Dennett and his followers have said very little about *how* we make these attributions and predictions, and one can imagine the process being subserved by either information-rich or information-poor mechanisms. We will discuss Dennett's theory in Section 3.4.4.

3.4.1. The scientific-theory theory

Since there is a lot going on in this section, we had best start with a quick overview of what's to come. We will begin our critique of the scientific-theory theory by focusing on two important mindreading skills that leading advocates of STT rarely mention and for which they offer no explanation. The skills are inference prediction and the attribution of large numbers of beliefs on the basis of no evidence. Our theory offers accounts of both of these—accounts which posit mechanisms that do not exploit the sorts of theoretical knowledge that are centre stage in STT. We will then turn to the mindreading skills of children. In that domain too there is an important phenomenon, the young child's capacity to produce detailed behaviour predictions, that advocates of STT never mention and cannot easily explain. After explaining the problem and sketching our own account of the mechanism that underlies the phenomenon, we will turn to the STT account of mindreading in very young children, and we will argue that the account of early mindreading preferred by leading scientific-theory theorists simply does not fit the facts. We will develop a number of criticisms of the STT account of the 'leap' in mindreading that occurs after the age of 3, and set out our own quite different explanation of that important developmental transition. Finally, we will briefly note another important cluster of facts about mindreading which advocates of STT do not attempt to explain—the puzzling pattern of mindreading deficits exhibited by individuals with autism.

Inference prediction

One of the items on our checklist of facts that a theory of mindreading needs to explain is that normal adults are very good at predicting the inferences of other people. On our account, this is explained by the hypothesis that the Inference Mechanism (which includes the UpDater) operates on representations in the PWB in much the same way that it operates on representations in the Belief Box. Thus a mindreader's own inferences and the predictions she makes about other people's inferences are subserved by the same mechanism. This is one of the places where our account borrows an idea from simulation theorists. Advocates of STT have been notably silent on the matter of inference prediction. Indeed, so far as we have been able to determine, no leading advocate of STT has even tried to offer an explanation of the fact that we are so good at predicting the inferences that other people make. And we are inclined to think that the reason for this omission is pretty clear. For a thoroughgoing STT enthusiast, the only available explanation of our inference prediction skills is *more theory*. If we are good at predicting how other people will reason, that must be because, by exploiting our general purpose theory acquisition skills, we have acquired a remarkably good theory about how people reason. But that account seems implausibly profligate. Why would Mother Nature go to the effort of arranging for us to have a *theory* about how the inference mechanism works when she could get the job done by using the inference mechanism itself? In his defence of simulation theory (1992), Paul Harris makes the simplicity of the simulation approach quite vivid by considering our capacity to predict the grammatical intuitions of someone who speaks the same language that we do.

To explain our success at this task, a hardline defender of STT would have to say that we have a *theory* about the processes subserving grammatical intuition production in other people. But that seems rather far-fetched. A much simpler hypothesis is that we rely on *our own* mechanisms for generating linguistic intuitions, and having determined what our own intuitions about a particular sentence are, we attribute them to the target. Although Harris's simplicity argument focuses on predicting grammaticality judgements, the argument plausibly extends to inference prediction as well.

Harris's *argument from simplicity* played an important role in convincing us that a comprehensive theory of mindreading would have to invoke many different sorts of processes, and that simulation processes would be among them (compare Stich and Nichols 1992 and 1995). However, we do not think that the argument from simplicity is the only reason to prefer our account of inference prediction over an STT account. Indeed, if the argument from simplicity were the only one available, a resolute advocate of STT might simply dig in her heels and note that the systems Mother Nature produces are often far from simple. There are lots of examples of redundancy and apparently unnecessary complexity in biological systems. So, the defender of STT might argue, the mere fact that a theory-based account of inference prediction would be less simple than a simulation style account is hardly a knock-down argument against it. Fortunately, there is another sort of argument that can be mounted against an STT approach to inference prediction. We think it is a particularly important argument since it can be generalized to many other mindreading skills, and thus it has been one of the more valuable tools in helping us to decide which aspects of mindreading are plausibly treated as simulation based.

This second argument, which we will call the *argument from accuracy*, begins with the observation that inference prediction is remarkably accurate over a wide range of cases, including cases that are quite different from anything that most mindreaders are likely to have encountered before. There is, for example, a rich literature in the so-called 'heuristics and biases' tradition in cognitive social psychology chronicling the ways in which people make what appear to be very bad inferences on a wide range of problems requiring deductive and inductive reasoning (see e.g. Kahneman et al. 1982; Nisbett and Ross 1980; Baron 2000; Samuels, Stich, and Faucher 2003). In all of this literature, however, there is no suggestion that people are bad at *predicting* inferences. This contrasts sharply with the literature on decision making that we discuss in Section 3.4.3, where it is often remarked how surprising and *un*predictable people's decisions are. Although it hasn't been studied systematically, we think it is quite likely that people typically predict just those bad inferences that they would make themselves, even on problems that are quite different from any they have encountered before. If that is indeed the case, it poses a problem for STT accounts: how do ordinary mindreaders manage to end up with such an *accurate* theory about how people draw inferences—a theory which supports correct predictions even on quite unfamiliar sorts of inference problems? The problem is made more acute by the fact that (as we will see in Section 3.4.3) there are other sorts of mindreading tasks on which people do very badly. Why do people learn the right theory about inference and the *wrong* theory about other mental processes? There is, of course, no puzzle at all in this if, as we have claimed, people use their own inference mechanism in predicting other people's inferences.

Obviously, the argument from accuracy is a two-edged sword. In those domains where we are particularly good at predicting what others will do in unfamiliar cases, the argument suggests that the prediction process is unlikely to be subserved by a theory. But in those cases where we are *bad* at predicting what people do in unfamiliar cases, the argument suggests that the prediction process is unlikely to be subserved by a *simulation* process. We recognize that there are various moves that might be made in response to the argument from accuracy, and thus we do not treat the argument as definitive. We do, however, think that the argument justifies a strong initial presumption that accurate mindreading processes are subserved by simulation-like processes and that inaccurate ones are not. And this is just the way we have used the argument in constructing our account of mindreading.

Before leaving the topic of inference prediction, we want to offer one further argument for preferring our account over the sort of account an STT advocate might offer. On our theory, the PWB and the inference mechanism are involved in *both* mindreading and hypothetical reasoning. Thus our theory predicts that there is a strong parallel between the answers people come up with in hypothetical reasoning tasks (like: Who would become President if the current President resigned?) and the predictions they make about what other people would infer if they believed the hypothesis was true (If Fred believes the current President has resigned, what inference will he draw about who will become President?). While the evidence for this parallel is largely anecdotal, if it does indeed exist, it poses yet another puzzle for advocates of STT, since on their account, there is no reason to suppose that the theory subserving inference prediction plays any role in the process of hypothetical reasoning. Thus the parallel is something of a mystery.

Default belief attribution

Another fact on our checklist is that normal adults readily attribute large numbers of beliefs to other people, even when they have no apparent evidence, and most of these attributions are correct. On our account default attribution plays a central role in explaining this skill. When building a model of a target in her PWB, a mindreader initially includes a large number of her own beliefs in the model. That is why we believe that the person we have just met at a party believes that the weather is warmer in summer than in winter. The process of default attribution is not plausibly viewed as theory mediated.[24] Thus it is not surprising that advocates of STT have said very little about the quite extra-ordinary fact that we attribute vast numbers of beliefs to people about whom we know next to nothing. To the best of our knowledge, no advocate of STT has ever proposed an explanation of the phenomenon.

The default attribution process does not, of course, offer a full explanation for the impressive accuracy of normal adult belief attribution. To explain that, two additional elements of our theory are required. First, there is a cluster of strategies for attributing discrepant beliefs, and while relatively little is known about the mechanisms subserving these strategies, it is certainly possible that the sort of theoretical information emphasized by STT plays a role in some of these strategies. But merely adding discrepant beliefs to the PWB model of a target would generate chaos if the model also contained most of the mindreader's own beliefs, since some of those beliefs will be incompatible with the discrepant beliefs of the target. To handle this problem, our theory posits that discrepant beliefs are 'clamped' and then the UpDater, which is part of the inference mechanism, cleans up the PWB model by eliminating the default attributed beliefs that are incompatible with the target's discrepant beliefs. This appeal to the UpDater—a mechanism which also plays a role in UpDating the mind-reader's own beliefs and in hypothetical reasoning—is another place in which a simulation-theoretic idea plays an important role in our theory. So on our account, three factors are involved in explaining the fecundity and accuracy of normal adult belief attribution: default attribution, discrepant belief attribution strategies, and the use of the UpDater. The sort of theoretical information that is the only tool in the monolithic STT toolkit is involved in no more than one of these.

Mindreading in children

We turn now to the STT account of mindreading in children. That account has several parts. First, advocates of STT maintain, there is an early mind-reading system, whose central component is a theory, sometimes called

[24] An advocate of STT might protest that default attribution *is* theory mediated, and that the relevant part of the theory is simply the proposition: (1) *Most people believe most of what I believe*. But (1) does not come close to explaining the subtlety and sophistication of the default attribution process. As emphasized in the following paragraph, on our account, when beliefs are default attributed, they are UpDated with previously recognized discrepant beliefs 'clamped'. This process removes from the PWB model of the target beliefs that are incompatible with the clamped discrepant beliefs. Obviously (1) could not begin to capture the complex pattern dis-played by the subset of the mindreader's beliefs that end up being default attributed. Nor is there any way of modifying (1) to do the job, without assuming that it includes an explicit account of the complex (and currently unknown!) strategy that the UpDater uses.

Desire-Perception Psychology (Gopnik and Wellman 1992, 1994), which invokes concepts of *desire* and *perception* that are 'non-representational' and thus importantly different from the concepts of *desire* and *perception* used in the theory subserving mindreading in older children and in adults. According to advocates of STT, the leap in mindreading that occurs after the age of 3 is importantly similar to the sort of theoretical change that occurs in science. As they get older, children encounter more and more evidence that is incompatible with their theory, and ultimately they come up with a new theory which includes new 'representational' concepts of *desire* and *perception* and a representational concept of *belief*. It is this new theory that guides mindreading in older children and adults. On our view, just about everything in this account is mistaken. To make our case for this claim, we will begin by noting one important aspect of early mindreading that cannot be explained simply by assuming that the child is using a Desire-Perception Psychology. After that, we will focus on the problems besetting the STT account of the transition from early to later mindreading.

Behaviour prediction in young children   According to leading advocates of STT, the theory that guides early mindreading enables young children to attribute goals or desires, and the attribution of desire can then lead to a prediction about how the target will behave (e.g. Bartsch and Wellman 1995). But these theorists have had relatively little to say about how the young mindreader goes from a desire attribution to a behaviour prediction, and no version of the STT accommodates the obvious fact that young children can make quite *detailed* predictions about the behaviour that targets will engage in while pursuing their goals. Gopnik and Wellman suggest that the young child exploits an early form of 'the practical syllogism' in order to make behaviour predictions, using the following principle: 'If an agent desires x, and sees that x exists, he will do things to get x' (Gopnik and Wellman 1994: 265). But what 'things' will the agent do to get x? If a 3-year-old knows that Mary wants an apple, how does the 3-year-old predict the way in which Mary will satisfy her desire? Will Mary slither on her stomach to the nearest apple? Will she telepathically have the nearest apple transported through the air? Gopnik and Wellman's account might explain how the young child can predict that the target will act so as to satisfy her desires (see also Wellman 1990; Bartsch and Wellman 1995). But that grossly understates the predictive capacities of the young child who can also predict that Mary will walk to the fridge, open the fridge door, pull open the appropriate drawer, pick an apple up with her hands (not with her feet or her elbows), and so on. Merely knowing that Mary desires an apple and sees that it exists does not provide the child with such a rich set of predictions. We have been unable to find any detailed discussion of the young child's capacity for this kind of rich behavioural prediction in the mindreading literature. But since one of us (Nichols) has a young child, we had an opportunity to explore

Box 3.2

Episode 1

FATHER. What if Sarah [Julia's older sister] wanted to get an apple? What would she do?

JULIA. NO RESPONSE.

FATHER. Where would she go? To the bathroom?

JULIA. No, to the fridgerator. (*The group proceeds to the kitchen, where Sarah (having been surreptitiously told what to do) walks up to the refrigerator, but does not open it.*)

FATHER. What will Sarah do now?

JULIA. Open the fridgerator. (*Sarah then opens the refrigerator.*)

FATHER. How will Sarah get the fruit out? (*Julia grabs an apple with her hands.*)

Episode 2

(*At the breakfast table, Julia watches her father put a bunch of grapes on a small tray, and then cover the tray with a large bowl.*)

FATHER. What would Mommy do if she wanted grapes?

JULIA. Lift up the bowl and get the grapes. (*Mommy then lifts the bowl.*)

FATHER. Like that?

JULIA. Yeah.

---

the capacity a bit. Box 3.2 presents two episodes involving Julia, who was 2 years and 10 months old at the time.

We have proposed that once a young mindreader detects the goal of the target, she uses the Planner, along with her own beliefs about the world, to predict how the target will achieve his goal. While some of the desire detection strategies that young children exploit might turn out to be similar to scientific theories in significant respects, we think it is much less plausible that the role we see for the Planner and for the child's own beliefs in the prediction process can be usefully viewed as just more theory, as a hardline theory–theory account would require. Of course, an obvious move for Gopnik and Wellman to make at this point is to appeal to a mechanism like our Planner *in addition to* the more theory-like elements of the early mindreading system. In so doing they would be moving away from the sort of monolithic theory–theory that they have advocated in the past, which, of course, we think would be a good thing.

The isolation of perception detection in early mindreading   We have maintained that young children have a Perception Detection Mechanism that enables them to pass various perspective-taking tasks (e.g. Level 1 tasks). This mechanism produces representations like 'Target sees the dog' or 'Target doesn't see the dog'. However, on our account, the early mindreading system *does not* rely on perception attribution to move from desire attribution to behaviour prediction. Desire detection, the Planner, and the child's own beliefs are all that is required. Thus our account can accommodate the desire-based behaviour predictions that young children make without appealing to the capacity for perception attribution.

By contrast, STT advocates regard perception attribution (and the 'perception-psychology' theory that, they maintain, underlies it) as a central part of the process that leads to behaviour predictions in early mindreading (see e.g. Wellman 1990; Gopnik and Meltzoff 1997). The point comes out particularly clearly in the following passage from Gopnik and Wellman (1994), in which they also elaborate on the idea that the Desire-Perception Psychology used by the young child is 'non-representational' and that it includes a 'first form' of the practical syllogism:

[D]esire and perception can be, and at first are, understood in non-representational terms...Desires at first are conceived simply as something like drives toward objects (Wellman & Woolley, 1990). Perceptions are first understood simply as awareness of or visual contact with objects (Flavell, 1988).... these very young children seem to treat desires and perception as simple causal links between the mind and the world.... These causal constructs [non-representational conceptions of desire and perception] are simple, but they have considerable predictive power. *In particular, together they allow the first form of 'the practical syllogism': 'If an agent desires x, and sees that x exists, he will do things to get x.' Even that form of the practical syllogism is a powerful inferential folk psychological law. It allows children to infer, for example, that if John wants a cookie and sees one in the cookie jar, he will go there for it. If he doesn't want it, or doesn't see it, he won't. And there is evidence that 2½-year olds make just such inferences (Wellman 1990, chap. 8).* (Gopnik and Wellman 1994: 265, emphasis added)

The problem with all this is that, as far as we can tell, *there is no evidence at all* that young children make these behaviour predictions that are simultaneously sensitive to perception and to desire. What the data do show (including especially the data reported in Wellman 1990: ch. 8) is that young children can make impressive behaviour predictions based on desire attributions. Other data show that young children and even infants can also make (less flexible) predictions based on perceptual attention (Baron-Cohen 1995; Spelke et al. 1995). But there is no evidence that these young children make predictions of action that are sensitive to desire and perception *at the same time*.[25] Indeed, the evidence indicates that the capacity for making and using desire attribution

---

[25] Alison Gopnik (personal communication) has suggested that the work of Wellman et al. (2000) might address this gap in the evidence. Wellman and his co-workers found that 2- and 3-year-old children can infer what a target is looking at by the target's emotional expression. For instance, in one experiment, subjects are shown two identical-looking boxes and shown that one has a toy in it and the other is empty. The boxes are closed, and one of the boxes is picked (without the child's knowing which) and put on the table. An accomplice comes in and opens the

pretty clearly precedes the capacity for perception attributions. Recent studies demonstrate that by the age of 18 months children have a surprisingly sophisticated appreciation of desire (Repacholi and Gopnik 1997; Meltzoff 1995). Yet children tend to make mistakes on simple perspective-taking tasks until after the age of 2 (Gopnik et al. 1995). So there seems to be no empirical reason to think that an understanding of perception plays a central role in the early mindreading system. And that is good news for our theory since we maintain that early behaviour prediction is subserved by the Desire and Plan system which does not rely on the Perception Detection Mechanisms. It is not such good news for Gopnik and Wellman, however, since they have offered no account of how behaviour prediction is possible, for the young mindreader, if perception attributions are unavailable.

From a 'non-representational' to a 'representational' understanding of desire One of the items on our checklist is the fact that young children show an understanding of desire before they show an understanding of belief. As noted earlier, the explanation offered by advocates of STT is part of their overall theory-revision strategy for explaining the leap in mindreading after the third birthday. Young children, they maintain, have a theory that invokes 'non-representational' concepts of *desire* and *perception*, and sometime between the ages of $2\frac{1}{2}$ and 4 this theory, which has an increasingly hard time explaining the evidence about minds and behaviour that children are acquiring, is replaced by a theory which utilizes 'representational' concepts of *desire* and *perception* and a representational concept of *belief*. The emergence of the new representational conception of desire is treated as a crucial piece of evidence in support of their claim that children use theory-building mechanisms like those employed in science to improve their theory of mind. There is, the story goes, a 'theoretical development' from one conception of desire to another (Wellman 1990; Bartsch and Wellman 1995; see also Gopnik and Meltzoff 1997; Flavell and Miller 1998).

On our view, an important change does indeed take place in what the child can *do* with attributions of desire between the ages of $2\frac{1}{2}$ and 4. However, we do not think that it is plausible to describe this change as the development of a new theory, nor do we think there is any interpretation of the term 'representational' on which it is plausible to describe the conception of desire that the older child has as 'representational' and the conception that the younger child has as

box. The accomplice either smiles and says 'Oh boy' or makes a sad face and says 'Oh no'. The child is then asked, 'What is Ann looking at?' Young children do quite well on this, saying that Ann is looking at the toy when Ann is smiling and that Ann is looking at the empty box when she is looking sad. This is, to be sure, a significant finding. But it surely does not show that children are exploiting the practical syllogism in predicting behaviour from perception and desire since the experiment does not involve any behaviour prediction at all.

'non-representational'. In support of these claims, we will begin by explaining why characterizing the change as a move from a 'non-representational' to a 'representational' understanding of desire is unmotivated. Then we will sketch our own view of what happens in this transition and why it is not plausibly viewed as the emergence of a new theory.

Perhaps the first thing to say about the idea that children move from a non-representational to a representational conception of desire is that it is not at all clear what it *means*. In both philosophy and cognitive science, there has been no shortage of attempts to define terms like 'represent' and 'representational' and related terms like 'intentional', but (to put it mildly) no consensus has emerged (Perry 1994; Schwartz 1994; Searle 1994; Stich and Warfield 1994; Von Eckardt 1999). The brief comments that advocates of STT make when they try to say what *they* mean do little to remedy the situation.[26] But rather than plunging into debates about the meaning of 'representational' we think it is more useful to focus on the sorts of *evidence* that these theorists offer in support of their claim that older children have a representational understanding of desire while young children have a non-representational understanding. This will enable us to offer a number of hypotheses about what the claim might mean. In each case, however, we will argue that if *that* is what they mean, then there is no good reason to think that the claim is *true*.[27]

We will begin with Astington and Gopnik (1991), who suggest that a subject has a representational understanding of desire if she appreciates that the same object can be desired by one person but not by another. So the crucial feature of a representational understanding on this account is the appreciation of the intersubjective *variability* of desires. This certainly is an important aspect of desire. However, if an appreciation of intersubjective variability counts as evidence that a subject's understanding of desire is representational, then the claim about the difference between younger and older children is not supported by the evidence, which suggests that children recognize the intersubjective variability of desire from a *very* young age. Indeed, as we noted earlier,[28] some of Gopnik's own experiments indicate that 18-month-old children appreciate that the same object can be desired by one person but not

---

[26] Here is an example from Bartsch and Wellman 1995: 65: '[D]esires are intentional, in the philosopher's sense, that is, they are about, for, or toward some object.... The object of a desire may be physical, but it could also be an action or complex states of affairs. John wants an apple, or he wants to raise his arm, or he wants to go home. John might even want an object that does not exist. He might want a unicorn or to be able to hold his breath for three hours. The object of such a desire must therefore be represented as a state of affairs in John's mind rather than in the world. It can be argued that all desires describe mental-content objects, internal states of affairs "as desired," rather than as they really are or really could be.'

[27] See Schwitzgebel (1999) for a related critique of the work on the child's development of a 'representational' understanding of desire.

[28] See the discussion of 'Some empirical evidence for (very) early mindreading' in Section 3.3.1.

by another person (Repacholi and Gopnik 1997; for additional evidence that young children appreciate the intersubjective variability of desire see also Wellman and Woolley 1990).

In Wellman's initial attempt to unpack the claim that young children have a 'nonrepresentational' notion of desire, he maintained that the young child has a 'Simple Desire Psychology', on which desires are 'attitudes about an actual object or state of affairs' (1990: 210). And, as the context makes clear, the 'actual' objects and states of affairs Wellman has in mind are specific physical objects like a nearby apple or toy, and states of affairs that actually obtain. However, as several critics have pointed out, this account does not support the claim that young children have only a non-representational understanding of desire, because young children can and do attribute desires for states of affairs that do not yet (and may never) actually obtain. So, for example, a young child can attribute to a target the desire to throw an apple, even though the apple in question is never thrown (Perner 1991: 279; Leslie 1994b: 138–9).[29]

This objection led Wellman to offer a revised account on which Early Desire Psychology is non-representational because the child sees 'the contents of a person's desires as *real* objects in the world'. 'In our proposed nonrepresentational understanding of desire, the intentional object of desire, for the 2-year-old, *really exists* in the world but is not necessarily visible, immediately available to the target person' (Bartsch and Wellman 1995: 151, 152, emphasis added). This, as we hardly need to point out, is not exactly a perspicuous doctrine. If the child believes that some target (perhaps the child herself) desires to be asleep but is not *now* asleep, what exactly could it *mean* to say that the object of this desire is a state of affairs which 'really exists' though it is not 'immediately available'? Our best guess about what Bartsch and Wellman have in mind is that 'real' actions and states of affairs are those that are *possible*. Some evidence for this interpretation is provided by the fact that, when illustrating the sorts of desires that can be attributed by someone with a full-blown representational account of desire, but not by someone with a non-representational account of desire, their examples are *wanting a unicorn* and *wanting to hold one's breath for three hours* (Bartsch and Wellman 1995: 65). We are, we should emphasize, struggling to give a charitable interpretation to Bartsch and Wellman's rather dark pronouncements. What they actually say is that 2-year-olds have a non-representational understanding of desire because they 'can imagine persons wanting things that 2-year-olds know to exist in the real world;

---

[29] Here is Perner's way of making the point: 'A simple conception of desires as proposed by Wellman (1990)...limits children's understanding of what Sam wants to being "an attitude about an actual object or state of affairs." This means that children could only understand "Sam wants the rabbit (which exists)." They could not have encoded "Sam wants to take the rabbit to school" because "taking the rabbit to school" is a nonexistent state of affairs and therefore, according to Wellman, beyond the simple conception of desire' (Perner 1991: 278–9).

but they cannot conceive of persons wanting things that 2-year-olds know to be nonexistent' (211). But taken literally, this simply cannot be true. For, as they acknowledge, a 2-year-old *can* conceive of a target child wanting to jump up and down now, even though the 2-year-old knows that the target is *not* jumping up and down now—and thus that the action which is the object of the target's desire is 'nonexistent'. If, as we are proposing, we interpret 'nonexistent' to mean 'not possible', then at least the claim they are making about young children is not patently false.

We are, of course, still not entirely out of the woods in trying to come up with a charitable interpretation of Bartsch and Wellman's view, since the notion of possibility, and thus the claim that 2-year-olds cannot conceive of persons wanting things that 2-year-olds know (or believe) to be impossible, is itself open to a variety of interpretations.[30] But we don't propose to dwell on this issue since as we see it, on any reasonable interpretation of possibility, the Bartsch and Wellman view confronts a pair of problems. First, as far as we can tell, there is exactly *no* evidence for the claim. Certainly no evidence is offered by Bartsch and Wellman. Second, it is very likely that the claim is *false*. If we look to the protocols of the group of four children that Bartsch and Wellman (1995) focus on, there are several examples in which young children seem to be attributing desires for things that they know are not possible. One striking example comes from Abe (Kuczaj and Maratsos 1975). At 2 years 9 months, the following exchange occurs between Abe and his mother:

ABE. I want to read the funny papers now.
MOTHER. Well it's not Sunday morning is it Abe? You have to be patient and wait for Sunday morning to get here.
ABE. I want the sun come up right now and then the funny papers come.

Abe presumably knows that what he wants is not possible. Similarly, at 2 years 11 months, Adam is playing with a small toy airplane and asks, 'do you want me get in?' The adult says, 'Yes. Can you fit in?' and Adam responds, 'I can't fit in' (Brown 1973). Here again it appears that Adam understands that what the adult wants is not possible.

In this section we have been struggling without success to find an interpretation of the claim that young children have a non-representational conception of desire that is both intelligible and not incompatible with available evidence. Perhaps some interpretation that we have not considered will do the trick. But until advocates of STT tell us what this interpretation is, we think the appropriate conclusion to draw is that they are simply mistaken (or

---

[30] So, for example, philosophers typically distinguish between nomological possibility, metaphysical possibility, and logical possibility.

confused) in claiming that sometime between the ages of $2\frac{1}{2}$ and 4 the child replaces a non-representational concept of *desire* with a representational concept. And since this alleged conceptual replacement is the central element in the argument that the leap in mindreading abilities during this period is a 'theoretical development' subserved by much the same processes that underlie theory change in science, we see no reason to accept this 'theory revision' account of the difference between early and later mindreading abilities.

An alternative account of the difference between the earlier and later understanding of desire   In the previous section we noted that advocates of STT invoke the alleged transition from a non-representational to a representational understanding of desire as an important piece of evidence in support of their view that mindreading is subserved by a succession of theories. But, as we saw, even when we attempt to interpret STT theorists as charitably as possible, the evidence simply does not support their claim that between the ages of $2\frac{1}{2}$ and 4, children move from a non-representational to a representational theory of mind. Although we do not believe that the $2\frac{1}{2}$-year-old has a 'non-representational' theory of desire, we agree that there *is* an important distinction between the younger and older child's understanding of desire and other mental states (e.g. Bartsch and Wellman 1995; Perner 1991; Leslie 1994*b*; Gopnik and Wellman 1994). On our view, what distinguishes the later understanding of desire is that desire attributions are profoundly affected by the addition of the PWB and various strategies of discrepant belief attribution to the mindreading system. In particular, the addition of the PWB and discrepant belief attribution mechanisms has a dramatic effect on the sorts of inferences that can be drawn concerning others' desires.

To rehearse a familiar philosophical point, even though Jocasta is Oedipus' mother, Oedipus might want to marry Jocasta without wanting to marry his mother. However, we propose that before the child is capable of using the PWB and discrepant belief attribution mechanisms, the child is condemned to less fine-grained attributions of desire. Before the child has these capacities, if he knows that Briar Rose is Princess Aurora,[31] and that Maleficent wants to harm Princess Aurora, the child will naturally infer that Maleficent wants to harm Briar Rose. As the child gains the capacity to attribute ignorance and to use the PWB for mindreading, he can recognize that Maleficent is ignorant of the fact that Briar Rose is Princess Aurora, and hence that Maleficent's desire to harm Princess Aurora will not lead her to desire to harm Briar Rose. More generally, we suggest that after the belief attribution mechanisms and PWB come on-line for mindreading, the child comes to recognize that the target's

---

[31] As one of us—the one who has young children—had to inform the other, Princess Aurora has yet another, and more familiar, name. She is the main character in *Sleeping Beauty*.

ignorance may warrant a blocking of certain inferences. Similarly, once the child can attribute false beliefs and use the PWB system for mindreading, the child can recognize that the target might have misdirected desires. For instance, if the child knows that Snow White falsely believes that the bearer of the apple is a kindly old woman (instead of the Wicked Queen), and adds this belief to her PWB model of Snow White's beliefs, then the inference mechanism, operating on the contents of the PWB might infer that the bearer of the apple is harmless and weak, and this will be added to the child's PWB model of Snow White. If the child believes that this is what Snow White believes, the child will infer that Snow White will want to help the bearer of the apple. But before the capacity to attribute false beliefs and use the PWB in mindreading emerges, the child will be unable to make these sorts of inferences, despite having an impressive understanding of desire.

As we noted earlier, some of the strategies of false and discrepant belief attribution that emerge between the ages of $2\frac{1}{2}$ and 4 *might* perhaps be subserved by theory-like information, and their acquisition might be usefully compared to the adoption of new theories. But the emergence of the capacity to use the PWB to build a model of a target's beliefs, and the role of the inference mechanism, which includes the UpDater, in the elaboration of PWB models is in no interesting way similar to the adoption of a new theory. So if the account we have sketched is on the right track, there is considerably more involved in the leap in mindreading skills that occurs after the third birthday than the STT can explain.

The mindreading deficits of individuals with autism

Our checklist includes three facts about individuals with autism:

1. autistic children do not exhibit the leap in mindreading abilities that normal children do at about the age of 3;
2. autistic children have some capacity for desire attribution despite their difficulties with belief attribution;
3. autistic children are deficient in their capacity for pretend play.

Advocates of STT rarely mention these facts and they have offered no systematic explanation for them.[32] Modularity theorists, on the other hand, have used the facts about autism as an important part of the evidence for their account of mindreading. Rather than setting out our own explanation of these facts here, we will save it for the following section where we will compare our explanation with the one offered by modularity theorists.

---

[32] Gopnik et al. 2000 try to sketch in broad strokes an STT approach to autism. But they offer no systematic explanation for the three facts listed above.

3.4.2. Modularity theory

Modularity theory, which is the other important information-rich account of mindreading, is defended principally in the work of Alan Leslie and his collaborators (Leslie 1991, 1994*b*, 1995, 2000; Leslie and Thaiss 1992; Leslie and Roth 1993; Scholl and Leslie 1999; see also Baron-Cohen 1995). In contrast with scientific-theory theorists, who think that the information used in mindreading is acquired, modified, and stored in much the same way that scientific and commonsense theories are, modularity theorists maintain that crucial parts of the information that guides mindreading is stored in one or more *modules*. Before we attempt to assess this claim, we will have to explain what modularity theorists think modules are and elaborate a bit on the role that Leslie and his collaborators think that modules play in mindreading.

The contemporary discussion of modularity in cognitive science can be traced to Jerry Fodor's highly influential book, *The Modularity of the Mind* (Fodor 1983). On Fodor's account, modules have most or all of the following characteristics:[33]

1. They are domain specific.
2. Their operation is mandatory.
3. There is only limited central access to the mental representations that modules compute.
4. Their operation is fast.
5. They are 'informationally encapsulated'. This, Fodor explains, means that modules have only limited access to information contained in other mental systems. In particular, he stresses that modules are insensitive to the cognitive agent's beliefs, desires, and expectations. Fodor clearly thinks that informational encapsulation is crucial for modularity. Indeed, in discussing 'input systems' like those subserving perception and language comprehension, he says 'informational encapsulation is *the essence of their modularity*' (1983: 71; emphasis added).[34]
6. Their outputs are shallow. This, according to Fodor, means that the information in the output of a module is restricted to relatively simple,

---

[33] Fodor has offered a number of slightly different characterizations of modules. The one that follows is based on the extended discussion in Fodor 1983: 47–101.

[34] Since the informational encapsulation of modules will play a central role in our argument, it will be useful to quote Fodor at some length:

The informational encapsulation of the input systems is, or so I shall argue, the essence of their modularity. It is also the essence of the analogy between the input systems and reflexes; reflexes are informationally encapsulated with bells on.

Suppose that you and I have known each other for many a long year (we were boys together, say) and you have come fully to appreciate the excellence of my character. In particular, you have come to know perfectly well that under no conceivable circumstances would low-level concepts. So, for example, a perceptual module might report on the shapes and colors of things, but it would not 'characterize visual stimuli in such terms as *proton trace*' (1983: 93; emphasis in the original).

7. They exhibit characteristic and specific breakdown patterns.
8. Their ontogeny exhibits a characteristic pace and sequencing.

While other writers have used the term 'module' in a bewildering variety of ways,[35] Leslie and his colleagues cite Fodor frequently and are clearly working with a notion of module that is, near enough, the same as the one Fodor introduced. Indeed, in a recent defence of the modularity account of mind-reading, Scholl and Leslie (1999) explicitly mention the first seven items on Fodor's list.

Though the account of mindreading offered by modularity theorists has become more complex and nuanced in the years since it was first proposed, it has never been as monolithic as the account urged by scientific-theory theorists. Modularity theorists have always recognized that non-modular mechanisms and processes play a significant role in adult mindreading. However, the core claim of the modularity theory is that at least one central part of the system subserving mindreading is modular and emerges fairly early in development. This modular component, which Leslie has dubbed 'ToMM' (for Theory-of-Mind-Mechanism), comes equipped with some basic mindreading concepts like *belief* and *desire*[36] and it performs many of the most basic mindreading functions—particularly those that emerge early in development. More specifically, 'ToMM ... is essentially a module which spontaneously and post-perceptually attends to behaviors and infers (i.e. computes) the mental states which contributed to them .... As a result, ToMM will provide the child with early intentional insight into the behaviors of others' (Scholl and Leslie 1999: 147). Somewhat later in development, Leslie and his colleagues maintain, another system, the Selection Processing (or 'SP') system develops.

I stick my finger in your eye. Suppose that this belief of yours is both explicit and deeply felt. You would, in fact, go to the wall for it. Still, if I jab my finger near enough to your eyes, and fast enough, you'll blink. To say, as we did above, that the blink reflex is mandatory is to say, inter alia, that it has no access to what you know about my character or, for that matter, to any other of your beliefs, utilities and expectations. For this reason the blink reflex is often produced when sober reflection would show it to be uncalled for; like panther-spotting, it is prepared to trade false positives for speed.

That is what it is like for a psychological system to be informationally encapsulated. If you now imagine a system that is informationally encapsulated in the way that reflexes are, but also computational in a way that reflexes are not, you will have some idea of what I'm proposing that input systems are like. (Fodor 1983: 71–2).

[35] See Segal 1996 and Samuels 2000.

[36] Leslie also includes *pretence* which, as we saw in Chapter 2, he takes to be a mindreading concept.

SP, which 'may be non-modular' (ibid.), plays a role in determining the exact content of mental states that a more mature mindreader attributes to targets. As we will see below, SP plays a central role in Leslie's account of how older children and adults succeed in attributing the right belief content in false belief tasks. Still later in development, the basic mindreading abilities that ToMM and SP make available 'are recruited by higher cognitive processes for more complex tasks, and the resulting higher-order [mindreading] activities may well interact (in a non-modular way) with other cognitive processes, and may not be uniform across individuals or cultures' (Scholl and Leslie 1999: 140). So, like us, Leslie and his colleagues view adult mindreading as 'a collection of multiple related capacities, each of which is cognitively realized by a distinct mechanism or processes' (Scholl and Leslie 1999: 140). Despite this, however, we find much to disagree with in modular accounts and we think there is ample reason to prefer our theory to any version of the modularity theory on offer.

One important area of disagreement centres on the process of default attribution. Leslie and his colleagues think that a modular ToMM can explain the fact that mindreaders attribute a vast number of their own beliefs to targets, but we will argue that this is a mistake. Moreover, as we will see, much the same problem that prevents modular mechanisms from explaining default attribution also makes it impossible for a modular mechanism to explain both detailed behaviour prediction and inference prediction. Why, then, should we think that modules play *any* major role in mindreading? Perhaps the most detailed answer is provided in Scholl and Leslie (1999). But we will argue that their answer is far from compelling. Indeed, most of the evidence they cite is *irrelevant* to the hypothesis that basic aspects of mindreading are subserved by a module. Though we do not think there is any reason to believe that modules play the sort of major role in mindreading that Leslie and his colleagues propose, we believe there is some evidence suggesting that one part of the complex mindreading system sketched in Figure 3.5—the Desire Detection System—might well be at least partly modular. We will review this evidence in the penultimate part of this section. In the final part, we will compare the modularity theorists' explanation of autism with the explanation that we favour, and argue that the experimental evidence cited by modularity theorists does not support their theory.

Default attribution

Modularity theorists, in contrast with scientific-theory theorists, have regularly noted that mindreaders typically attribute many of their own beliefs to targets, and Leslie has offered an explanation that, at first blush, sounds similar to the one that we have proposed. Here is a passage in which he

explains, quite correctly we think, why default belief attribution is generally
a good strategy:

> It is useful to understand why belief attribution has a default bias. If *desires* set an
> agent's goals, *beliefs* inform the agent about the state of the world. A belief that
> misinforms an agent is a useless, even a dangerous, thing: beliefs *ought* to be true.
> Therefore, the optimal default strategy for the belief attributer is to assume that an
> agent's beliefs *are* true. Apparently, this is the strategy followed by the three-year-old.
> (Leslie 2000: 1242)

But, as Leslie goes on to note, there will also be occasions—false belief tasks,
for example, and their real-life equivalents—in which this default strategy
will lead to a mistaken belief attribution. In these circumstances, the default
strategy must be inhibited or overridden, and some other content must be
selected. On Leslie's theory, both the overriding and the selecting are handled
by the Selection Processing system. However, that system matures later than
the mechanism that leads to default attribution, and until SP is in place, the
child gets false belief tasks wrong.[37]

So far, this all sounds plausible enough. But let's look more carefully at the
default strategy which, according to Leslie, the 3-year-old always uses and
older mindreaders use except when it is overridden by the SP system. What
is the mechanism that makes these default contents available? The answer,
Leslie tells us, is the modular Theory-of-Mind-Mechanism, ToMM: 'ToMM
always makes the current situation available as a possible and even preferred
content because (a) the current situation is a truer picture of the world, and
(b) beliefs tend to be true' (Scholl and Leslie 1999: 147).[38] Now the first thing
to say about this idea is that Scholl and Leslie are obviously being a bit careless
when they say that 'ToMM always makes the current situation available'.
Since ToMM is not omniscient, it cannot always know the current situation.
So what they must really mean is that ToMM always makes available *what
the mindreader believes the current situation to be*. Thus ToMM must have
basically unrestricted access to everything that the mindreader believes about
the world. And if that is the case, then Leslie's theory is in serious trouble.
For, as we have seen, an *essential* characteristic of modules is that they
are *informationally encapsulated*, and thus they are largely *insensitive* to

---

[37] '[F]alse belief tasks require that the default strategy be over-ridden. According to the
ToMM-SP model, to do so requires inhibition of the pre-potent attribution. The older child's
success shows that he manages this inhibition' (Leslie 2000: 1242). 'SP's job is thus essentially
to *inhibit* competing possible contents for the belief.... [T]o infer the content of somebody's
belief when that content is false, SP is required to select among the possible contents that ToMM
makes available' (Scholl and Leslie 1999: 147).

[38] Since the point will loom large in our critique, it is worth emphasizing that Leslie makes
exactly the same claim in a number of places. In Leslie (2000: 1240), for example, he notes that
Leslie and Thais (1992) 'argue that the ToMM by default attributes a belief with a content that
reflects current reality'.

information about the mindreader's beliefs. Indeed, a cognitive system that has unrestricted access to all of the mindreader's beliefs would be a paradigm case of a *non-modular* system. So ToMM cannot do what Leslie says it does—it cannot explain the phenomenon of default attribution—*unless it is non-modular.*[39]

One reaction we have encountered to this argument, and those to come about detailed behaviour prediction and inference prediction, is the suggestion that a different interpretation of the notion of encapsulation is appropriate when considering 'central' modules like ToMM. Peter Carruthers (personal communication) has argued that while default attribution, as we characterize it, clearly violates the requirement of informational encapsulation, it is entirely compatible with what Botterill and Carruthers (1999: 69) call 'processing encapsulation'. Informational encapsulation, according to Botterill and Carruthers, is determined by the extent to which 'information from elsewhere in cognition can *enter* a modular processor', while processing encapsulation is determined by the extent to which 'the *processing* which the module does can be influenced by other parts of the system' (1999: 69, emphasis in the original). (In conversation, Jerry Fodor made what we took to be a similar suggestion. Or perhaps it was the even stronger suggestion that processing encapsulation is the only sort of encapsulation required for both central and peripheral modules!) While we agree that default attribution may well be processing encapsulated, we don't think that advocates of modularity should take much comfort from this, since as far as we can see, processing encapsulation is an *extremely weak* constraint to place on a component of the mind, so weak, in fact, that it is hard to think of interesting systems that violate the constraint. So if processing encapsulation is the essential feature of modules, then just about *every* component of the mind that does any information processing will pass the test, and the notion of a module will turn out to be much less interesting.

To see the point, consider the decision-making (or practical reasoning) system. On our account, this is a processing component that has access to all of the cognitive agent's beliefs and desires, and its primary job is the daunting one of generating both decisions about what to do and 'instrumental desires' that will be needed to get it done. Obviously, the practical reasoning system is informationally *un*encapsulated (with bells on!). Indeed, practical reasoning

---

[39] The requirement that the outputs of a module must be 'shallow' (i.e. restricted to relatively simple, low-level concepts) poses yet another problem for the claim that default attribution is subserved by a modular ToMM, since we often default attribute beliefs involving quite sophisticated concepts. For example, default attribution leads us to believe that our new colleague down the hall believes that George W. Bush lost the popular vote but won the Presidency in the Electoral College. And while we're not at all sure how 'low level' a 'shallow' concept must be, we are reasonably confident that concepts like *winning in the Electoral College* don't count.

has long been one of Fodor's favourite examples of a process that is *not* subserved by a module. How does the practical reasoning system work? No one
really knows, of course. But one obvious speculation is that it runs a complex
programme that embodies an elaborate logic of decision (along with some
fancy algorithms for searching for relevant information in the Belief Box and
Desire Box). The outputs of this complex programme—the decisions and
instrumental desires it produces—are, of course, a function of what it finds in
the Belief and Desire Boxes. But it is plausible to suppose that the *programme
itself* is not affected by what the cognitive agent believes and desires. If that's
right, then the practical reasoning mechanism is processing encapsulated. And
if processing encapsulation, not informational encapsulation, is what's important for modularity, then practical reasoning may well be subserved by a module. Apparently, Botterill and Carruthers are entirely comfortable with this
idea. '[N]othing,' they write, 'counts against the idea of some sort of practical
reasoning module, which takes as its inputs both current beliefs and current
desires, and operates in such a way as to formulate as output intentions to act'
(1999: 69). A few pages later, they suggest that scientific reasoning, which is
Fodor's other favourite example of a process that is *not* subserved by a module, may be the product of 'a dedicated science module' (72–3).

To summarize: if informational encapsulation is an essential feature of
modules, then default attribution cannot be subserved by a module. We do not
deny that default attribution may be subserved by a 'mental module' if the sort
of encapsulation that is essential for modularity is *processing* encapsulation
rather than *informational* encapsulation. But when the notion of encapsulation is interpreted in this way, it is far from clear that there are *any* mental
processes that are not subserved by 'encapsulated' mechanisms.

Detailed behaviour predictions

As we saw in Section 3.4.1, young children can often offer detailed predictions about how a target will go about accomplishing a goal. Adults can do this
too, of course. To the best of our knowledge, modularity theorists have offered
no explanation of this skill. On our account, young children generate these
detailed predictions by using their Planners and the information stored in their
own beliefs to figure out the best way to accomplish the target's goal. Older
children and adults have a more sophisticated strategy in which the Planner
uses the information in the PWB model of the target when it determines the
best way to satisfy the target's desires. Though the details of our account may
turn out to be incorrect, it is hard to see how any account can be given of the
young child's predictive skills that does not rely heavily on what the child
believes about the world. In the first episode described in Box 3.2 above, for
example, Julia predicts that her sister will go to the 'fridgerator', open the

door and take an apple with her hands. How could she possibly make this prediction without relying on her own beliefs about where apples are kept and
how to get them? But if the process that leads to detailed behaviour predictions
in young children does indeed rely on all sorts of information drawn from the
child's own beliefs, it can't be the case that this process is subserved by a module, since modules are informationally encapsulated and thus they don't have
unrestricted access to the information stored in the child's beliefs. Consider,
now, the detailed behaviour predictions made by adults. In this case, if we are
right, it is the PWB that drives the Planner, and a great deal of the information
in the PWB is derived from the mindreader's own beliefs via default attribution. Here again, we may be wrong about the details, but there can be no doubt
that in crafting her detailed predictions about a target's behaviour, an adult
mindreader often relies on her own beliefs about the world. And, to repeat the
now familiar point, informationally encapsulated modular systems cannot do
that. So neither ToMM nor any other informationally encapsulated modular
mechanism can explain the fact that both young children and adults can make
detailed predictions about how a target will behave.

Inference prediction

We turn, now, to inference prediction. On our account, this is explained by the
Inference Mechanism operating on a model of the target that the mindreader
builds up in her PWB. This is, of course, an 'information-poor' process of a
piece with those proposed by simulation theorists. Since modularity theorists
focus on the role of 'information-rich' modules, it might be thought that
their only option would be to posit a module that contained lots of information about the way in which people make inferences, and that this account
would be threatened by the arguments from simplicity and accuracy set out in
Section 3.4.1. But actually the situation is a bit more interesting and complicated. For, as we saw in Chapter 2, Leslie has suggested that both pretence and
mindreading are subserved by 'decoupled' representations, and the notion of a
collection of decoupled representations is, near enough, equivalent to the idea
of a functionally separate workspace like our PWB. Since Leslie prefers to
think of these decoupled representations as housed in the Belief Box, rather
than in a separate workspace, it would be quite natural for him to assume that
the Inference Mechanism can operate on these decoupled representations,
much as it operates on the ordinary representations that subserve the mindreader's belief about the non-mental world. This would, of course, introduce a
simulation-like element into Leslie's theory, though it is, we think, very much
in the spirit of his approach. But if this is how Leslie would explain inference
prediction, he is still not out of the woods. To see why, consider the case in
which a mindreader predicts that a target who believes that the President has

resigned will infer that the Vice-President will become President. On Leslie's account, the episode begins with the mindreader having a representation of the form *Target believes that the President has resigned* in his Belief Box. The embedded content sentence, *the President has resigned*, is a decoupled representation on which the Inference Mechanism can operate. But, of course, there isn't much that the Inference Mechanism can infer from this *by itself*. In order to infer that *the Vice-President will become President*, the mindreader must also attribute to the target a cluster of other beliefs like:

> When the President resigns the office of the Presidency is vacant.
>
> When the office of the Presidency is vacant, ordinarily the Vice President becomes President.
>
> There is nothing in the current situation that would block or prevent the Vice President from becoming President.

and perhaps some others. But where do *these* beliefs about the target's beliefs come from? As far as we can see, the only even remotely plausible answer would appeal to a process, similar to default attribution, which attributes to the target some of the mindreader's own beliefs about the world. And here we are back with our familiar problem: processes like default attribution cannot be subserved by a module, because modules are informationally encapsulated and they don't have free access to the mindreader's beliefs. At this point, since we have already assumed that Leslie might happily embrace the simulation-inspired idea that the Inference Mechanism works on decoupled representations, we might suggest that he also adopt something like our (*very non-modular*) account of default attribution. If he does adopt default attribution to explain where the 'extra premisses' come from in cases like the one we have been considering, then his account of inference prediction would begin to look very much like a notational variant of our own.

Modularity and innateness

Let us pause for a moment to take stock of where our discussion of modularity has taken us so far. In the first part of this section, we focused on default attribution and argued that the module-based explanation offered by Leslie and his collaborators cannot be correct. Then we looked at two other central aspects of mindreading—detailed behaviour prediction and inference prediction—which modularity theorists have not attempted to explain, and we argued that no module-based explanation is possible for either. In light of these arguments, one might well begin to wonder why modularity theorists think that modular mental mechanisms play a central role in mindreading. An important part of the answer, we believe, can be found in an argument that focuses on reasons for thinking that the mechanisms subserving mindreading are *innate*. That argument has recently been set out in considerable detail in a paper by Scholl and Leslie (1999). However, it is our contention that their argument is seriously confused and provides no reason at all to think that *any* aspect of mindreading is subserved by a module.

Scholl and Leslie refer approvingly to Fodor's (1983) account of modularity. Importantly, they also embrace Fodor's view on which feature of modularity is essential:

> The essence of architectural modularity is a set of restrictions on information flow.... The standard examples are visual illusions. In the Müller-Lyer illusion, for example, you still fall prey to the mistaken percept that one line is longer than the other, even though you may have convinced yourself (say, by use of a ruler) that they are in fact the same length. This is to be explained by appeal to informational encapsulation: the processes which the module uses to construct your percept are encapsulated *with respect to your beliefs. A cognitive function is architecturally modular to the degree that it is informationally 'encapsulated' in this way*. (Scholl and Leslie 1999: 133, emphasis added)

After telling us a bit more about their conception of 'architectural modularity' and giving a list of 'symptoms of modularity' that includes most of the items on Fodor's list, Scholl and Leslie launch their argument for the modularity of the mechanism underlying 'the basic ToM [i.e. mindreading] abilities' (1999: 140) with a remark which, for reasons we will explain shortly, we find deeply puzzling.[40] For future reference, we'll label it the *modularity entails innateness thesis*, or *(M→I)*.

> (M→I): Our application of the notion of modularity to the domain of ToM results in the following claim: *ToM has a specific innate basis*. (Scholl and Leslie 1999: 134; emphasis in the original)

Scholl and Leslie then set out their case for thinking that certain core concepts used in mindreading, including 'BELIEF, PRETENCE and DESIRE' (137) are innate, and they explain in some detail—and very plausibly, in our view— why the evidence in the developmental literature, which indicates that mindreading skills develop over time, is fully compatible with the claim that these basic mindreading concepts are innate.

Now what we find so puzzling about (M→I) is that on Scholl and Leslie's own account (and on Fodor's), the 'essence' of modularity is informational

---

[40] A note on terminology: for Leslie and his colleagues, 'theory of mind' or 'ToM' 'refers to the capacity to interpret, predict and explain behaviour in terms of their underlying mental states' (Scholl and Leslie 1999: 132). Elsewhere, Leslie says 'theory of mind' refers to 'our ability to explain, predict, and interpret behaviour in terms of mental states, like *wanting, believing*, and *pretending*' (Leslie 2000: 1235). So 'theory of mind' or 'ToM' is, near enough, a synonym for 'mindreading', as we have been using that term. 'ToMM' refers to the hypothesized modular mechanism that underlies basic mindreading abilities.

encapsulation, and *there is no reason to think that an informationally encapsulated system must be innate*. Indeed, at the end of their article Scholl and Leslie refer approvingly to Karmiloff-Smith's suggestion that many sorts of specialized expertise 'such as bird-watching or wine-tasting' may be 'simply learned by induction' and 'only later come to exhibit some of the symptoms of modular encapsulation' (1999: 149) But this is only *half* of the puzzle posed by (M→I) and the use Scholl and Leslie make of it. For even if there were some reason to think that a modular mechanism has to be innate,[41] *surely there is no reason to think that an innate mechanism must be modular. Still less is there any reason to think that a mechanism which invokes innate concepts is modular.* It is, for example, plausible to suppose that the Inference Mechanism and the Planner (or important parts of them) are innate. But these are exactly the sorts of completely *un*encapsulated mechanisms that Fodor and Leslie would classify as *non*-modular. And Scholl and Leslie themselves emphasize that the (allegedly) innate ToM concepts 'may eventually be recruited by higher cognitive processes for more complex tasks, and the resulting higher-order ToM activities may well interact (in a non-modular way) with other cognitive processes' (1999: 140). Yet, with a single exception that we will consider below, *all* of the arguments that Scholl and Leslie offer are aimed at showing that the basic concepts invoked in ToM are innate. But even if we grant that this is true, it tells us exactly nothing about the informational encapsulation or modularity of *any* of the cognitive mechanisms that apply or use these concepts. Thus, as best we can see, all the evidence that Scholl and Leslie marshal in support of the claim that ToM invokes innate concepts is simply *irrelevant* to the question of whether or not *any part* of mindreading is subserved by a modular mechanism.

Some evidence for the modularity of part of the Desire Detection system

In this section we want to consider the one argument in Scholl and Leslie's paper that is not aimed at defending the idea that the basic concepts used in mindreading are innate. Though we do not think that the argument lends any support to the claim that there is a modular ToMM subserving many core aspects of mindreading, we think that it does provide some evidence suggesting that at least part of the Desire Detection system may be modular. Since their argument is very brief, we will quote it in full.

We will assume that the normal acquisition of ToM is at least in part due to the operation of a ToM-specific architectural module. At a minimum, ToM interpretations,

---

[41] Or perhaps just a reason to think that a modular mechanism that can explain aspects of mindreading must be innate.

explanations, and predictions seem to be relatively domain specific (they seem to involve specialized sorts of representations and computations), fast (they typically occur without lengthy and effortful reasoning), and mandatory (you can't decide *not* to interpret lots of situations as involving intentional agents although you can ignore the interpretation; cf. Dasser, Ulbaek, & Premack, 1989; Heider & Simmel 1944). (Scholl and Leslie 1999: 134–5)

The *only* data that Scholl and Leslie cite are the striking results produced by Heider and Simmel (1944) and Dasser and colleagues (Dasser et al. 1989).[42] As we noted in Section 3.3.5, Heider and Simmel demonstrated that subjects tend to offer mentalistic interpretations of the behaviour of geometric objects in a film clip. Before attempting to draw any conclusions about whether this supports the existence of a modular ToMM, however, let's take a closer look at what subjects say. Here is the beginning of a typical example of a subject's description that Heider and Simmel offer: 'A man has planned to meet a girl, and the girl comes along with another man. The first man tells the second to go; the second tells the first, and he shakes his head. Then the two men have a fight' (Heider and Simmel 1944: 246–7). It is singularly implausible to claim that everything in this interpretation of the stimuli is mandatory, since many of the details (e.g. gender) are obviously inessential, and other subjects offered significantly different interpretations. Nor is it in the least plausible that this interpretation does not draw heavily on the subject's background beliefs about social situations.

Interestingly, however, there are a few points on which the interpretations offered by Heider and Simmel's subjects did converge. Out of twelve scenes, there were three that were interpreted the same way in almost all reports. In one scene, the big triangle and the little triangle fight; in another scene, the big triangle 'tries to get out' of the box, and in a third scene, the big triangle chases the little triangle and the circle (1994: 247). Notice that all these are descriptions of actions or goals. Hence, these examples fit fairly well with the evidence discussed in Section 3.3.1 suggesting that infants and children attribute goals to computer-generated stimuli (Gergely et al. 1995; Csibra et al. 1999; Dasser et al. 1989). These findings lend no support at all to the hypothesis that there is a modular ToMM which subserves people's basic skills in attributing belief, desire, and pretence. But they do at least suggest that the mind-reading system *may* include modular mechanisms for *goal detection* or perhaps *desire detection* and thus that the Goal/Desire Detection system we discussed in Section 3.3.1 includes a modular component. Another possibility, which might account for the fact that subjects generate mentalistic interpretations for many stimuli which they know do not have minds, is that there is a modular front-end to the mindreading system, perhaps something like an Agency

---

[42] Baron-Cohen also discusses these data (Baron-Cohen 1995: 35–8).

Detector (discussed in Section 3.3.5), which picks out elements in the environment that the remainder of the mindreading system must then try to interpret. The bottom line, we submit, is that what little evidence there is about the modularity of the mechanisms subserving mindreading is fully compatible with our theory, which proposes that some parts of the Desire Detection system may be modular, though there is no reason at all to think that other aspects of mindreading are subserved by a modular mechanism.

Autism

Scientific-theory theorists have had little to say about autism, and they offer no systematic explanation for the three items on our checklist that mention the abilities and deficits of people who are afflicted with the disease. Modularity theorists, by contrast, have a great deal to say about autism. Leslie, along with Baron-Cohen and Frith was one of the discoverers of the fact that autistic children fail the false belief task, and this important finding led to an explosion of research on the mindreading skills of autistic children and children with other developmental disorders, like Williams syndrome (see e.g. Baron-Cohen et al. 1985; Baron-Cohen 1995; Baron-Cohen et al. 2000; Tager-Flusberg et al. 1997). Early on, modularity theorists suggested that there was a single modular system subserving both mindreading and pretence, and that this system was impaired in autism. As their theory evolved, however, modularity theorists put forward a variety of more complex accounts positing modules and non-modular systems that mature and become operative at different times.

As we saw in Section 3.2.2, normal children acquire the ability to attribute desires before they acquire the ability to attribute beliefs, and autistic children have much more difficulty with belief attributions than with desire attributions. To explain these two facts, modularity theorists have proposed that there is an early maturing module which subserves the sort of understanding of desire that has been demonstrated in young children, and that this module is spared in autism (Baron-Cohen 1995; Leslie 1994*b*). Following Astington and Gopnik (1991), Baron-Cohen maintains that this early maturing module leads to an understanding of desire that is 'non-representational' (see Phillips et al. 1995). ToMM, the central modular component of the mindreading system, develops somewhat later. This component, which Baron-Cohen, following Leslie, characterizes as 'processing representations of propositional attitudes' facilitates the understanding of belief as well as a representational understanding of desire (Baron-Cohen 1995: 51; Leslie 1994*b*: 122). As we saw in Chapter 2, Leslie also maintains that mindreading is central to pretence and he holds that ToMM plays a central role in the capacity for pretence (Leslie

1987). It is ToMM, according to Leslie and his colleagues, that does not develop normally in people with autism.[43]

If this theory is correct, it would explain why autistic children have a serious deficit in their capacity for pretend play. It would also lead us to expect that normal young children and much older autistic children both have a non-representational understanding of desire. We are sceptical about both points. In Chapter 2 we offered an extended argument against Leslie's claim that mindreading is central to pretence. If that argument is correct, it undercuts the modularity theorist's explanation of the deficits that autistic children have in pretend play. We think that our theory provides a more promising approach to the explanation of these deficits. On our view, the PWB system is implicated in sophisticated mindreading and in pretence, so the fact that both capacities are damaged might best be explained by the hypothesis that something is damaged in the PWB system. However, on our theory it is quite an open question *where* the breakdown is in the PWB system. It may be in the mechanisms that insert the representations into the PWB; it may be in the capacity to store representations in the PWB; or it may be in the connection between the PWB and the Planner. Also, it is entirely possible, on our account, that there is no unitary account of autism and that different individuals diagnosed with the condition have different problems with the PWB system.

Let us turn, now, to the claim that both normal young children and older autistic children have a non-representational understanding of desire. In Section 3.4.1 we argued at some length against the claim that normal young children have a non-representational understanding of desire. So here we will focus on the parallel claim about autistic children. The best-developed argument for that claim comes from Phillips, Baron-Cohen, and Rutter (1995), who adopt Astington and Gopnik's (1991) characterization of 'representational' desire. On a representational understanding of desire, Phillips et al. tell us, 'the same entity (object, event, situation) can appear desirable to one person, while at the same time being undesirable to another. According to Astington and Gopnik (1991), to understand this fact requires a concept of desire that includes its personal, subjective nature' (Phillips et at. 1995: 160–1).

---

[43] There is, we think, something rather puzzling about this theory. If it is indeed the case that there is an early developing module that makes available a non-representational understanding of desire, what becomes of this module in normal individuals after the ToMM matures and makes available a representational conception of desire? Do normal individuals then have *two* distinct desire attribution modules, one of which attributes ordinary 'representational' desires while the other attributes 'non-representational' desires? Or does the first one shut down at some later point in development? And if the first one does shut down, why doesn't it shut down in people with autism? So far as we know, modularity theorists have never addressed these issues. In what follows, we propose to ignore this puzzle, since as we see it there are much more serious problems with the modularity theorists' account of early mindreading and autism.

To establish that autistic children do not understand this feature of desire, and thus that they lack a representational understanding of desire, Phillips et al. present several experiments.

In their experiments, they find that autistic children have greater difficulty than their mental age peers with complex features of desire. In one experiment, subjects are told stories and they need to figure out the goals of characters from fairly subtle cues. For instance, the children were shown two three-panel cartoons. In both cartoons, the first panel shows a boy standing next to a pool, and the third panel shows a boy dripping wet, standing next to the pool. In one strip, the second frame shows a boy jumping into the pool, and in the other strip the second frame shows a boy falling into the pool. The children are asked, 'which boy meant to get wet?' (1995: 157). In another experiment, the subject had to recognize that the subject's desires changed because of the circumstances. For example, in one such Desire Change task they are told about a boy who wants to give a dog a bit of food, but the dog growls at him and he subsequently eats it himself (1995: 162). The researchers found that autistic children did significantly worse on these tasks than normal children and mentally handicap children matched for mental age.

These results are important and interesting, but we think that the tasks are much too hard to address the basic question of whether autistic children recognize that the same entity can be 'desirable to one person, while at the same time being undesirable to another'. For instance, in the Desire Change tasks, the subject has to recognize that the target acquires a new *belief* about an unexpected feature of environment (e.g. the dog growled) that leads to a change in desire. If the autistic children's PWB system is compromised, as we maintain, then it is not surprising that they have difficulty with the task.

A much simpler and more direct way to explore whether autistic children understand that something can be desirable to one person and not to another would be to appeal to simple preferences. For example, an experiment might let subjects observe two people, one of whom indicates disgust after tasting a cookie and delight after tasting lettuce, and the other does the opposite. Subjects could then be asked which food the targets want. As we have seen (Section 3.3.1), young children perform well on somewhat similar tasks. If autistic children also perform well on this task, that would clearly indicate that they understand that a cookie can be desirable to one person and undesirable to another. Another simple way to approach the autistic child's understanding of desire change is by exploring their understanding of satiation. For instance, one might have subjects watch a target eat ravenously at snack-time until he is sated. Then the subjects could be asked whether the target is hungry now and whether he was hungry when they first started watching him. If autistic children perform well on this, that indicates that they do have some understanding of desire change.

The upshot of all of this is that we see no reason to think that autistic children do not understand that the same entity can be desirable to one person and not desirable to another, and thus that they have a 'non-representational' understanding of desire. Indeed, we think there is good reason to be optimistic about the abilities of autistic children in this domain, and we suspect that those parts of the normal capacity for desire attribution that do not rely on the PWB system are largely *intact* in autism. So we see little reason to accept the modularity theorists' hypothesis that there is a later maturing modular ToMM that plays an important role in the attribution of beliefs and 'representational' desires which does not develop normally in autism.

3.4.3. Simulation theory

Before we attempt to compare our theory with the sorts of theories urged by simulation theorists, we will have to spend a few pages trying to clarify the rather messy terminological situation that has led to considerable confusion in this area. Perhaps the best way to proceed is to sketch a bit of the history that gave rise to the current terminological muddles.

A central goal of cognitive science has always been to explain complex cognitive capacities like the ability to produce and understand natural language or the ability to manipulate and predict the behaviour of middle-sized physical objects (Chomsky 1965; McClosky 1983). From the earliest days of cognitive science, the dominant explanatory strategy was to posit the existence of an internally represented 'knowledge structure'—a body of information about the domain in question—which serves to guide the execution of the capacity to be explained. Our ability to produce and understand natural language, for example, is widely thought to depend, in part, on an internally represented grammar, and on the standard accounts, our ability to predict the behaviour of physical objects is guided by an internally represented folk physics. Against this background, it is not surprising that when cognitive scientists sought explanations of mindreading they assumed that, in this area too, our skill was guided by an internally represented body of information. As we have seen, both scientific-theory theorists and modularity theorists adopt this 'information rich' approach.

However, in 1986, Robert Gordon and Jane Heal independently introduced an important new explanatory strategy that was quickly adopted by a number of leading philosophers and psychologists including Alvin Goldman, Paul Harris, and Gregory Currie. The basic idea was that, since mindreaders and their targets typically have very similar cognitive systems, some mindreading tasks might be accomplished by using part of the mindreader's own cognitive system to simulate the activity of the analogous system in the target. This strategy, it was argued, required nothing like the rich body of information about the mind that was posited by earlier approaches to mindreading. In contrast with both scientific-theory theorists and modularity theorists, advocates of this new approach suggested that we might be able to give an 'information poor' explanation for many mindreading skills. In early publications exploring the simulation approach, the most carefully worked out proposal focused on predicting decisions by taking the practical reasoning mechanism off-line, as in Figure 2.3, though it quickly became clear that the idea could be generalized in a variety of ways.

In those early days of simulation theory, two things happened that sowed the seeds of much later confusion. First, many writers, ourselves included, began to characterize debates over the plausibility of these new accounts as part of a *two-sided* battle in which either simulation theory or the 'theory theory' (a term used for *all* information-rich accounts) would 'win'. Though understandable enough in the context of those early debates, this proved to be a very unfortunate way of characterizing the theoretical landscape, since it ignored the possibility that the correct account of mindreading might be provided by a *hybrid* theory in which some aspects of mindreading are explained by processes like those in Figure 2.3, some by information-rich processes (invoking either modules or a theory-like information base) and some by processes which do not fit comfortably into either of those two categories. The theory we have proposed in this volume is, of course, just such a hybrid. Second, and in part, we suspect, because the debate was conceived as one in which simulation theory would either win or lose, advocates of simulation theory argued that just about any process or phenomenon that could plausibly be described as a 'simulation' *in some sense or other* supported their side, despite the fact that many of the processes and phenomena they mentioned had little or nothing in common. Since this dialectical turn is quite important in understanding the prevailing terminological confusion, it will be useful to offer a brief (and far from complete) survey of the sorts of things to which the 'simulation' label has been applied.

1. First, of course, was the decision prediction process depicted in Figure 2.3, in which the decision-making or practical reasoning mechanism is taken off-line and provided with 'pretend' inputs that are importantly different from the inputs it gets when it is running 'on-line' (e.g. Gordon 1986; Goldman 1989; Currie 1995*b*).

2. In Stich and Nichols (1995), inspired by some comments in Harris (1992), we suggested that a very similar process, in which the inference mechanism is taken off-line and provided with non-standard inputs, might explain inference prediction.

3. On the basis of findings suggesting that normal visual processing and visual imagery 'employ substantial parts of the same central-processing

system but have different inputs and outputs' Currie (1995*d*: 29) suggested that visual imagery is a simulation process, though as he recognized, the inputs and outputs in visual imagery are quite different from the inputs and outputs in processes like (1) and (2).

4. Harris (1992) and Heal (1996) both use the term 'simulation' for a prediction process in which predictors literally place themselves in situations that are similar to the one the target confronts, and use their own inferences or judgements as a basis for predicting what the target will infer or judge. In Heal's example, we predict the answer a target will offer to an arithmetic problem by solving the problem ourselves. Note that there is nothing here that corresponds to the 'pretend' inputs of (1) and (2), nor is any cognitive system taken 'off-line'. In Stich and Nichols (1997) we called this 'actual-situation-simulation' to distinguish it from very different processes like (1) and (2) which we called 'pretence-driven-off-line-simulation'.

5. Goldman (1989: 170) proposes that one strategy we use to attribute desires is to assume that others 'have the same basic likings that I have: for food, love, warmth and so on', and he describes this as a simulation process. Here, however, there are no 'pretend' inputs, and there is no processing mechanism being taken off-line; indeed, there is no processing mechanism involved at all.

6. In a similar vein, following a suggestion of Harris's we ourselves proposed that the process we have been calling 'default belief attribution' could be viewed as a kind of simulation (Harris 1992; Stich and Nichols 1997).

7. A number of psychologists have proposed that we predict the likely outcome of many processes having nothing to do with mindreading by running through the processes in imagination or thought and making various different assumptions about the initial state of the system of interest. Kahneman and Tversky (1982*b*: 201) note, quite rightly, that this process 'resembles the running of a simulation model', and they offer examples of its use that include predicting what the likely consequences would be if civil war breaks out in Saudi Arabia. Both Goldman (1989) and Currie (1995*b*) suggest that, since this is an example of 'mental simulation' it somehow lends support to their simulation theory of mindreading, despite the fact that simulations like those Kahneman and Tversky discuss would be impossible unless the person engaging in the simulation had a rich body of information about the process being simulated. Thus these information-rich simulations are fundamentally different from information-poor simulations like those proposed in (1) and (2).

8. According to Goldman, 'from your perceptual situation, I infer that you have certain experiences or beliefs, the same ones I would have in your situation' (1989: 170). This, he maintains, is yet another example of a phenomenon that can be explained by simulation. It is hard to see how this

process could work, however, unless mindreaders have access to a fairly rich body of information about the ways in which perceptual situations lead to beliefs, at least in their own case. So this 'simulation' process, too, is information rich rather than information poor.

9. Heal (1998) argues that there is an important sense of 'simulation' on which the claim that simulation is involved in mindreading is not an empirical thesis at all. Rather, she maintains, it is an a priori truth that 'simulation is central in thinking about the thoughts of others' (477). Heal labels this kind of simulation 'co-cognition', which is 'just a fancy name for the everyday notion of thinking about the same subject matter' (Heal 1998: 483). So, for Heal, whenever a mindreader and a target think about the same subject matter, the mindreader is simulating the target.

10. Robert Gordon was one of the original proponents of simulation theory. In recent years he has elaborated a version of the theory that invokes notions like 'imaginative identification' (Gordon 1995a), 'imaginative transformation into the other' (Gordon 1996), and 'a certain conception of people: peepholes through which the world reappears, possibly transformed' (Gordon 2000: 102). Gordon makes it clear that he is not committed to the existence of off-line simulation processes like those in (1) and (2), but he is (to put it mildly) less than clear about what he *is* committed to. Along with many other readers, we simply have no idea how to interpret his remarks about 'imaginative transformation' and 'peepholes'.

In reaction to the apparently irresistible tendency to use the word 'simulation' as a label for almost *anything*, we have for some years been arguing that the term 'simulation' needs to be retired because 'the diversity among the theories, processes and mechanisms to which advocates of simulation theory have attached the label "simulation" is so great that the term itself has become quite useless. It picks out no natural or theoretically interesting category' (Stich and Nichols 1997: 299; see also Nichols and Stich 1998: 500). And we were pleased to learn that at least one of the originators of the simulation theory, Jane Heal, now wholeheartedly agrees with us (Heal 1998: 496).

All of this, of course, creates a major obstacle when it comes to comparing our account of mindreading with the accounts urged by simulation theorists, since it is not at all clear what we are supposed to be comparing our theory with. So what we propose to do, in this section, is to explicitly adopt a policy that we have been tacitly using throughout this book, and to anchor *our* use of 'simulation' by taking pretence-driven off-line processes like (1) and (2) as prototypes. Using the term in this way, we can ask which components of our theory are significantly similar to these simulation prototypes, which are importantly different, and for those that are different, why is our approach preferable to a simulation approach. Taking (1) and (2) as prototypes of simulation still leaves considerable vagueness about *how similar* to a prototype something must be to count as a simulation process, but for the project at hand, we don't think this will pose much of a problem.

Which components of our theory are similar to prototypical simulation processes, and which are not?

The most obvious simulation process included in our theory is the one subserving inference prediction. On our account this is accomplished by allowing the inference mechanism to run on representations in the Possible World Box. In the simulation-prototype inference prediction process, the inference mechanism is said to be provided with 'pretend' belief inputs from a 'pretend belief generator',[44] but since the notion of a pretend belief generator was never explained in any detail, it is impossible to say whether our PWB should be viewed as an elaboration of that idea.

The other feature of our theory that bears obvious similarities to the simulation prototypes is the use of the Planner in generating predictions about how targets will go about satisfying their desires, and about what instrumental desires they will acquire. In Figure 2.3, the Practical Reasoning Mechanism is taken off-line and provided with inputs from a 'pretend belief and desire generator'. On our account, the Planner uses information from the PWB which, as just noted, might be viewed as a more detailed elaboration of the pretend belief generator. But there is nothing in our account that corresponds to a 'pretend desire generator'. Rather, information about the target's desires is assembled in the mindreader's Belief Box—they are just beliefs about the target's desires—and this information is passed on to the Planner by the Mindreading Coordinator. Despite the differences, however, we think that the use we see for the Planner in mindreading is a reasonably close cousin to the simulation prototypes.

We turn, now, to the components of our theory that clearly do not bear much similarity to the simulation prototypes. There are three categories of these.

Mechanisms subserving perception attribution   Our account posits the existence of innate Perception Detection Mechanisms which begin to come on-line fairly early. These are the mechanisms that form beliefs about what a target does and does not perceive on the basis of information about the target (the direction of her gaze, for example, and whether her eyes are open) and about the target's environment. We don't think there is *any* way to explain these belief-forming processes that relies on mechanisms akin to the simulation

---

[44] See e.g. Figure 5.3 in Stich and Nichols (1995).

prototypes. Rather, we maintain, perception detection is an information-rich process, and the mechanisms that subserve the process must have access to a fair amount of information about how perception works. There is also a fair amount of information about perception that the Perception Detection Mechanisms *do not* have, and this *lack* of information explains the fact that our ability to predict many perceptual states (for example those produced by perceptual illusions) is quite limited. This sort of inaccuracy is, of course, one of the symptoms indicating that the process is not simulation-like.

Mechanisms subserving desire attribution   On our account, there are a number of different processes that can give rise to beliefs about a target's desires. One of these, which attributes instrumental desires for sub-goals required to carry out a plan, makes use of the Planner and thus it counts as a simulation mechanism.[45] Our theory also posits a cluster of Desire Detection Mechanisms which, we maintain, are information rich and do not depend on mechanisms that resemble the simulation prototypes. These mechanism generate beliefs about targets' desires from information about the targets' verbal and non-verbal behaviour, and their facial expressions. They also generate beliefs about targets' desires based on what other people say about the target and, no doubt, based on a variety of other cues and sources of data (Section 3.3.1). As we saw in Section 3.4.2, there is some reason to think that a few of these mechanisms may be modular. We have two quite different reasons for our claim that these mechanisms exploit information-rich processes rather than simulation processes.

SYSTEMATIC INACCURACIES IN DESIRE ATTRIBUTION   First, the Desire Detection system exhibits a pattern of systematic inaccuracy and that, as we argued in Section 3.4.1, supports at least an initial presumption that the process does not resemble the simulation prototypes. In Section 3.2.1 we sketched Milgram's famous experiments in which persistent instructions from the experimenter generated a desire to comply which, in most cases, overwhelmed the subject's desire not to harm the person they believed to be on the receiving end of the electric shock apparatus. We also noted that in Bierbrauer's (1973) re-enactment subjects failed to predict this effect, even when they themselves played the role of the person instructed to deliver the shocks. In another experiment, Nuttin and Beckers (1975) had an attractive young woman ask male Belgian college students to give a television speech in *favour* of a hated exam system, to which they were subjected. A strenuous protest movement *against* the system was supported by virtually all students. All of the eleven students who were asked to give the television speech complied. When twenty-two fellow

---

[45] See Section 3.3.1.

students were asked how many students would comply with such a request, the majority thought less than 5 per cent, and the most cynical guessed 30 per cent! So in this case too, people were very bad at predicting the effect of the experimenter's request on the desires of the eleven subjects.

There is a large literature in cognitive social psychology detailing many other cases in which desires and preferences, and the actions they give rise to, are affected in remarkable and unexpected ways by the circumstances subjects encounter and the environment in which they are embedded. The important point, for present purposes, is that people typically find these results surprising and occasionally quite unsettling, and the fact that they are surprised (even after seeing or getting a detailed description of the experimental situation) indicates that the mental mechanisms they are using to predict the subjects' desires and preferences are systematically inaccurate. In many of these cases, it is people's actions and the decisions that lead to those actions that are most alarming. But we think it is clear that our inability to predict those actions is rooted in our inability to predict the way in which their situation affects their motivations—their preferences and desires—since if we were told that subjects in Milgram experiments typically developed strong desires to comply with the instructions of the experimenter (and if we believed it) it would be much easier to predict what they do. Though this is not the place for an extended survey of the many examples in the literature, we cannot resist mentioning one more of our favourites.[46]

In a recent study, Loewenstein and Adler (1995) looked at the ability of subjects to predict *their own* preferences when those preferences are influenced by a surprising and little-known effect. The effect that Loewenstein and Adler exploit is the *endowment effect*, a robust and rapidly appearing tendency for people to set a significantly higher value for an object if they actually own it than they would if they did not own it (Thaler 1980). Here is how Loewenstein and Adler describe the phenomenon.

In the typical demonstration of the endowment effect (see, e.g., Kahneman, Knetsch and Thaler 1990), one group of subjects (sellers) are endowed with an object and are given the option of trading it for various amounts of cash; another group (choosers) are not given the object but are given a series of choices between getting the object or getting various amounts of cash. Although the objective wealth position of the two groups is identical, as are the choices they face, endowed subjects hold out for significantly more money than those who are not endowed. (Loewenstein and Adler 1995: 929–30)

In an experiment designed to test whether 'unendowed' subjects could predict the value they would set if they were actually to own the object in question,

---

[46] For an excellent review of the literature, see Ross and Nisbett (1991).

the experimenter first allowed subjects (who were members of a university class) to examine a mug engraved with the school logo. A form was then distributed to approximately half of the subjects, chosen at random, on which they were asked 'to imagine that they possessed the mug on display and to predict whether they would be willing to exchange the mug for various amounts of money' (Loewenstein and Adler 1995: 931).[47] When the subjects who received the form were finished filling it out, *all* the subjects were presented with a mug and given a second form with instructions analogous to those on the prediction form. But on the second form it was made clear that they actually could exchange the mug for cash, and that the choices they made on this second form would determine how much money they might get. 'Subjects were told that they would receive the option that they had circled on one of the lines—which line had been determined in advance by the experimenter' (Loewenstein and Adler 1995: 931). The results showed that subjects who had completed the first form substantially underpredicted the amount of money for which they would be willing to exchange the mug. In one group of subjects, the mean predicted exchange price was $3.73, while the mean actual exchange price for subjects (the same ones who made the prediction) was $5.40! Moreover, there seemed to be an 'anchoring effect' in this experiment which depressed the actual exchange price, since the mean actual exchange price for subjects who did not make a prediction about their own selling price was even higher at $6.46. Here again we find that people are systematically inaccurate at predicting the effect of the situation on desires, and in this case the desires they fail to predict are their own![48]

THE IMPLAUSIBILITY OF SIMULATION-BASED EXPLANATIONS OF DESIRE ATTRIBUTION
Our second reason for thinking that the Desire Detection Mechanisms exploit an information-rich process rather than one similar to the simulation prototypes is that it is hard to see how the work done by these mechanisms *could* be accomplished by a mechanism like those used in the simulation prototypes. Indeed, so far as we know, simulation theorists have made only one proposal about how some of these desire detection tasks might be carried out,

---

[47] The exact wording of the form was as follows: 'We are interested in your opinion about the mug displayed at the front of the room. Imagine that we gave you a mug exactly like the one you can see, and that we gave you the opportunity to keep it or trade it for some money. Below are a series of lines marked "Keep mug___ Trade it for $amount___." On each line check whether you would think that you would prefer to keep the mug or to trade it in for the amount of money written on the line. Check one or the other on every line.' The remainder of the page consisted of 40 lines in which the amount of money for which the mug might be traded increased from 25 cents to 10 dollars, in 25 cent increments.

[48] When discussing this experiment in an earlier paper (Nichols et al. 1995) we treated it as a failure of decision prediction without noting that the failed decision prediction was the result of a failure in preference prediction. But it seems clear that the inability to predict the decision

and it is a proposal that we find singularly implausible. The proposal, endorsed by both Gordon (1986) and Goldman (1989) begins with the fact that simulation processes like the one sketched in Figure 2.3 can be used to make behaviour predictions, and goes on to suggest that they might also be used to generate beliefs about the desires and beliefs that give rise to observed behaviour by exploiting something akin to the strategy of analysis-by-synthesis (developed by Halle and Stevens (1962) for phoneme recognition). In using the process in Figure 2.3 to predict behaviour, hypothetical or 'pretend' beliefs and desires are fed into the mindreader's decision-making system (being used 'off-line' of course), and the mindreader predicts that the target would do what the mindreader would decide to do, given those beliefs and desires. In an analysis-by-synthesis account of the generation of beliefs about desires and beliefs, the process is, in effect, run backwards. It starts with a behavioural episode that has already occurred and proceeds by trying to find hypothetical beliefs and desires which, when fed into the mindreader's decision mechanism, will produce a decision to perform the behaviour we want to explain.

An obvious problem with this strategy is that it will generate too many candidates, since typically there are endlessly many possible sets of beliefs and desires that would lead the mindreader to decide to perform the behaviour in question. Gordon is well aware of the problem, and he seems to think he has a solution:

No matter how long I go on testing hypotheses, I will not have tried out all candidate explanations of the [agent's] behavior. Perhaps some of the unexamined candidates would have done at least as well as the one I settle for, if I settle: perhaps indefinitely many of them would have. But these would be 'far fetched', I say intuitively. Therein I exhibit my inertial bias. The less 'fetching' (or 'stretching', as actors say) I have to do to track the other's behavior, the better. I tend to feign only when necessary, only when something in the other's behavior doesn't fit.... This inertial bias may be thought of as a 'least effort' principle: the 'principle of least pretending'. It explains why, other things being equal, I will prefer the less radical departure from the 'real' world—i.e. from what I myself take to be the world. (Gordon 1986: 164)

Unfortunately, it is not at all clear what Gordon has in mind by an inertial bias against 'fetching'. The most obvious interpretation is that attributions are more 'far-fetched' the further they are, on some intuitive scale, from one's

---

is a result of a failure to predict the effect of the circumstances on preferences since, as in the Milgram case, if we told subjects that 'endowment' led people to value the mug almost twice as much (and if they believed it), it would be much easier for them to make a more accurate prediction. We got a bit clearer on this in Stich and Nichols 1997. Our slowness in seeing that this is an example of a failure in the desire and preference prediction system is all the more embarrassing since Loewenstein and Adler were clear on the point from the beginning. Their paper was titled 'A bias in the prediction of *tastes*'.

own mental states. But if that's what Gordon intends, it seems clear that the suggestion won't work. For in many cases we explain behaviour by appealing to desires or beliefs (or both) that are *very* far from our own desires. I might, for example, explain the cat chasing the mouse by appealing to the cat's desire to eat the mouse. But there are indefinitely many desires that would lead me to chase a mouse that are intuitively much closer to my actual desires than the desire to eat a mouse! Simulation theorists have offered no other proposal for narrowing down the endless set of candidate beliefs and desires that the analysis-by-synthesis strategy would generate, and without some plausible solution to this problem the strategy looks quite hopeless. So it is perhaps not surprising that accounts of this sort have largely disappeared from the simulation theory literature over the last decade.

Mechanisms subserving belief attribution   On our theory, belief attribution is subserved by three quite different sorts of mechanisms. Many beliefs are default attributed, and though some authors suggest that default attribution is a *kind* of simulation (Harris 1992; Heal 1998; and (alas) Stich and Nichols 1995), it is, we think, quite radically different from our simulation prototypes, since there is no process which is being run off-line and provided with non-standard inputs. The use of the inference mechanism to UpDate the model of a target in the PWB is a second process subserving belief attribution, and that one, of course, *is* a simulation process. Finally, our theory posits a cluster of processes for attributing discrepant beliefs to targets including:

- a process that infers discrepant beliefs from beliefs about the target's perceptual states;
- a process that attributes discrepant beliefs on the basis of information about the way the world usually is (though the mindreader knows that the world does not happen to be that way now);
- a process that attributes discrepant beliefs on the basis of the target's behaviour along with beliefs about the target's desires;
- a process that attributes discrepant beliefs on the basis of what the target says about the world;
- a process that attributes discrepant beliefs on the basis of third-person reports.

All of these, we maintain, are subserved by information-rich mechanisms, rather than by a mechanism similar to the simulation prototypes. Our reasons are largely parallel to the ones we offered for the Desire Detection Mechanism. First, there is abundant evidence that the discrepant belief attribution system exhibits systematic inaccuracies of the sort we would expect from an information-rich system that is not quite rich enough and does not contain information about the processes generating certain categories of discrepant beliefs. Second, there is no plausible way in which prototypical simulation mechanisms could do what the discrepant belief attribution system does.

One particularly disquieting example of a systematic failure in discrepant belief attribution comes from the study of belief perseverance. In the psychology laboratory, and in everyday life, it sometimes happens that people are presented with fairly persuasive evidence that they have some hitherto unexpected trait. In the light of that evidence people typically form the belief that they do have the trait. What will happen to that belief if, shortly after this, people are presented with a convincing case discrediting the first body of evidence? Suppose, for example, that what convinced them were some psychological test results and they are then convinced that the test results were actually someone else's, or that no real test was conducted at all. Most people expect that the undermined belief will simply be discarded. And that view was shared by a generation of social psychologists who duped subjects into believing all sorts of things about themselves, observed their reactions, and then 'debriefed' the subjects by explaining the ruse. They assumed that no enduring harm could be done because once the ruse was explained the induced belief would be discarded. But in a widely discussed series of experiments, Ross and his co-workers have demonstrated that this is simply not the case. Once a subject has been convinced that she is very good at telling real from fake suicide notes, for example, showing her that the evidence was completely phoney does not succeed in eliminating the belief (Nisbett and Ross 1980: 175–9). The part of the discrepant belief attribution system that led both psychologists and everyone else to expect that these discrepant beliefs would be discarded after debriefing apparently has no information about belief perseverance in these cases, and thus it leads to systematically mistaken belief attribution.

Another example, with important implications for public policy, is provided by the work of Loftus (1979) and others on the effect of 'postevent interventions' on what people believe about events they have witnessed. In one experiment subjects were shown a film of an auto accident. A short time later they were asked a series of questions about the accident. For some subjects, one of the questions was, 'How fast was the white sports car traveling when it passed the barn while traveling along the country road?' Other subjects were asked, 'How fast was the white sports car traveling while traveling along the country road?' One week later all the subjects were asked whether they had seen a barn. Though there was no barn in the film that the subjects had seen, subjects who were asked the question that mentioned the barn were five times more likely to believe that they had seen one. In another experiment, conducted in train stations and other naturalistic settings, Loftus and her students staged a 'robbery' in which a male confederate pulled an object from a bag that two female students had temporarily left unattended and stuffed it under his coat. A moment later, one of the women noticed that her bag had been tampered with and shouted, 'Oh my God, my tape recorder is missing.' She went on to lament that her boss had loaned it to her and that it was very expensive. Bystanders, most of whom were quite cooperative, were asked for their phone numbers in case an account of the incident was needed for insurance purposes. A week later, an 'insurance agent' called the eye-witnesses and asked about details of the theft. Among the questions asked was 'Did you see the tape recorder?' More than half of the eye-witnesses remembered having seen it, and nearly all of these could describe it in detail—this despite the fact that *there was no tape recorder*! On the basis of this and other experiments, Loftus concludes that even casual mention of objects that were not present or of events that did not take place (for example, in the course of police questioning) can significantly increase the likelihood that the objects or events will be incorporated into people's beliefs about what they observed. One central theme in Loftus's work is that the legal system should be much more cautious about relying on eye-witness testimony. A major reason why the legal system is *not* as cautious as it should be is that our discrepant belief attribution system lacks information about the postevent processes of belief formation that Loftus has demonstrated.

As in the case of the Desire Detection Mechanisms, we see no plausible way in which the work done by the Discrepant Belief system could be accomplished by anything like a prototypical simulation mechanism. Here again, the only proposal that simulation theorists have offered is the analysis-by-synthesis account, and that strategy won't work any better for belief attribution than it does for desire attribution.

3.4.4. Rationality theories

In philosophical discussions of mindreading, one prominent idea has been that we attribute mental states and predict behaviour in accordance with an assumption of rationality. This view is associated with Davidson (1980) and especially Dennett (1978a, 1987). According to Dennett, when we ascribe beliefs and desires, we are adopting the 'intentional stance' which requires that we attribute to the target the beliefs and desires that it would be rational for the target to have in her situation. Similarly, when we adopt the intentional stance to predict behaviour, we predict that the target will do what it would be rational for her to do in that situation. Though rationality-based theories have not played a large role in the empirical literature on mindreading, a few prominent researchers have adverted to Dennett's account. For instance, Gergely et al. 1995 write

As Dennett argued, taking the intentional stance allows one to generate specific action predictions only on the basis of a general assumption of rationality: one assumes that a rational agent will choose to perform that particular instrumental action which, given his beliefs about the situation, will lead to his goal in the most rational manner. (Gergely et al. 1995: 171–2; see also Baron-Cohen 1995: 21 ff.)

Since these researchers say little about the role of the rationality assumption in the attribution of mental states, it is not clear to what extent they are really committed to Dennett's programme. Nor is it clear what sort of mental mechanism Dennett and his followers think subserves rationality-based attributions and predictions. Perhaps the most natural way to elaborate a rationality-based account of mindreading would be to posit an internally represented theory of rationality, and indeed from time to time Dennett suggests that the information subserving mindreading 'must be organized into something rather like a theory' (Dennett 1987: 100). But both modular mechanisms and information-poor simulation-style mechanisms might also yield attributions and predictions that accord with principles of rationality. Since the advocates of rationality-based theories don't tell us much about the mechanism, we propose to leave the matter open and to interpret Dennett and his followers as claiming merely that there is *some mechanism or other* that generates mental state attributions and behaviour predictions in accordance with 'a general assumption of rationality'. It is our contention that even this rather noncommittal version of the theory is singularly implausible.[49]

Dennett makes two importantly different claims about the intentional stance. (1) The intentional stance will be or should be adopted in an adequate *science* of mind. (2) The intentional stance (or something close to it) provides an accurate characterization of the strategy that people actually use in everyday mindreading. Though we believe that both of these claims are mistaken, we will restrict our attention to the second claim, since that is the one that is directly relevant to our concerns in this book.[50]

On Dennett's account of intentional state attribution and behaviour prediction, we judge what it is rational for the target to do, believe, or want. Then we attribute those mental states and predict those actions. Perhaps Dennett's most explicit explanation of the process is to be found in the following passage:

We approach each other as *intentional systems* . . . , that is, as entities whose behavior can be predicted by the method of attributing beliefs, desires and rational acumen according to the following rough and ready principles:

(1) A system's beliefs are those it *ought to have*, given its perceptual capacities, its epistemic needs, and its biography. Thus, in general, its beliefs are both true and relevant to its life . . .

---

[49] Dennett's views on the intentional stance have been roundly criticized over the last twenty years. See e.g. Cherniak 1986, Fodor 1981, Goldman 1989, Stich 1981, Webb 1994. We think that many of the criticisms are quite persuasive and we will borrow liberally from them in the remainder of this section.   [50] For some criticisms of the former claim, see Stich 1981.

(2) A system's desires are those it *ought to have*, given its biological needs and the most practicable means of satisfying them. Thus intentional systems desire survival and procreation, and hence desire food, security, health, sex, wealth, power, influence, and so forth, and also whatever local arrangements tend (in their eyes—given their beliefs) to further these ends in appropriate measure ...

(3) A system's behavior will consist of those acts that *it would be rational* for an agent with those beliefs and desires to perform. (Dennett 1987: 49; all italics are in the original)

Unfortunately, as Dennett himself admits, he has never been very clear about what 'rationality' is: 'for ten years I have hedged and hinted and entertained claims that I have later qualified or retracted. I didn't know what to say, and could see problems everywhere I turned' (1987: 94). His notion of rationality, he suggests is 'flexible' (1987: 94) and 'slippery' (1987: 97). Though the elusiveness of Dennett's notion of rationality poses some obvious problems, we think a plausible case can be made that mindreading does *not* depend on an assumption of rationality, on any reasonable construal of rationality. To make the case, we will start by noting a major shortcoming in Dennett's explanation of the intentional stance. We will then argue that, even if the problem is patched along the lines we will suggest, there are still many, many cases in which the theory fails to account for the mental states that are attributed in everyday mindreading.

A striking feature of Dennett's sketch of the intentional stance, quoted above, is that it doesn't even *mention* how we might arrive at intentional attributions by *observing behaviour*. Rather, on this account, the intentional stance is used to attribute the beliefs and desires that a system ought to have, given its circumstances and its biological needs. We might call this a 'top-down' approach to intentional attribution. But often we attribute mental states from the 'bottom up'—on the basis of what the target *does* (see especially Webb 1994). For instance, if we see Bill go to the fridge and reach for an orange, we typically form the belief that Bill wants an orange. But it is absurd to suggest that we arrive at this attribution by considering what it would be rational for Bill to want, given his 'biological needs and the most practicable means of satisfying them'.

There is an obvious way in which Dennett might try to bring these kinds of cases into the fold of his rationality-based theory. He might concede that the top-down strategy is only part of the story but maintain that bottom-up attributions also depend on an assumption of rationality. Of course, the rationality assumption would have to play a rather different role in the bottom-up strategy. When we see Bill reach for the orange, rationality theory doesn't explain why it is rational for him to desire an orange. Rather, the appeal to rationality lies in attributing a desire that 'makes sense' of the behaviour. That is, it would be rational for Bill to reach for the orange if Bill wanted an orange. From this along with the background assumption that Bill is rational, we might infer that Bill reached for the orange because he wanted an orange. We are inclined to think that this is the best way to elaborate Dennett's theory to accommodate the obvious problem posed by behaviour-based mental state attributions, and what little textual evidence we can find in Dennett's writings seems to support this reading.[51] But even if the theory is elaborated in this way, it still faces a major problem, because often the top-down approach and the bottom-up approach will come into conflict, and it is not at all clear how Dennett's theory can explain which strategy should be privileged (Webb 1994). For instance, suppose that for several years John has had violently allergic reactions immediately after he eats chocolate, and that both you and John know this. Suppose further that you see John methodically unwrap a chocolate bar, wolf it down without any sign of hesitation, and then smile contentedly. Since eating chocolate will produce a violent allergic reaction in John, and he knows that it will, there is a powerful top-down reason to think that it is irrational for John to want to eat the chocolate. Yet the fact that John methodically unwraps the chocolate and eats it with no hesitation provides bottom-up evidence that John wants to eat it, since this is the rational thing to do if he wants to eat it.[52] Thus, Dennett's rationality-based theory leads to two conflicting attributions—according to top-down considerations, John does not want to eat the chocolate, and according to bottom-up considerations, he does. Though Dennett's theory gives us no way to decide between these conflicting attributions, commonsense mindreading often does not see these cases as in the least problematic. If asked whether John wants to eat the chocolate, we think a typical mindreader would say that he does, and we expect that John would agree. Of course both John and those observing him might also say that this desire is unwise or irrational, and the fact that John has strong irrational desires poses a serious problem for him. It also poses a problem for Dennett's theory.

An entirely analogous problem arises for *belief* attribution. Perhaps the most abundant source of vivid examples comes from the 'heuristics and biases' tradition in cognitive social psychology. For over thirty years, researchers in that tradition have been exploring the many ways in which ordinary human subjects come to hold *irrational* beliefs on the basis of *irrational* reasoning processes.[53] Consider, for example, Kahneman and

---

[51] See e.g. Dennett 1987: 53–4.

[52] Here a critic might object that even if John wants to eat the chocolate, it is *not* rational for him to eat it, since presumably he also has a very strong desire not to have a violent allergic reaction. We have considerable sympathy with this objection. But since we are trying to interpret Dennett as charitably as possible we will ignore it and assume that on the slippery and flexible interpretation of rationality that Dennett has in mind, it *is* rational for John to eat the chocolate. Without this charitable assumption it is hard to see how Dennett's theory could even begin to handle the vast number of cases in which people have foolish or irrational desires which lead them to do foolish or irrational things.

[53] For good surveys see Kahneman, Slovic, and Tversky 1982 and Baron 2000.

Tversky's (1982*a*) famous 'feminist bank teller' experiment. Subjects in this experiment were presented with the following task:

Linda is 31 years old, single, outspoken, and very bright. She majored in philosophy. As a student, she was deeply concerned with issues of discrimination and social justice, and also participated in anti-nuclear demonstrations.

Please rank the following statements by their probability, using 1 for the most probable and 8 for the least probable.

   (a) Linda is a teacher in elementary school.
   (b) Linda works in a bookstore and takes Yoga classes.
   (c) Linda is active in the feminist movement.
   (d) Linda is a psychiatric social worker.
   (e) Linda is a member of the League of Women Voters.
   (f) Linda is a bank teller.
   (g) Linda is an insurance sales person.
   (h) Linda is a bank teller and is active in the feminist movement.

Kahneman and Tversky found that 89 per cent of subjects who had no background in statistics judged that statement (h) was more probable than statement (f), although of course one cannot be a feminist bank teller without being a bank teller. This faulty pattern of reasoning has been called the 'conjunction fallacy', and the result has been replicated numerous times. How does Dennett react to cases like this? Sometimes, it appears, he is inclined to take a hard line and insist that the subjects in these experiments don't really believe that (h) is more probable than (f). But along with many other critics of Dennett's theory, we find this hard line hard to take seriously.[54] On other occasions, Dennett seems to suggest that these cases can be accommodated by his theory in much the same way that it can accommodate John's desire to eat the chocolate. If a subject believes that (h) is more probable than (f), then (in these circumstances) it is rational for the subject to say so. And since the subject *does* say that (h) is more probable than (f), we can use the rationality assumption to infer that he believes it. But, of course, if Dennett adopts this line he faces the same problem for belief attribution that we noted earlier for desire attribution: the theory leads to two conflicting attributions with no way of deciding between them.[55]

Before moving on, we want to note a rather different way in which the feminist bank teller and other heuristics and biases examples may pose a problem for Dennett. In addition to the fact that we regularly attribute

---

[54] See e.g. Goldman 1989: 165. For a more detailed critique of Dennett's 'hard line' see Stich 1981.

[55] Yet another way for Dennett to handle these cases would be to insist, along with Gigerenzer (2000) and other advocates of 'ecological rationality', that subjects who believe that (h) is more probable than (f) are *not* being irrational. As far as we know, Dennett has never flirted with this option.

irrational beliefs to subjects who give the most common answers in these experiments, we suspect that people can often *predict* the inferences that other people will make and the beliefs that they will form, since just about everyone feels the tug of the irrational reasoning heuristic. Stephen J. Gould makes the point with characteristic panache:

I am particularly fond of [the Linda] example, because I know that the [conjunction] is least probable, yet a little homunculus in my head continues to jump up and down, shouting at me—'but she can't just be a bank teller; read the description.' ... Why do we consistently make this simple logical error? Tversky and Kahneman argue, correctly I think, that our minds are not built (for whatever reason) to work by the rules of probability. (Gould 1992: 469)

Although it hasn't been systematically studied as far as we know, we think it is quite likely that even subjects who get the right answer on the Linda task can often predict the mistake that others will make. For there is an important sense in which the mistake is perfectly natural, as the Gould quote nicely illustrates. Furthermore, we expect that much the same is true for a wide range of findings in the heuristics and biases tradition. That is, we expect that many of the rationally faulty inferences charted by social psychologists are perfectly natural inferences for us to draw, and, further, even when people are sophisticated enough to avoid these errors by invoking socially acquired principles of reasoning, they may well be able to predict that others will make the errors. If this is right, then once again Dennett's rationality-based theory of mindreading is in serious trouble. On our theory, by contrast, this is just what we would expect, since according to us inference prediction is subserved by the same mechanism that subserves ordinary unreflective inference.

In the cases we have considered so far, Dennett's rationality-based theory provides *too many* mental state attributions and no principled way of choosing between them. We think that there is an even more direct threat to Dennett's account. There are lots of cases in which we attribute mental states on the basis of cues that have no rational link to behaviour, even when the notion of rationality is construed in Dennett's slippery and flexible way. When playing object-hiding games with children, adults often infer the location of the hidden object by noting the child's gaze direction, which indicates where the child believes the object is hidden. Since the child wants to keep the location of the object a secret, it is hardly rational for her to look at the hiding location. So it is hard to see how Dennett's theory can provide any account of mindreading episodes like this. We typically don't expect adults to make these kinds of mistakes. But the pervasive phenomenon of lying provides lots of examples of people inferring an adult's beliefs in ways that a rationality-based theory cannot explain. In his work on lying, Paul Ekman has developed a number of sophisticated techniques for determining whether someone is lying. However, he notes that there are many ways that ordinary people detect liars, because liars often betray themselves with what Ekman calls 'deception clues' (1985: 39). To take some obvious examples, nervousness often gives liars away, as does covering one's mouth or avoiding eye contact. These kinds of deception cues are particularly likely to be picked up by close friends and family members. And there is a wide range of such cues: 'Deception clues or leakage may be shown in a change in the expression on the face, a movement of the body, an inflection to the voice, a swallowing in the throat, a very deep or shallow breath, long pauses between words, a slip of the tongue, a micro facial expression, a gestural slip' (Ekman 1985: 43). In these cases of gleaning beliefs from behaviour, there is no rational link between the cue and the belief. Indeed, in most such cases there is an obvious sense in which it is quite *irrational* for the liar to exhibit the behaviour he does and thereby betray the beliefs he is attempting to conceal.

There are also many ways in which mindreaders attribute *desires* on the basis of behaviour that has no rational link to the desire. From a young age, toddlers recognize that when a person displays facial expressions of disgust towards an object, that person typically does not desire the object. Adults draw the same conclusion. But it is utterly implausible to suggest that an appeal to rationality plays a role in cases like this. The mindreading child or adult doesn't typically infer that the target is scrunching up his nose because that is the *rational* thing to do if one dislikes the food. Similarly, there is a wide range of cases in which mindreaders attribute emotions to a target on the basis of cues that have no rational link to the emotion. When a child sees someone crying, the child infers that the person is sad. But it is hardly plausible to suppose that the child reasons that the target is probably sad because it would be rational for him to cry if he is sad. The problem is perhaps even clearer if we consider *blushing*. If we see a person blush, we typically come to believe that the person is embarrassed by something. But we may also recognize that the person has no reason to communicate his embarrassment. Indeed, in many cases, blushing people have good reasons *not* to betray their embarrassment.

It would be easy enough to marshal many more examples of mindreading that cannot plausibly be explained by rationality-based theories like Dennett's. But we are inclined to think that those we have already discussed, along with the many objections raised in the extensive literature critical of Dennett's approach, are more than adequate to show that rationality-based theories are not serious competitors to the theory of mindreading that we have sketched in this chapter.

5. Conclusion

In this chapter we have set out an integrated hybrid theory of third-person mindreading which includes components congenial to three of the major competing theories. The Desire Detection Mechanisms are information rich, and some of them may be modular; the Discrepant Belief Attribution Mechanisms are also information rich, and most of them are non-modular; the strategies used for inference and plan prediction are similar to the paradigmatic simulation strategies. Our theory also includes some important features—the PWB and the process of selective default belief attribution—that have not been important elements in any competing theory. Mindreading is a complex and multifaceted process, and it has been our contention that our eclectic hybrid theory does a better job of explaining a broad range of mindreading phenomena than any of the more monolithic accounts that have been offered. There can be little doubt that both critical scrutiny and new empirical findings will reveal that there are many ways in which our theory needs to be elaborated and modified. We offer it not as the last word on third-person mindreading, but only as a first pass at a detailed and integrated theory. We will be well satisfied if our efforts inspire other authors to produce empirically well-informed accounts of mindreading that are clearer or more detailed than ours, and that deal with even more aspects of mindreading than we have, even if those accounts offer good reasons to reject parts of the theory we have assembled. We don't pretend to be the rocket scientists of mindreading; our goal has been to build a better launching pad.

4

Reading One's Own Mind

4.1. Introduction

The idea that we have special access to our own mental states has a distinguished philosophical history. Philosophers as different as Descartes and Locke agreed that we know our own minds in a way that is quite different from the way in which we know other minds. In the latter half of the twentieth century, however, this idea came under serious attack, first from philosophy (Sellars 1956) and more recently from researchers working on mindreading.[1] In the previous chapter, we developed an account of how people read *other peoples'* minds. This has been the focus of most of the work on mindreading. However, a number of psychologists and philosophers have also proposed accounts of the mechanisms underlying the attribution of mental states to *oneself*. This process of *reading one's own mind* or *becoming self-aware* will be our primary concern in this chapter.

We will start by examining what is probably the account of self-awareness that is most widely held among psychologists, an account which we will call the 'theory theory of self-awareness' (TTSA). The two basic ideas of this account are (1) that one's access to one's own mind depends on the same cluster of cognitive mechanisms that underlie the capacity to attribute mental states to others, and (2) that those mechanisms include a rich body of information about the mind which plays a central role in both third-person and first-person mindreading. Though many authors have endorsed the theory theory of self-awareness (Gopnik 1993; Gopnik and Wellman 1994; Gopnik and Meltzoff 1994; Perner 1991; Wimmer and Hartl 1991; Carruthers 1996; Frith 1994; Frith and Happé 1999), it is our contention that advocates of this account have left their theory seriously underdescribed. In the next section, we will suggest three different ways in which the theory might be elaborated, all of which have significant shortcomings. In Section 4.3, we will present our own theory of self-awareness, the Monitoring Mechanism theory, and compare its merits to those of the TTSA. Advocates of the TTSA argue that it is supported by

---

[1] For more on Sellars's role in this challenge to the traditional view, see Stich and Ravenscroft (1994).

evidence about psychological development and psychopathologies. In Section 4.4 we will review the developmental arguments and try to show that none of the evidence favours the TTSA over our Monitoring Mechanism theory. Indeed, we will maintain that a closer look at the evidence on development actually provides arguments *against* the TTSA. In Section 4.5 we will review the arguments from psychopathologies and we will argue that none of the evidence favours the TTSA over our Monitoring Mechanism theory. Then, in Section 4.6, we will marshal some additional evidence on psychopathologies to provide an argument in favour of the Monitoring Mechanism theory. On our account, but not on the TTSA, it is possible for the mechanisms subserving self-awareness and reading other people's minds to be damaged independently. And, we will suggest, this may well be just what is happening in certain cases of schizophrenia and autism. After making our case against the theory theory of self-awareness and in favour of our theory, we will consider two other theories of self-awareness to be found in the recent literature. The first of these, discussed in Section 4.7, is Robert Gordon's 'ascent routine' account (Gordon 1995*b*, 1996), which, we will argue, is clearly inadequate to explain the full range of self-awareness phenomena. The second is Alvin Goldman's (1993*a*, *b*, 1997, 2000) phenomenological account which, we maintain, is also under-described and admits of two importantly different interpretations. On both of these interpretations, we'll argue, the theory is singularly implausible. That's where we're headed. But before we do any of this, there is a good deal of background that needs to be set in place.

We begin by drawing a distinction that was left implicit in preceding chapters. Mindreading skills, in both the first-person and the third-person cases, can be divided into two categories which, for want of better labels, we will call *detecting* and *reasoning*.

- *Detecting* is the capacity to attribute *current* mental states to someone.
- *Reasoning* is the capacity to use information about a person's mental states (typically along with other information) to make predictions about the person's *past and future mental states*, her *behaviour*, and her *environment*.

So, for instance, one might *detect* that another person wants ice cream and that the person thinks the closest place to get ice cream is at the corner shop. Then one might *reason* from this information that, since the person wants ice cream and thinks that she can get it at the corner shop, she will go to the shop. The distinction between detecting and reasoning is an important one because some of the theories we will be considering offer integrated accounts on which detecting and reasoning are explained by the same cognitive mechanism. Other theories, including ours, maintain that in the first-person case, these two aspects of mindreading are subserved by different mechanisms.

Like the other authors we'll be considering, we take it to be a requirement on theories of self-awareness that they offer an explanation for:

1. the obvious facts about self-attribution (e.g. that normal adults do it easily and often, that they are generally accurate, and that they have no clear idea of how they do it);
2. the often rather un-obvious facts about self-attribution that have been uncovered by cognitive and developmental psychologists.

However, we *do not* take it to be a requirement on theory building in this area that the theory address philosophical puzzles that have been raised about knowledge of one's own mental states. In recent years, philosophers have had a great deal to say about the link between content externalism and the possibility that people can have privileged knowledge about their own propositional attitudes (e.g. McLaughlin and Tye 1998; Wright et al. 1998).[2] These issues are largely orthogonal to the sorts of questions about underlying mechanisms that we will be discussing in this chapter, and we have nothing at all to contribute to the resolution of the philosophical puzzles posed by externalism. But in the unlikely event that philosophers who worry about such matters agree on solutions to these puzzles, we expect that the solutions will fit comfortably with our theory.

4.2. The Theory Theory of Self-Awareness

As noted earlier, among psychologists the theory theory of self-awareness is the prevailing account. And, of course, two of the leading accounts of how we understand *other people's* minds are also 'theory theories'.[3] Before setting out TTSA, it will be useful to review in broad outline how theory theory accounts of third-person mindreading propose to explain our capacity to read other people's minds, stressing some important points on which the scientific-theory theory of third-person mindreading and the modular account of third-person mindreading *agree*.

According to both the scientific-theory theory and the modularity theory, the capacity to *detect* other people's mental states relies on inferences that

---

[2] Content externalism is the view that the content of one's mental states is determined at least in part by factors external to one's mind. In contemporary analytic philosophy, the view was motivated largely by Putnam's Twin Earth thought experiments (Putnam 1975) that seem to show that two molecule-for-molecule twins can have thoughts with different contents or meanings, apparently because of their different external environments.

[3] As we noted in the previous chapter (Section 3.4), the term 'theory theory' has been used both as a label for what we have been calling the 'scientific-theory theory' and as a label for *all* information-rich accounts of mindreading, including modular theories. In this book we have adopted the latter, more inclusive, reading of 'theory theory'.

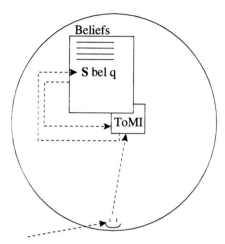

Fig. 4.1   Theory theory of detecting others' mental states

invoke a rich body of information about the mind. For scientific-theory theorists, this information is acquired and stored in much the same way that scientific theories are, while for modularity theorists, the information is innate and stored in a mental module. Although this distinction was quite important to the concerns of the previous chapter, in the present chapter little turns on the distinction and thus it can be safely ignored. So in this chapter we will often use 'ToMI' to refer to the body of information about the mind (the 'Theory of Mind Information') that is exploited in third-person mind-reading, regardless of whether this information is akin to a scientific theory or housed in a module.[4] According to theory theorists of both stripes, when we detect another person's mental state, the process involves an information-mediated (or 'theory-mediated') inference that makes use of the information in ToMI. The inference can also draw on perceptually available information about the behaviour of the target and about her environment, and information stored in memory about the target and her environment. A sketch of the mental mechanisms invoked in this account is given in Figure 4.1.

Both versions of the theory theory also maintain that ToMI is both the information about the mind that underlies the capacity to *detect* other people's mental states and the information about the mind that underlies the capacity to *reason* about other people's mental states and predict their behaviour. So for theory theorists, reasoning about other people's mental states and predicting

---

[4] We will also sometimes use 'ToMI' as a label for the mental mechanism or mechanisms that house and exploit this information. Where the distinction is important, the context will make clear which is intended.

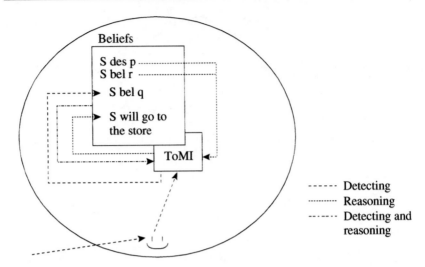

Fig. 4.2   Theory theory of detecting and reasoning about others' mental states

their behaviour is also a theory-mediated inference process, where the inferences draw on beliefs about (*inter alia*) the target's mental states. Of course, some of these beliefs will themselves have been produced by detection inferences. When detecting and reasoning are depicted together we get Figure 4.2.

In Chapter 3 we argued that both versions of the theory theory of third-person mindreading are inadequate, because simulation-style processing is also crucial to mindreading. For the first six sections of this chapter, however, we will try to simplify matters by ignoring our critique and assuming, for argument's sake, that some version of the account of third-person mindreading depicted in Figure 4.2 is correct. We maintain that even if *all* third-person mindreading depends on ToMI, that still will not provide the advocates of TTSA with the resources to accommodate the facts about self-awareness. So we ask the reader to bear in mind that, until Section 4.7, we will be assuming that all third-person mindreading depends on ToMI.[5]

4.2.1. Reading one's own mind: three versions of the TTSA

The theory theory account of how we read other minds can be extended to provide an account of how we read our own minds. Indeed, both the theory

---

[5] Though the argument is a bit messier, the case against TTSA is even stronger if one drops the simplifying assumption that all third-person mindreading invokes ToMI. The details are left as an exercise for the reader.

theory for understanding other minds and the theory theory for self-awareness seem to have been first proposed in the same article by Wilfrid Sellars (1956). The core idea of the theory theory account of self-awareness is that the process of reading one's own mind is largely or entirely parallel to the process of reading someone else's mind. Advocates of the TTSA maintain that knowledge about one's own mind, like knowledge about other minds, comes from theory-mediated (or information-mediated) inferences, and the information that mediates these inferences is the same for self and other—it is ToMI. In recent years many authors have endorsed this idea; here are two examples:

Even though we seem to perceive our own mental states directly, this direct perception is an illusion. In fact, our knowledge of ourselves, like our knowledge of others, is the result of a theory.... (Gopnik and Meltzoff 1994: 168)

... if the mechanism which underlies the computation of mental states is dysfunctional, then self-knowledge is likely to be impaired just as is the knowledge of other minds. The logical extension of the ToM deficit account of autism is that individuals with autism may know as little about their own minds as about the minds of other people. This is not to say that these individuals lack mental states, but that in an important sense they are unable to reflect on their mental states. Simply put, they lack the cognitive machinery to represent their thoughts and feelings as thoughts and feelings. (Frith and Happé 1999: 7)

Unfortunately, advocates of the theory theory account of self-awareness are much less explicit than one would like, and unpacking the view in different ways leads to significantly different versions of the theory. But all of them share the claim that the processes of reasoning about and detecting one's own mental states will parallel the processes of reasoning about and detecting others' mental states. Since the process of *detecting* one's own mental states will be a central concern in what follows, it is especially important to be very explicit about the account of detection suggested by the theory theory of self-awareness. According to the TTSA:

1. Detecting one's own mental states is an information-mediated or theory-mediated inferential process. The information, here as in the third-person case, is ToMI.
2. As in the third-person case, the information-mediated or theory-mediated process which enables people to detect their own mental states draws on perceptually available information about one's own behaviour and environment. The inference also draws on information stored in memory about oneself and one's environment.

At this point the TTSA can be developed in at least three different ways. So far as we know, advocates of the TTSA have never taken explicit note of these distinctions. Thus it is difficult to determine which version a given theorist would endorse.

TTSA version 1

TTSA version 1 (for which our code name is *the crazy version*) proposes to maintain the parallel between detecting one's own mental states and detecting another person's mental states quite strictly. The *only* information used as evidence for the inference involved in detecting one's own mental state is the information provided by perception (in this case, perception of oneself) and by one's background beliefs (in this case, background beliefs about one's own environment and previously acquired beliefs about one's own mental states). This version of TTSA is sketched in Figure 4.3.

Of course, we typically have much more information about our own behaviour and our own prior mental states than we do about the behaviour and prior mental states of others, so even on this version of the TTSA we may well have a better grasp of our own mind than we do of other minds (see e.g. Gopnik 1993: 94). However, the mechanisms underlying self-awareness are supposed to be the same mechanisms that underlie awareness of the mental states of others. Thus this version of the TTSA denies the widely held view that an individual has some kind of special or privileged access to his own mental states.

We are reluctant to claim that anyone actually advocates this version of the TTSA, since we think it is a view that is hard to take seriously. Indeed, the claim that *perception of one's own behaviour* is the prime source of information on which to base inferences about one's own mental states reminds us of the old joke about the two behaviourists who meet on the street. One says to

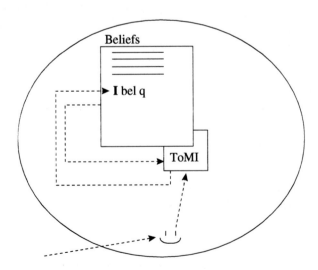

Fig. 4.3   Theory theory of self-awareness, version 1

the other, 'You're fine. How am I?' The reason the joke works is that it seems patently absurd to think that perception of one's behaviour is the best way to find out how one is feeling. It seems obvious that people can sit quietly without exhibiting any relevant behaviour and report on their current thoughts. For instance, people can answer questions about current mental states like 'what are you thinking about?' Similarly, after silently working through a problem in their heads, people can answer subsequent questions like 'how did you figure that out?' And we typically assume that people are correct when they tell us what they were thinking or how they just solved a problem. Of course, it is not just one's current and immediately past *thoughts* that one can report. One can also report one's own current desires, intentions, and imaginings. It seems that people can easily and reliably answer questions like: 'what do you want to do?'; 'what are you going to do?'; 'what are you imagining?' People who aren't exhibiting much behaviour at all are often able to provide richly detailed answers to these questions.

These more or less intuitive claims are backed by considerable empirical evidence from several research programmes in psychology. Using 'think aloud' procedures, researchers have been able to corroborate self-reports of current mental states against other measures. In typical experiments, subjects are given logical or mathematical problems to solve and are instructed to 'think aloud' while they work the problems.[6] For instance, people are asked to think aloud while multiplying 36 times 24 (Ericsson and Simon 1993: 346–7). Subjects' responses can then be correlated with formal analyses of how to solve the problem, and the subject's answer can be compared with the correct answer. If the subject's think-aloud protocol conforms to the formal task analysis, that provides good reason to think that the subject's report of his thoughts is accurate (Ericsson and Simon 1993: 330). In addition to these concurrent reports, researchers have also explored retrospective reports of one's own problem solving.[7]

---

[6] To give an idea of how this works, here is an excerpt from Ericsson and Simon's instructions to subjects in think-aloud experiments: 'In this experiment we are interested in what you think about when you find answers to some questions that I am going to ask you to answer. In order to do this I am going to ask you to THINK ALOUD as you work on the problem given. What I mean by think aloud is that I want you to tell me EVERYTHING you are thinking from the time you first see the question until you give an answer.' (Ericsson and Simon 1993: 378.)

[7] For retrospective reports, immediately after the subject completes the problem, the subject is given instructions like the following: 'Now I want to see how much you can remember about what you were thinking from the time you read the question until you gave the answer. We are interested in what you actually can REMEMBER rather than what you think you must have thought. If possible I would like you to tell about your memories in the sequence in which they occurred while working on the question. Please tell me if you are uncertain about any of your memories. I don't want you to work on solving the problem again, just report all that you can remember thinking about when answering the question. Now tell me what you remember.' (Ericsson and Simon 1993: 378.)

For instance Ericsson and Simon discuss a study by Hamilton and Sanford in which subjects were presented with two different letters (e.g. R–P) and asked whether the letters were in alphabetical order. Subjects were then asked to say how they solved the problem. Subjects reported bringing to mind strings of letters in alphabetical order (e.g. LMNOPQRST), and reaction times taken during the problem solving correlated with the number of letters subjects recollected (Ericsson and Simon 1993: 191–2).

So, both commonsense and experimental studies confirm that people can sit quietly, exhibiting next to no overt behaviour, and give detailed, accurate self-reports about their mental states. In light of this, it strikes us as simply preposterous to suggest that the reports people make about their own mental states are being inferred from perceptions of their own behaviour and information stored in memory. For it is simply absurd to suppose that there is enough behavioural evidence or information stored in memory to serve as a basis for accurately answering questions like 'what are you thinking about now?' or 'how did you solve that math problem?' Our ability to answer questions like these indicates that version 1 of the TTSA cannot be correct since it cannot accommodate some central cases of self-awareness.

TTSA version 2

Version 2 of the TTSA (for which our code name is *the underdescribed version*) allows that in using ToMI to infer to conclusions about one's own mind there is information available *in addition to* the information provided by perception and one's background beliefs. This additional information is available only in the first-person case, not in the third-person case. Unfortunately, advocates of the TTSA tell us very little about what this alternative source of information is. And what little they do tell us is unhelpful to put it mildly. Here, for instance, is an example of the sort of thing that Gopnik has said about this additional source of information:

One possible source of evidence for the child's theory may be first-person psychological experiences that may themselves be the consequence of genuine psychological perceptions. For example, we may well be equipped to detect certain kinds of internal cognitive activity in a vague and unspecified way, what we might call *'the Cartesian buzz'*. (Gopnik 1993: 11, emphasis added)

We have no serious idea what the 'Cartesian buzz' is, or how one would detect it. Nor do we understand how detecting the Cartesian buzz will enable the ToMI to infer to conclusions like: *I want to spend next Christmas in Paris* or *I believe that the Brooklyn Bridge is about eight blocks south of the Manhattan Bridge*. Figure 4.4 is our attempt to sketch version 2 of the TTSA.

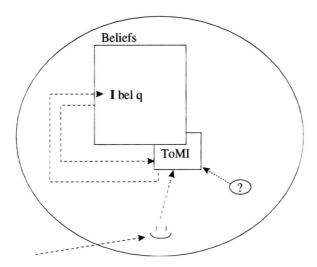

Fig. 4.4   Theory theory of self-awareness, version 2

We won't bother to mount a critique against this version, apart from observing that without some less mysterious statement of what the additional source(s) of information are, the theory is too incomplete to evaluate.

TTSA version 3

There is, of course, one very natural way to spell out what is missing in version 2. What is needed is some source of information that would help a person form beliefs (typically true beliefs) about his own mental states. The obvious source of information would be the mental states themselves. So, on this version of the TTSA, the ToMI has access to information provided by perception, information provided by background beliefs, *and information about the representations contained in the Belief Box, the Desire Box, etc.* This version of the TTSA is sketched in Figure 4.5.

Now at this juncture one might wonder why the ToMI is *needed* in this story. If the mechanism subserving self-awareness has access to information about the representations in the various attitude boxes, then ToMI has no serious work to do. So why suppose that it is involved at all? That's a good question, we think. And it is also a good launching pad for our theory. Because on our account Figure 4.5 has it wrong. In detecting one's own mental states, the flow of information is *not* routed through the ToMI system. Rather, the process is subserved by a separate self-monitoring mechanism.

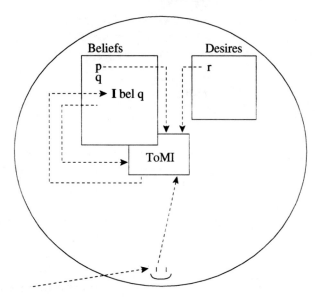

Fig. 4.5   Theory theory of self-awareness, version 3

4.3. Reading One's Own Mind: The Monitoring Mechanism Theory

In constructing our theory about the process that subserves self-awareness we have tried to be, to borrow a phrase from Nelson Goodman (1983: 60), 'refreshingly non-cosmic'. What we propose is that we need to add another component or cluster of components to our account of cognitive architecture, a mechanism (or mechanisms) that serves the function of monitoring one's own mental states.

4.3.1. The Monitoring Mechanism and propositional attitudes

Recall what the theory of self-awareness needs to explain. The basic facts are that when normal adults believe that *p*, they can quickly and accurately form the belief *I believe that p*; when normal adults desire that *p*, they can quickly and accurately form the belief *I desire that p*; and so on for other basic propositional attitudes like *intend* and *imagine*.[8] In order to implement this ability, no sophisticated body of information about the mind like ToMI is required. To have beliefs about one's own beliefs, all that is required is that there be a Monitoring Mechanism (MM) that, when activated, takes the representation *p* in the Belief

---

[8] There are, of course, much more complicated propositional attitudes like disappointment and *Schadenfreude*. We postpone discussion of these 'thick' propositional attitudes until Chapter 5 (see Section 5.1.2).

Box as input and produces the representation *I believe that p* as output. This mechanism would be trivial to implement. To produce representations of one's own beliefs, the Monitoring Mechanism merely has to copy representations from the Belief Box, embed the copies in a representation schema of the form: *I believe that* ___, and then place the new representations back in the Belief Box. The proposed mechanism (or perhaps a distinct but entirely parallel mechanism) would work in much the same way to produce representations of one's own desires, intentions, and imaginings.[9] Although we propose that the MM is a special mechanism for detecting one's own mental states, we maintain that there is no special mechanism for what we earlier called *reasoning about* one's own mental states. Rather, reasoning about one's own mental states depends on the same ToMI as reasoning about others' mental states.[10] As a result, our theory (as well as the TTSA) predicts that, *ceteris paribus*, where the ToMI is deficient or the relevant information is unavailable, subjects will make mistakes in reasoning about their own mental states as well as others'. Our account of the process subserving self-awareness for beliefs is sketched in Figure 4.6.

Since our theory maintains that reasoning about one's own mental states relies on ToMI, we can readily accommodate findings like those presented by Nisbett and Wilson (1977). They report a number of studies in which subjects make mistakes about their own mental states. However, the kinds of mistakes that are made in those experiments are typically not mistakes in *detecting* one's own mental states. Rather, the studies show that subjects make mistakes in *reasoning about* their own mental states. The central findings are that subjects sometimes attribute their behaviour to inefficacious beliefs and that subjects sometimes deny the efficacy of beliefs that are, in fact, efficacious. For instance, Nisbett and Schacter (1966) found that subjects were willing to tolerate more intense shocks if they were given a drug (actually a placebo) and told that the drug would produce heart palpitations, irregular breathing, and butterflies in the stomach. Although being told about the drug had a significant effect on the subjects' willingness to take shocks, most subjects denied this. Nisbett and Wilson's explanation of these findings is, plausibly enough, that subjects have an incomplete theory regarding the mind and that the subjects' mistakes reflect the inadequacies of their theory (Nisbett and Wilson 1977). This explanation of the findings fits well with our account too. For on

---

[9] Apart from the cognitive science trappings, the idea of an internal monitor goes back at least to David Armstrong (1968) and has been elaborated by William Lycan (1987) among others. However, much of this literature has become intertwined with the attempt to determine the proper account of consciousness, and that is not our concern at all. Rather, on our account, the monitor is just a rather simple information-processing mechanism that generates explicit representations about the representations in various components of the mind and inserts these new representations in the Belief Box.

[10] Recall that, for simplicity in evaluating TTSA, we are ignoring the role of processes that don't exploit ToMI in third-person mindreading and assuming that all third-person mindreading depends on ToMI.

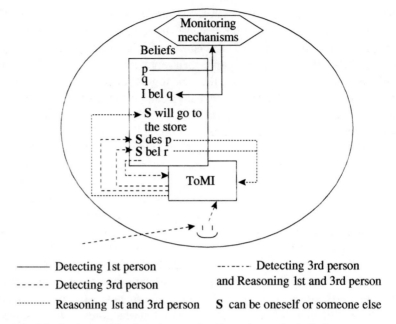

Fig. 4.6   Monitoring mechanism theory of self-awareness for beliefs

our account, when trying to figure out the *causes* of one's own behaviour, one must reason about mental states, and this process is mediated by the ToMI. As a result, if the ToMI is not up to the task, then people will make mistakes in reasoning about their own mental states as well as others' mental states.

In this chapter, we propose to remain agnostic about the extent to which the information about the mind in ToMI is innate. However, we do propose that the MM (or cluster of MMs) is innate and comes on-line fairly early in development—significantly before ToMI is fully in place. During the period when the Monitoring Mechanism is up and running but ToMI is not, the representations that the MM produces can't do much. In particular, they can't serve as premisses for reasoning about mental states, since reasoning about mental states is a process mediated by ToMI. So, for example, ToMI provides the additional premisses (or the special purpose inferential strategies) that enable the mind to go from premisses like *I want q* to conclusions like: *If I believed that doing A was the best way to get q, then (probably) I would want to do A.* Thus our theory predicts that young children can't reason about their own beliefs in this way.

Although we take no stand on the extent to which ToMI is innate, we maintain (along with many theory theorists) that ToMI comes on-line only gradually. As it comes on-line, it enables a richer and richer set of inferences from the representations of the form *I believe (or desire) that p* that are produced by the MM. Some might argue that early on in development, these representations of the form *I believe that p* do not really count as having the content *I believe that p*, since the concept (or 'proto-concept') of *belief* is too inferentially impoverished. On this view, it is only after a rich set of inferences becomes available that the child's *I believe that p* representations really count as having the content *I believe that p*. To make a persuasive case for or against this view, one would need a well-motivated and carefully defended theory of content for concepts. And we don't happen to have one. (Indeed, one of us is inclined to suspect that much recent work aimed at constructing theories of content is deeply misguided (Stich 1992, 1996).) But, with this caveat, we don't have any objection to the claim that early *I believe that p* representations do not have the content *I believe that p*. If that's what your favourite theory of content says, that's fine with us. Our proposal can be easily rendered consistent with such a view of content by simply replacing the embedded mental predicates (e.g. *'believe'*) with technical terms 'bel', 'des', 'pret', etc. We might then say that the MM produces the belief that *I bel that p* and the belief that *I des that q*; and that at some point further on in development, these beliefs acquire the content *I believe that p, I desire that q*, and so forth. That said, we propose to ignore this subtlety for the rest of the chapter.

The core claim of our theory is that the MM is a distinct mechanism that is specialized for detecting one's own mental states.[11] However, it is important to note that on our account of mindreading, the MM is not the *only* mental mechanism that can generate representations with the content *I believe that p*. Representations of this sort can also be generated by ToMI. Thus it is possible that in some cases, the ToMI and the MM will produce *conflicting* representation of the form *I believe that p*. For instance, if ToMI is deficient, then in some cases it might produce an inaccurate representation with the content *I believe that p* which conflicts with accurate representations generated by the MM. In these cases, our theory does not specify how the conflict will be resolved or which representation will guide verbal behaviour and other actions. On our view, it is an open empirical question how such conflicts will be resolved.

4.3.2. The Monitoring Mechanism and perceptual states

Of course, the MM theory is not a complete account of self-awareness. One important limitation is that the MM is proposed as the mechanism underlying self-awareness of one's propositional attitudes, and it is quite likely that the

---

[11] As we have presented our theory, the MM is a mechanism that is distinct from ToMI. But it might be claimed that the MM that we postulate is just a *part* of the ToMI mechanism. Here the crucial question to ask is whether it is a 'dissociable' part which could be selectively

account cannot explain awareness of one's own perceptual states. Perceptual states obviously have phenomenal character, and there is a vigorous debate over whether this phenomenal character is fully captured by a representational account (e.g. Tye 1995; Carruthers 2000; Block 2003). If perceptual states can be captured by a representational or propositional account, then perhaps the MM can be extended to explain awareness of one's own perceptual states. For, as noted above, our proposed MM simply copies representations into representation schemas; for example, it copies representations from the Belief Box into the schema 'I believe that ___'. However, we are sceptical that perceptual states can be entirely captured by representational accounts, and as a result, we doubt that our MM theory can adequately explain our awareness of our own perceptual states. Nonetheless, we think it is plausible that some kind of monitoring account (as opposed to a TTSA account) might apply to awareness of one's own perceptual states. Since it will be important to have a sketch of such a theory on the table, we will provide a brief outline of what the theory might look like.

In specifying the architecture underlying awareness of one's own perceptual states, the first move is to posit a 'Percept Box'. This device holds the percepts produced by the perceptual processing systems. We propose that the Percept Box feeds into the Belief Box in two ways. First and most obviously, the contents of the Percept Box lead the subject to have beliefs about the world around her, by what we might call a Percept-to-Belief Mediator. For instance, if a normal adult looks into a quarry, her perceptual system will produce percepts that will, *ceteris paribus*, lead her to form the belief that *there are rocks down there*. Something at least roughly similar is presumably true in dogs, birds, and frogs. Hence, there is a mechanism (or set of mechanisms) that takes percepts as input and produces beliefs as output. However, there is also, at least in normal adult humans, another way that the Percept Box feeds into the Belief Box—we form beliefs *about our percepts*. For example, when looking into a quarry I might form the belief that *I see rocks*. We also form beliefs about the similarity between percepts—for example, *this toy rock looks like that real rock*. To explain this range of capacities, we tentatively propose that there is a set of Percept-Monitoring Mechanisms that take input from the Percept Box and produce beliefs about the percepts. We represent this account in Figure 4.7. Note that the PMM will presumably be a far more complex mechanism than the MM. For the PMM must take perceptual experiences and produce representations about those perceptual experiences. We have no idea how to characterize this further in terms of cognitive mechanisms, and as a result, we are much less confident about this account than we are about the MM account.

damaged or selectively spared. If the answer is no, then we will argue against this view in Section 4.6. If the answer is yes (MM is a dissociable part of the ToMI mechanism) then there is nothing of substance left to fight about. That theory is a notational variant of ours.

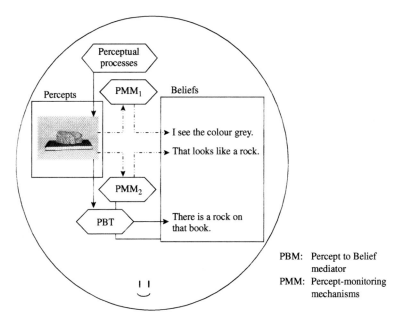

Fig. 4.7   Percept-monitoring mechanism theory

4.4. Developmental Evidence: The Theory Theory of Self-Awareness *vs.* the Monitoring Mechanism Theory

In this section and the one to follow, we will discuss the empirical arguments for and against the theory theory account of self-awareness. But before we present those arguments, it may be useful to provide a brief reminder of the problems we have raised for various versions of the TTSA:

1. Version 1 looks to be hopelessly implausible; it cannot handle some of the most obvious facts about self-awareness.
2. Version 2 is a mystery theory; it maintains that there is a special source of information exploited in reading one's own mind, but it leaves the source of this additional information unexplained.
3. Version 3 faces the embarrassment that if information about the representations in the Belief Box & Desire Box is available, then no rich body of information about the mind is needed to explain self-awareness; ToMI has nothing to do.

We think that these considerations provide an important prima-facie case against the TTSA, though we also think that, as in any scientific endeavour, solid empirical evidence might outweigh the prima-facie considerations.

However, it is our contention that the empirical evidence produced by advocates of TTSA does not support their theory over our Monitoring Mechanism
theory. Rather, we shall argue, in some cases both theories can explain the
data about equally well, while in other cases the Monitoring Mechanism
theory has a clear advantage over the TTSA.

The best-known and most widely discussed argument for the theory theory
of self-awareness comes from developmental work charting the relation
between performance on mindreading tasks for oneself and for others. The
TTSA predicts that subjects' performance on mindreading tasks should be
about equally good (or equally bad) whether the tasks are about one's own
mental states or the mental states of another person. In perhaps the most systematic and interesting argument for the TTSA, Gopnik and Meltzoff maintain that there are indeed clear and systematic correlations between
performance on mindreading tasks for self and for others (see Table 4.1,
reproduced from Gopnik and Meltzoff 1994: table 10.1). For instance,
Gopnik and Meltzoff note that children succeed at perceptual mindreading
tasks for themselves and others before the age of 3. Between the ages of 3 and 4,
children begin to succeed at desire mindreading tasks for self and for others.
And at around the age of 4, children begin to succeed at the false belief task
for self and for others. 'The evidence', Gopnik and Meltzoff maintain,

suggests that there is an extensive parallelism between children's understanding of
their own mental states and their understanding of the mental states of others.... In
each of our studies, children's reports of their own immediately past psychological

Table 4.1 Children's knowledge of their own mental states and those of others

States	Others	Self
Easy		
Pretence	Before age 3	Before age 3
	(Flavell et al. 1987)	(Gopnik and Slaughter 1991)
Imagination	Before age 3	Before age 3
	(Wellman and Estes 1986)	(Gopnik and Slaughter 1991)
Perception	Before age 3	Before age 3
(Level 1)	(Flavell et al. 1981)	(Gopnik and Slaughter 1991)
Intermediate		
Desire	Age 3–4	Age 3–4
	(Flavell et al. 1990)	(Gopnik and Slaughter 1991)
Difficult		
Source of belief	After age 4	After age 4
	(O'Neill et al. 1992)	(Gopnik and Graf 1988)
False belief	After age 4	After age 4
	(Wimmer and Perner 1983)	(Gopnik and Astington 1991)

Source: From Gopnik and Meltzoff 1994: 180.

states are consistent with their accounts of the psychological states of others. When they can report and understand the psychological states of others, in the cases of pretense, perception, and imagination, they report having had those psychological states themselves. When they cannot report and understand the psychological states of others, in the case of false beliefs and source, they do not report that they had those states themselves. Moreover, and in some ways most strikingly, the intermediate case of desire is intermediate for self and other. (1994: 179–80)

This 'extensive parallelism' is taken to show that 'our knowledge of ourselves, like our knowledge of others, is the result of a theory' (Gopnik and Meltzoff 1994: 168). Thus the argument purports to establish a broad-based empirical case for the theory theory of self-awareness. However, on our view quite the opposite is the case. In the pages to follow we will try to show that the data don't provide *any* support for the TTSA over the Monitoring Mechanism theory that we have proposed, and that some of the data that are comfortably compatible with MM cannot be easily explained by the TTSA. Defending this claim is rather a long project, but fortunately the data are intrinsically fascinating.

4.4.1. The parallelism prediction

Before we proceed to the data, it is important to be clear about the structure of Gopnik and Meltzoff's argument and of our counter-argument in favour of the Monitoring Mechanism theory. If Gopnik and Meltzoff are right that there is an 'extensive parallelism', that would support the TTSA because the TTSA *predicts* that there will be parallel performance on parallel mindreading tasks for self and other. According to the TTSA, in order to determine one's own mental states, one must exploit the same ToMI that one uses to determine another's mental states. So, if a child's ToMI is not yet equipped to solve certain third-person tasks, then the child should also be unable to solve the parallel first-person tasks.

By contrast, for many of the tasks we will consider, our theory simply doesn't make a prediction about whether there will be parallel performance on self- and other-versions of the tasks. On our theory, the special purpose mechanisms for detecting one's own mental states (MM & PMM) are quite independent from ToMI, which plays a central role in processes of reasoning about mental states and detecting the mental states of others. Hence, the ability to detect one's own mental states and the ability to detect another's mental states need not show similar developmental trajectories, though in some cases they might. What our theory does predict is that the capacity to detect one's own mental states, though not necessarily the capacity to reason about them, should emerge quite early, since the theory claims that the MM and the PMM are innate and on-line quite early in development. Also, as noted in

Section 4.3, our theory allows for the possibility that the ToMI *can* be used in attributing mental states to oneself. So it may well turn out that sometimes subjects produce inaccurate self-attributions because they are relying on the ToMI. Since our theory provides no a priori reason to expect extensive parallel performance in detecting mental states in oneself and others, if there is extensive parallelism our theory would be faced with a major challenge—it would need to provide some additional and independently plausible explanation for the existence of the parallelism in each case where it is found. But if, as we shall argue, the parallelism is largely illusory, then it is the TTSA that faces a major challenge—it has to provide some plausible explanation for the fact that the parallelism it predicts does not exist.

4.4.2. TTSA meets data

Gopnik and Meltzoff argue for the TT by presenting a wide range of cases in which, they maintain, subjects show parallel performance on self and other versions of mindreading tasks, and at first glance the parallels look very impressive indeed. However, we will argue that on closer inspection this impression is quite misleading. In some cases, there really is parallel performance, but these cases do not support the TTSA over our MM theory, since in these cases both theories do about equally well in explaining the facts; in some cases, the evidence for parallel performance is dubious; and in several other cases, there is evidence that performance is *not* parallel. These cases are of particular importance since they are compatible with the MM account and prima facie *in*compatible with the TTSA. In the remainder of this section we will consider each of these three classes of cases.

Cases where the parallelism is real

The 'easy' tasks   There is a range of tasks that Gopnik and Meltzoff classify as *easy for other and easy for self*. They claim that pretence, imagination, and perception (level 1 perspective taking) are understood for both self and other before age 3. At least on some tasks, this claim of parallel performance seems to be quite right. Simple perceptual tasks provide perhaps the clearest example. Lempers and colleagues (Lempers et al. 1977) found that $2\frac{1}{2}$-year-old children succeeded at 'level 1' perspective-taking tasks, in which the children had to determine whether another person could see an object or not. As we noted in Section 3.3.3, if a young child is shown that a piece of cardboard has a picture of a rabbit on one side and a picture of a turtle on the other, and if the child is then shown the turtle side, the child can correctly answer that the person on the other side of the cardboard sees the picture of the rabbit. Using similar tasks, Gopnik and Slaughter (1991) found that

3-year-old children could also successfully report their own past perceptions. As Gopnik and Meltzoff characterize it, this task is 'easy' for other and 'easy' for self, and Gopnik and Meltzoff put forward such cases as support for the TTSA.

As we see it, however, the fact that level 1 perspective-taking tasks are easy for other and for self does not count as evidence for the TTSA over our MM theory. To see why, let us consider first the *self* case and then the *other* case. On our account, MM is the mechanism responsible for self-awareness of propositional attitudes and, we have tentatively suggested, another mechanism (or family of mechanisms), the Percept-Monitoring Mechanism, underlies awareness of one's own perceptual states. The PMM, like the MM, is hypothesized to be innate and to come on-line quite early in development. Thus the PMM is up and running by the age of $2\frac{1}{2}$, well before ToMI is fully in place. So our theory predicts that quite young children should be able to give accurate reports about their own perceptual states. Let's turn now to the *other* case. Both the TTSA and our theory maintain that the detection of mental states in others depends on ToMI and, like advocates of TTSA, we think that evidence on visual perspective taking (e.g. Lempers et al. 1977) shows that part of ToMI is on-line by the age of $2\frac{1}{2}$. It is of some interest to determine why the part of ToMI that subserves these tasks emerges as early as it does, though neither the TTSA nor our theory currently has any explanation to offer. For both theories it is just a brute empirical fact. So here's the situation: our theory predicts that awareness of one's own perceptions will emerge early, and has no explanation to offer for why the part of ToMI that subserves the detection of perceptual states in others emerges early. By contrast, TTSA predicts that both self and other abilities will emerge at the same time, but has no explanation to offer for why they both emerge early. By our lights this one is a wash. Neither theory has any clear explanatory advantage over the other.

Much the same reasoning shows that Gopnik and Meltzoff's cases of pretence and imagination do not lend any significant support to the TTSA over our theory. There is some evidence that by the age of 3 children have some understanding of pretence and imagination in others (e.g. Wellman and Estes 1986), though as we will see in Section 4.4.2, there is also some reason for scepticism. However, whatever the ontogeny is for detecting pretence and imagination in others, the TTSA account can hardly offer a better explanation than our account, since we agree with advocates of TTSA that ToMI is centrally involved in this process, and neither we nor the defenders of TTSA have any explanation to offer for the fact that the relevant part of ToMI emerges when it does. As in the case of perception, our theory does have an explanation for the fact that the ability to detect one's own pretences and imaginings emerges early, since on our view this process is subserved by the MM which is up and running by the age of $2\frac{1}{2}$, but we have no explanation for the fact (if indeed it is a fact) that the part of ToMI that subserves the detection of pretences and imaginings in others also emerges early. The TTSA, on the other hand, predicts that self and other abilities will both emerge at the same time, but does not explain why they both emerge early. So here, as before, neither theory has any obvious explanatory advantage over the other.

Sources of belief   A suite of studies by Gopnik, O'Neill, and their colleagues (Gopnik and Graf 1988; O'Neill and Gopnik 1991; O'Neill et al. 1992) show that there is a parallel between performance on source of belief tasks for self and for others. In the self-versions of these tasks, children came to find out which objects were in a drawer either by seeing the object, being told, or inferring from a simple cue. After establishing that the child knows what is in the drawer, the child is asked 'How do you know that there's an x in the drawer?' This question closely parallels the question used to explore children's understanding of the sources of another's belief (O'Neill et al. 1992). O'Neill and her colleagues found that while 4-year-olds tended to succeed at the other-person version of the task, 3-year-olds tended to fail it; similarly, Gopnik and Graf (1988) found that 4-year-olds tended to succeed at the self-version of the task, but 3-year-olds tended to fail it. For instance, 3-year-olds often said that their knowledge came from seeing the object when actually they had been told about the object, and 3-year-olds made similar errors when judging the source of another person's knowledge.

These results are interesting and surprising, but they are orthogonal to the issue at hand. The Monitoring Mechanism posited in our theory is a mechanism for *detecting* mental states, not for reasoning about them. But questions about the sources of one's beliefs or knowledge cannot be answered merely by *detecting* one's own mental states. Rather, questions about how you gained knowledge fall into the domain of *reasoning* about mental states, and that job, we are assuming, is performed by the ToMI. So, on our theory, questions about sources will implicate the ToMI both for self and other. Hence, our theory, like the TTSA, predicts that there will be parallel performance on tasks like the source tasks.

The relevant but dubious data

In Gopnik and Meltzoff's table displaying extensive parallelism, there are two remaining cases that cannot be dismissed as irrelevant. However, we will argue that the cases fall far short of clear support for the TTSA.

False belief   In Chapter 3, we discussed at length the well-known finding that young children fail the 'false belief task' (see Sections 3.2.2 and 3.3). On closely matched tasks, Gopnik and Astington (1988) found a correlation between failing the false belief task for another and failing it for oneself. Gopnik and Astington (1988) presented children with a candy box and then let the children see that there were really pencils in the box. Children were asked, 'What will Nicky think is in the box?' and then, 'When you first saw the box, before we opened it, what did you think was inside it?' Children's ability to answer the question for self was significantly correlated with their ability to answer the question for other. Thus, here we have a surprising instance of parallel performance on tasks for self and other.[12] This is, of course, just the outcome that the TTSA would predict. For the TTSA maintains that ToMI is crucial both in the detection of other people's beliefs and in the detection of one's own. Thus if a child's ToMI has not yet developed to the point where it can detect other people's beliefs in a given situation, it is to be expected that the child will also be unable to detect her own beliefs in that context. And this, it appears, is just what the experimental results show.

What about our theory? What explanation can it offer for these results? The first step in answering this question is to note that in the *self* version of the false belief task, the child is not actually being asked to report on her *current* belief, but rather to recall a belief she had in the recent past. Where might such memories come from? The most natural answer, for a theory like ours, is that when the child first sees the box she believes that there is candy in it, and the MM produces a belief with the content *I believe that there is candy in the box*. As the experiment continues and time passes that belief is converted into a past tense belief whose content is (roughly) *I believed that there was candy in the box*. But, of course, if that were the end of the story, it would be bad news for our theory, since when asked what she believed when she first saw the box, the child reports that she believed *that there were pencils in the box*. Fortunately, that is *not* the end of the story. For, as we noted in Section 4.3.1, in our theory MM is not the only mechanism capable of generating beliefs with the content *I believe(d) that p*. ToMI is also capable of producing such beliefs, and sometimes ToMI may produce a belief of that form that will conflict with a belief produced by MM. That, we propose, is exactly what is happening in the Gopnik and Astington experiment when younger children fail to report their own earlier false belief. As the results in the other-version of the task indicate, the ToMI in younger children has a strong tendency to attribute beliefs that the child actually believes to be true. So when asked what she believed at the beginning of the experiment, ToMI mistakenly concludes that *I believed that there were pencils in the box*.[13] Thus, on our account, there

---

[12] Similarly, Baron-Cohen (1991a) found that in people with autism, there are correlations between failing the false belief task for other and failing the task for self.

[13] Some theorists, most prominently Fodor (1992), have explained the results in the other-version of the task by claiming that young children do not use the ToMI in these tasks. They

will be two competing and incompatible representations in the child's Belief Box. And to explain the fact that the child usually relies on the mistaken ToMI-generated belief, rather than on the correct MM-generated belief, we must suppose that the memory trace is relatively weak, and that when the child's cognitive system has to decide which belief about her past belief to rely on, the MM-generated memory trace typically loses.

At this point, we suspect, a critic might protest that this is a singularly unconvincing explanation. There is, the critic will insist, no reason to think that the MM-generated memory will typically be weaker than the ToMI-generated belief; it is just an ad hoc assumption that is required to get our theory to square with the facts. And if this were the end of the story, the critic would be right. Fortunately for us, however, this is not the end of the story. For there is evidence that provides independent support for our explanation and under-cuts the TT account. Recent work by German and Leslie exploring perform-ance on self- and other-versions of the false belief task indicates that *if memory enhancements are provided, young children's performance on self-versions improves, while their performance on other-versions stays about the same.* German and Leslie devised a task in which a child would hide a biscuit and then search for it in the wrong place, because it had been moved when the child was behind a screen. In one condition, the child was then shown a videotape of the entire sequence of events—hiding, moving, and searching—and asked, at the appropriate point, 'Why are you looking there?' and then, 'When you were looking for the biscuit, where did you think the biscuit was?' In another condition, after the same hiding, moving, and searching sequence, the videotape was 'accidentally' rewound too far, and the child watched another child in an identical situation. At the appropriate point, the child was asked, 'Why was she looking there?' and 'When she was looking for the bis-cuit, where did she think the biscuit was?' German and Leslie found that chil-dren who were shown their own mistaken search were much more likely to offer a false belief explanation and to attribute a false belief than were chil-dren who were shown another's mistaken search (German and Leslie, forth-coming). This fits nicely with our proposed explanation for why young children fail the false belief task for the self. However, it is difficult to see how an advocate of the TTSA could explain these results. For according to the TTSA, if the child has a defective or immature ToMI, the child should make the same mistakes for himself that he does for another. If there is no MM to generate a correct belief which becomes a correct memory, then giving memory enhancements should not produce differential improvement.

arrive at their answer, Fodor argues, by using a separate reality-biased strategy. We need take no stand on this issue, since if Fodor is correct then it is plausible to suppose that the same reality-biased strategy generates a mistaken *I believed that there were pencils in the box* representation in the self-version of the task.

Desire   Another source of data that might offer support to the TTSA comes from work on understanding desires. Gopnik and Meltzoff maintain that 3-year-olds are just beginning to understand desire in others, and Gopnik and Slaughter found that a significant percentage of children make mistakes about their own immediately past desires. The Gopnik and Slaughter own-desire tasks were quite ingenious. In one of the tasks, they went to a daycare centre just before snack time and asked the child whether he was hungry. The hungry child said 'Yes' and proceeded to eat all the snack he desired. Then the experimenter asked, 'When I first asked you, before we had the snack, were you hungry then?' (1991: 102). Gopnik and Slaughter found that 30–40 per cent of the 3-year-olds mistakenly claimed that they were in their current desire state all along. This surprising result is claimed to parallel Flavell et al.'s (1990) finding that a significant percentage of 3-year-olds make mistakes on desire tasks for others. In the Flavell tasks, the child observes Ellie make a disgusted look after tasting a cookie, and the child is asked 'Does Ellie think it is a yummy tasting cookie?' (Flavell et al. 1990: 918). Gopnik and Meltzoff remark that the 'absolute levels of performance were strikingly similar' to the results reported by Flavell et al. (Gopnik and Meltzoff 1994: 179), and they cite this as support for the parallel performance hypothesis.

The central problem with this putative parallel is that it is not at all clear that the tasks are truly parallel. In Gopnik and Slaughter's tasks, 3-year-olds are asked about a desire that they don't currently have because it was recently satisfied. It would be of considerable interest to couple Gopnik and Slaughter's own-desire version of the hunger task with a closely matched other-person version of the task. For instance, the experiment could have a satiated child watch another child beginning to eat at snack time and ask the satiated child, 'Is he hungry?' If the findings on this task paralleled findings on the own-desire version, that would indeed be an important parallel. Unfortunately, the putatively parallel task in Flavell et al. that Gopnik and Meltzoff cite is quite different from the Gopnik and Slaughter task. In the Flavell tasks, the child is asked whether the target thinks the cookie is 'yummy tasting' (Flavell et al. 1990: 918). The task doesn't explicitly ask about desires at all. Flavell and his colleagues themselves characterize the task as exploring children's ability to attribute value *beliefs*. Further, unlike the Gopnik and Slaughter task, the Flavell et al. tasks depend on expressions of disgust. Indeed, there are so many differences between these tasks that we think it is impossible to draw any conclusions from the comparison.

In this section we have considered the best cases for the TTSA, and it is our contention that the data we have discussed do not provide much of an argument in favour of the TTSA. For there are serious empirical problems with both cases, and even if we ignore these problems, the data certainly don't establish the 'extensive parallelism' that the TTSA predicts. Moreover, as we

will see in the next section, there are results not discussed by Gopnik and
Meltzoff which, we think, strongly suggest that the parallelism on which their
argument depends simply does not exist.

Evidence against the self-other parallelism

In this section we will review a range of data indicating that often there is *not*
a parallel between performance on self and other versions of mindreading
tasks. We are inclined to think that these data completely uproot Gopnik and
Meltzoff's parallelism argument, and constitute a major challenge to the
theory theory of self-awareness.

Knowledge vs. *ignorance*   In knowledge versus ignorance experiments,
Wimmer and colleagues found a significant difference between performance
on closely matched tasks for self and other (Wimmer et al. 1988). After let-
ting children in two conditions either look in a box or not look in a box, the
researchers asked them, 'Do you know what is in the box or do you not know
that?' The 3-year-olds performed quite well on this task. For the other-person
version of the task, they observed another who either looked or didn't look
into a box. They were then asked: 'Does [name of child] know what is in the
box or does she [he] not know that?' (1988: 383). Despite the almost verbatim similarity between this question and the self-version, the children did significantly worse on the other-version of this question (see also Nichols 1993).
Hence, we have one case in which there is a significant *difference* between
performance on a mindreading task for self and performance on the task for
other. And there's more to come.

Pretence and imagination   Gopnik and Meltzoff maintain that children
under age 3 understand pretence for others and for self. Although there are
tasks on which young children exhibit some understanding of pretence (e.g.
Wellman and Estes 1986), the issue has turned out to be considerably more
complicated. It is clear from the literature on pretend play that from a young
age, children are capable of reporting their own pretences. Indeed, Gopnik
and Slaughter (1991) show that 3-year-old children can easily answer questions about their past pretences and imaginings. Despite this facility with their
own pretences, it doesn't seem that young children have an adequate 'theory'
of pretence. For instance, Lillard's (1993) results suggest that children as old
as 4 years think that someone can pretend to be a rabbit without knowing anything about rabbits. More importantly for present purposes, although young
children have no trouble detecting and reporting their own pretences (e.g.
Leslie 1994*a*), children seem to be significantly worse at recognizing pretence in others (Flavell et al. 1987; Rosen et al. 1997). Indeed, recent results

from Rosen et al. (1997) indicate that young children have a great deal of difficulty characterizing the pretences of others. Rosen and his colleagues had subjects watch a well-known television show in which the characters were sitting on a bench but pretending to be on an airplane. The researchers asked the children: 'Now we're going to talk about what everyone on *Barney* is thinking about. Are they thinking about being on an airplane or about sitting on a bench outside their school?' (1997: 1135). They found that 90 per cent of the 3-year-olds answered incorrectly that everyone was thinking about sitting on a bench. By contrast, in Gopnik and Slaughter's experiments, 3-year-old children did quite well on questions about what they themselves were pretending or imagining. In one of their pretence tasks, the child was asked to pretend that an empty glass had orange juice in it; the glass was turned over, and the child was subsequently asked to pretend that it had hot chocolate in it. The child was then asked, 'When I first asked you.... What did you pretend was in the glass then?' (Gopnik and Slaughter 1991: 106). Children performed near ceiling on this task. In Gopnik and Slaughter's imagination task, the children were told to close their eyes and think of a blue doggie, then they were told to close their eyes and think of a red balloon. The children were then asked, 'When I first asked you...., what did you think of then? Did you think of a blue doggie or did you think of a red balloon?' (Gopnik and Slaughter 1991: 106). Over 80 per cent of the 3-year-olds answered this correctly. Although the Gopnik and Slaughter pretence and imagination tasks aren't exact matches for the Rosen et al. task, the huge difference in the results suggests that children do much better on pretence and imagination tasks for self than they do on pretence and imagination tasks for another person. Hence, it seems likely that children can detect and report their own pretences and imaginings before they have the theoretical resources to detect and characterize pretences and imaginings in others.[14]

Perspective taking   As we noted earlier, children as young as $2\frac{1}{2}$ years are able to succeed at 'level 1' perspective-taking tasks both for others and for themselves. However, there is a cluster of more difficult perspective-taking tasks, 'level 2' tasks, in which young children do significantly better in the self-version than in the other-version. These tasks require the child to figure

---

[14] In Chapter 2, we argued against Leslie's view that the young child has a notion of PRETEND, and in this chapter we maintain that the young child has an early-emerging capacity to detect her own pretences. However, there is no inconsistency here. For Leslie's notion of PRETEND is explicitly the ToMI notion that one uses to ascribe pretence to *others*. Our claim in Chapter 2 is that, contra Leslie, there is no reason to think that the 18-month-old child has the ToMI *pretend* concept. Although there is no good reason to think that young children have the ToMI *pretend* concept, in this chapter our claim is that there is reason to think that 3-year-olds have a concept of *pretend* that is delivered by the monitoring mechanism. And there is no reason to think that even *this* concept is available to the 18-month-old.

out how an object looks from a perspective that is different from her own current perspective. In one task, for example, the child is shown a drawing of a turtle that looks to be lying on its back when viewed from one position and standing on its feet when viewed from another position. The child is asked whether the turtle is on its back or on its feet; then the child is asked how the person across the table sees the turtle: on its back or on its feet. Children typically don't succeed at these tasks until about the age of 4. However, contrary to the parallel performance hypothesis, Gopnik and Slaughter (1991) found that 3-year-olds did well on a self-version of the task. They had the child look at the drawing of the turtle and then had the child change seats with the experimenter. The child was subsequently asked, 'When I first asked you, before we traded seats, how did you see the turtle then, lying on his back or standing on his feet' (1991: 106). Gopnik and Slaughter were surprised at how well the 3-year-olds did on this task. They write, 'Perhaps the most surprising finding was that performance on the level 2 perception task turned out to be quite good, and was not significantly different from performance on the pretend task. Seventy-five percent of the 3-year-olds succeeded at this task, a much higher level of performance than the 33% to 50% reported by Masangkay et al. (1974) in the other person version of this task' (Gopnik and Slaughter 1991: 107). Here, then, is another example of a mindreading task in which the self-version of the task is significantly easier for subjects than the other-version of the task. So we have yet another case in which the TTSA's prediction of extensive parallelism is disconfirmed.[15]

4.4.3. What conclusions can we draw from the developmental data?

We now want to step back from the details of the data to assess their implications for the debate between the TTSA and our Monitoring Mechanism theory. To begin, let's recall what each theory predicts, and why. The TTSA maintains that ToMI is centrally involved in detecting and reasoning about both

---

[15] Gopnik and Meltzoff have also produced results that suggest a disparity between performance on self- and other-versions of a very simple perspective-taking task. They found that when 24-month-olds were asked to hide an object from the experimenter, they 'consistently hid the object egocentrically, either placing it on the experimenter's side of the screen or holding it to themselves so that neither they nor the experimenter could see it' (reported in Gopnik and Meltzoff 1997: 116). Given that Gopnik and Meltzoff characterize the child's performance as 'egocentric', it seems quite likely that the children would succeed at versions of this task that asked the child to hide the object from herself. Hence, one expects that children would perform significantly better on a self-version of the task than on the other-version of the task. If in fact the 2-year-old child can't solve the hiding task for another person, but can solve it for self, then this looks like another case that counts against the extensive parallelism predicted by the TTSA.

one's own mental states and other people's. But the TTSA makes no claims about when in the course of development various components of ToMI are acquired or come on-line. Thus TTSA makes no predictions about when specific mindreading skills will emerge, but it does predict that any given mindreading skill will appear at about the same time in self and other cases. MM, by contrast, maintains that ToMI is involved in detecting and reasoning about other people's mental states and in reasoning about one's own mental states, but that a separate Monitoring Mechanism (or a cluster of such mechanisms) is typically involved when we detect our own mental states. MM also claims that the Monitoring Mechanism(s) come on-line quite early in development. Thus MM predicts that children will be able to detect (but not necessarily reason about) their own mental states quite early in development. But it does not predict any particular pattern of correlation between the emergence of the capacity to detect one's own mental states and the emergence of the capacity to detect other people's mental states.

Which theory does better at handling the data we have reviewed? As we see it, the answer is clear: MM is compatible with all the data we have reviewed, while some of the data are seriously problematic for the TTSA. To make the point as clearly as possible, let's assemble a list of the various mindreading phenomena we have reviewed:

1. *Level 1 perspective taking*. This emerges early for both self and other. TTSA predicts the parallel emergence and is compatible with, but does not predict, the early emergence. MM predicts the early emergence in the self case and is compatible with but does not predict the early emergence in the other case. Neither theory has an advantage over the other.

2. *Pretence and imagination*. It is clear that self-detection emerges early, as MM predicts. However, there is some recent evidence indicating that detection and understanding of pretence in others does not emerge until much later. If this is right, it is a problem for TTSA, though not for MM.

3. *Sources of belief*. The ability to identify sources of belief emerges at about the age of 4 in both the self and the other case. Since this is a reasoning problem not a detection problem, both theories make the same prediction.

4. *False belief*. Recent evidence indicates that if memory enhancements are provided, young children do better on the self-version of false belief tasks than on the other-version. This is compatible with MM but quite problematic for TTSA.

5. *Desire*. The evidence available does not use well-matched tasks, so no conclusions can be drawn about either TTSA or MM.

6. *Knowledge* vs. *ignorance*. Three-year-olds do much better on the self-version than on the other-version. This is compatible with MM but problematic for TTSA.

7. *Level 2 perspective taking.* Here again, 3-year-olds do better on the self-version than on the other-version, which is a problem for TTSA but not for MM.

Obviously, the extensive parallelism between self and other cases on which Gopnik and Meltzoff rest their case for the theory theory of self-awareness is not supported by the data. Conceivably a resourceful advocate of TTSA could offer plausible explanations for each of the cases in which the parallel predicted by TTSA breaks down. But in the absence of a systematic attempt to provide such explanations we think it is clear that the developmental evidence favours our theory of self-awareness over the TTSA.

4.5. The Evidence from Autism: The Theory Theory of Self-Awareness *vs.* The Monitoring Mechanism Theory

In addition to the developmental arguments, several authors have appealed to evidence on autism as support for a theory theory account of self-awareness (Baron-Cohen 1989; Carruthers 1996; Frith and Happé 1999). On our view, however, the evidence from autism provides no support at all for TTSA. Before we consider these arguments, we need to provide a bit of background to explain why data from autism are relevant to the issue of self-awareness. Studies of people with autism have loomed large in the literature in mind-reading ever since Baron-Cohen, Leslie, and Frith (1985) reported some now famous results on the performance of autistic individuals on the false belief task. As we noted in Section 3.2.2, Baron-Cohen and colleagues compared performance on false belief tasks in normal children, autistic children, and children with Down's syndrome. They found that autistic subjects with a mean chronological age of about 12 and mean verbal and non-verbal mental ages of 9 years, 3 months, and 5 years, 5 months respectively failed the false belief task (Baron-Cohen et al. 1985). These subjects answered the way normal 3-year-olds do. By contrast, the control group of Down's syndrome subjects matched for mental age performed quite well on the false belief task. One interpretation of these results is that autistic individuals lack a properly functioning ToMI mechanism. Although in Chapter 3 we argued that this does not provide an adequate explanation of the mindreading deficits in autism, in this section we propose to assume, for argument's sake, that the interpretation is correct. Our strategy will be to argue that *even if it is granted that people with autism have an impaired ToMI mechanism*, the arguments to be considered in favour of TTSA *still* are not plausible.

Now, if we assume that individuals with autism have an impaired ToMI, then, since the theory theory account of self-awareness claims that ToMI is implicated in the formation of beliefs about one's own mental states, the TTSA predicts that autistic individuals should have deficits in this domain as well. If people with autism lack a properly functioning ToMI mechanism and that mechanism is required for self-awareness, then autistic individuals should be unable to form beliefs about their own beliefs and other mental states. In recent papers both Carruthers (1996) and Frith and Happé (1999) have maintained that autistic individuals do indeed lack self-awareness, and that this supports the TTSA account. In this section we will consider three different arguments from the data on autism. One argument depends on evidence that autistic children have difficulty with the appearance/reality distinction. A second argument appeals to introspective reports of adults with Asperger's syndrome (autistic individuals with near normal IQs), and a third, related, argument draws on autobiographical testimony of people with autism and Asperger's syndrome.

4.5.1. Autism and the appearance/reality distinction

Both Baron-Cohen (1989) and Carruthers (1996) maintain that the performance of autistic children on appearance/reality tasks provides support for the view that autistic children lack self-awareness, and hence provides evidence for the TTSA. The relevant studies were carried out by Baron-Cohen (1989), based on the appearance/reality tasks devised by Flavell and his colleagues. Using those tasks, Flavell and his colleagues found that children have difficulty with the appearance/reality distinction until about the age of 4 (Flavell et al. 1986). For instance, after playing with a sponge that visually resembles a piece of granite (a 'Hollywood rock'), most 3-year-olds claim that the object both is a sponge and looks like a sponge. Baron-Cohen found that autistic subjects also have difficulty with the appearance/reality distinction. When they were allowed to examine a piece of fake chocolate made out of plastic, for example, they thought that the object both looked like chocolate and really was chocolate. 'In those tasks that included plastic food,' Baron-Cohen reports, 'the autistic children alone persisted in trying to eat the object long after discovering its plastic quality. Indeed, so clear was this perseverative behavior that the experimenter could only terminate it by taking the plastic object out of their mouths' (Baron-Cohen 1989: 594).

Though we find Baron-Cohen and Flavell et al.'s work on the appearance/ reality distinction intriguing, we are deeply puzzled by the suggestion that the studies done with autistic subjects provide support for the theory theory account of self-awareness. And, unfortunately, those who think that these studies do support the TTSA have never offered a detailed statement of how the argument is supposed to go. At best they have provided brief hints like the following:

[T]he mind-blindness theory would predict that autistic people will lack adequate access to their own experiences as such . . . , and hence that they should have difficulty in negotiating the contrast between *experience* (appearance) and *what it is an experience of* (reality). (Carruthers 1996: 260–1)

[Three-year-old children] appear unable to represent both an object's real and apparent identities simultaneously. . . . Gopnik and Astington (1988) argued that this is also an indication of the 3-year-old's inability to represent the distinction between their representation of the object (its appearance) and their knowledge about it (its real identity). In this sense, the A-R distinction is a test of the ability to attribute mental states to oneself. (Baron-Cohen 1989: 591)

The prediction that this would be an area of difficulty for autistic subjects was supported, and this suggests that these children . . . are unaware of the A-R distinction, and by implication unaware of their own mental states. These results suggest that when perceptual information contradicts one's own knowledge about the world, the autistic child is unable to separate these, and the perceptual information overrides other representations of an object (Baron-Cohen 1989: 595)

How might these hints be unpacked? What we have labelled *the A/R Argument* is our best shot at making explicit what Carruthers and Baron-Cohen might have had in mind. Though we are not confident that this is the right interpretation of their suggestion, it is the most charitable reading we have been able to construct. If this *isn't* what they had in mind (or close to it) then we really haven't a clue about how the argument is supposed to work.

A/R Argument

If the theory theory of self-awareness is correct then ToMI plays a crucial role in forming beliefs about one's own mental states. Thus, since autistic subjects do not have a properly functioning ToMI mechanism they should have considerable difficulty in forming beliefs about their own mental states. So autistic people will typically not be able to form beliefs with contents like:

    (1) I believe that that object is a sponge.

and

    (2) I am having a visual experience of something that looks like a rock.

Perhaps (2) is too sophisticated, however. Perhaps the relevant belief that they cannot form but that normal adults can form is something more like:

    (2a) That object looks like a rock.

By contrast, since ToMI is *not* involved in forming beliefs about the non-mental part of the world, autistic subjects should not have great difficulty in forming beliefs like:

    (3) That object is a sponge.

To get the correct answer in an appearance/reality task, subjects must have beliefs with contents like (3) and they must also have beliefs with contents like (2) or (2*a*). But if the TTSA is correct then autistic subjects cannot form beliefs with contents like (2) or (2*a*). Thus the TTSA predicts that autistic subjects will fail appearance/reality tasks. And since they do in fact fail, this counts as evidence in favour of the TTSA.

Now what we find puzzling about the A/R Argument is that, while the data do indeed indicate that autistic subjects fail the appearance/reality task, they fail it in exactly the *wrong way*. According to the A/R Argument, autistic subjects should have trouble forming beliefs like (2) and (2*a*) but should have no trouble in forming beliefs like (3). In Baron-Cohen's studies, however, just the opposite appears to be the case. After being allowed to touch and taste objects made of plastic that looked like chocolate or eggs, the autistic children gave no indication that they had incorrect beliefs about what the object *looked like*. Quite the opposite was the case. When asked questions about their own perceptual states, autistic children answered *correctly*. They reported that the fake chocolate looked like chocolate and that the fake egg looked like an egg. Where the autistic children apparently did have problems was just where the A/R Argument says they should *not* have problems. The fact that they persisted in trying to eat the plastic chocolate suggests that they had not succeeded in forming beliefs like (3)—beliefs about *what the object really is*. There are lots of hypotheses that might be explored to explain why autistic children have this problem. Perhaps autistic children have difficulty updating their beliefs on the basis of new information; perhaps they perseverate on first impressions;[16] perhaps they privilege visual information over the information provided by touch and taste; perhaps the task demands are too heavy. But whatever the explanation turns out to be, it is hard to see how the sorts of failures predicted by the TTSA—the inability to form representations like (1), (2), and (2*a*)—could have any role to play in explaining the pattern of behaviour that Baron-Cohen reports.

All this may be a bit clearer if we contrast the performance of autistic children on appearance/reality tasks with the performance of normal 3-year-olds. The 3-year-olds also fail the task. But unlike the autistic children who make what Baron-Cohen calls 'phenomenist' errors (Baron-Cohen 1989: 594), normal 3-year-olds make what might be called 'realist' errors on the same sorts of tasks. Once they discover that the Hollywood rock really is a sponge, they report that it *looks like* a sponge. Since there is reason to believe that ToMI is not yet fully on-line in 3-year-olds, one might think that the fact that 3-year-olds make 'realist' errors in appearance/reality tasks supports a

---

[16] It is worth noting that perseveration is quite common in autistic children in other domains as well.

theory theory account of self-awareness. Indeed, Alison Gopnik appears to defend just such a view. The appearance/reality task, she argues,

is another case in which children make errors about their current mental states as a result of their lack of a representational theory [i.e. a mature ToMI]... Although it is not usually phrased with reference to the child's current mental states, this question depends on the child's accurately reporting an aspect of his current state, namely, the way the object looks to him. Children report that the sponge-rock looks to them like a sponge. To us, the fact that the sponge looks like a rock is a part of our immediate phenomenology, not something we infer.... The inability to understand the idea of false representations... seems to keep the child from accurately reporting perceptual appearances, even though those appearances are current mental states. (Gopnik 1993: 93)

For our current purposes, the crucial point here is that Gopnik's argument, unlike the A/R Argument, is perfectly sensible. Three-year-olds are not at all inclined to make 'phenomenist' errors on these tasks. Once they have examined the plastic chocolate, they no longer believe that it really is chocolate, and they have no inclination to eat it. Where the 3-year-olds go wrong is in reporting what plastic chocolate and Hollywood rocks look like. And this is just what we should expect if, as the TTSA insists, ToMI is involved in forming beliefs about one's own perceptual states.

At this point, the reader may be thinking that we have jumped out of the frying pan and into the fire. In using Gopnik's argument to highlight the shortcomings of the A/R Argument, have we not also provided a new argument for TTSA, albeit one that does not rely on data about autistic subjects? Our answer here is that Gopnik's argument is certainly one that must be taken seriously. But her explanation is not the only one that might be offered to account for the way in which 3-year-olds behave in appearance/reality tasks. The hypothesis we favour is that though the Percept-Monitoring Mechanisms that we posited in Section 4.3.2 are in place in 3-year-olds, 3-year-olds fail the task because of heavy information-processing demands in the standard appearance/reality task. As it happens, there are the beginnings of such a theory in the literature, and some nice evidence supporting it (Rice et al. 1997). In the standard appearance/reality task, the successful subject must keep in mind several things at once. She must have in mind the reality of the object—it's a sponge; she must also have in mind the typical appearance of sponges; further, she must have in mind the typical appearance of rocks. This constitutes a serious informational load, and perhaps the informational demands lead younger children to fail. If so, then easing the informational load should improve the young child's performance. In fact, this is exactly what Rice and colleagues found. They first presented subjects with a standard appearance/reality task. Subjects were then shown an ordinary rock and asked to identify the object. After identifying the object, the subject was told to pick it up and feel it. The rock was placed on the table and the subjects were asked

'So, what is this really and truly?' The same procedure was then done with an ordinary sponge and finally with the sponge-rock. At the end, all three objects were on the table, with the sponge-rock in the middle. The experimenter then pointed to the sponge-rock and asked, 'Now, for real, is this really and truly a rock or is this really and truly a sponge?' and 'Now, when you look at this with your eyes right now, does it look like a sponge or does it look like a rock?' The results of this experiment were impressive: 74 per cent of the 3-year-olds passed the task. This seems to support the information-processing explanation for why young children fail the appearance/reality task. For in the Rice et al. experiment, the child does not need to keep in mind the typical appearance of rocks and the typical appearance of sponges. She can simply consult the rock and the sponge that are flanking the sponge-rock. More importantly for our purposes, the experiment indicates that children do indeed have access to their percepts and can form beliefs about them. For if they lacked such access, presumably the information-processing aids would not help them to perform well on the task.

Let us briefly sum up this section. Our major conclusion is that, while the data about the performance of autistic subjects on appearance/reality tasks are fascinating, they provide no evidence at all for the TTSA. Moreover, while some of the data about the performance of normal 3-year-olds on appearance/reality tasks is compatible with the TTSA, more recent data suggest that the difficulty that young children have with some of these tasks can be traced to heavy information-processing requirements they impose. So none of the findings reviewed in this section suggests that TTSA is preferable to our MM theory.

4.5.2. Introspective reports and autobiographies from adults with Asperger's syndrome

The next two arguments we will consider are much more direct arguments for the TTSA, but, we maintain, no more convincing. Carruthers (1996) and Frith and Happé (1999) both cite evidence from a recent study on introspective reports in adults with Asperger's syndrome (Hurlburt et al. 1994). People with Asperger's syndrome have normal intelligence levels, but they have a cluster of social deficits that has led researchers to regard Asperger's syndrome as a type of autism (e.g. Frith 1991). The study on introspective reports is based on a technique for 'experience sampling' developed by Russell Hurlburt. Subjects carry around a beeper and are told, 'Your task when you hear a beep is to attempt to "freeze" your current experience "in mind," and then to write a description of that experience in a...notebook which you will be carrying. The experience that you are to describe is the one that was occurring at the instant the beep began...' (Hurlburt 1990: 21).

Hurlburt and his colleagues had three adults with Asperger's syndrome carry out this experience sampling procedure (Hurlburt et al. 1994). All three of the subjects were able to succeed at simple mindreading. The researchers found that the reports of these subjects were considerably different from reports of normal subjects. According to Hurlburt and colleagues, two of the subjects reported only visual images, whereas it is common for normal subjects also to report inner verbalization, 'unsymbolized thinking',[17] and emotional feelings. The third subject didn't report any inner experience at all in response to the beeps.

Carruthers maintains that these data suggest 'that autistic people might have severe difficulties of access to their own occurrent thought processes and emotions' (1996: 261). Frith and Happé also argue that the evidence 'strengthens our hypothesis that self-awareness, like other awareness, is dependent on ToM' (Frith and Happé 1999: 14).

As further support for the theory theory account of self-awareness, Frith and Happé appeal to several autobiographical essays written by adults with autism or Asperger's syndrome (1999). They argue that these autobiographies indicate that their authors have significant peculiarities in self-consciousness. Here are several examples of autobiographical excerpts quoted by Frith and Happé:

'When I was very young I can remember that speech seemed to be of no more significance than any other sound. ... I began to understand a few single words by their appearance on paper...' (Jolliffe et al. 1992: 13, quoted in Frith and Happé 1999: 15)

'I had—and always had had, as long as I could remember—a great fear of jewellery ... I thought they were frightening, detestable, revolting.' (Gerland 1997: 54, quoted in Frith and Happé 1999: 16)

'It confused me totally when someone said that he or she had seen something I had been doing in a different room.' (Gerland 1997: 64, quoted in Frith and Happé 1999: 17)

4.5.3. What conclusions can we draw from the data on introspection in autism?

We are inclined to think that the data cited by Carruthers (1996) and Frith and Happé (1999) provide a novel and valuable perspective on the inner life of

---

[17] Hurlburt and colleagues describe 'unsymbolized thoughts' as 'clearly-apprehended, differentiated thoughts that occurred with no experience of words, images, or others symbols that might carry the meaning. Subjects sometimes referred to the phenomenon as "pure thought". In such samples the subjects could, in their sampling interviews, say clearly what they had been thinking about at the moment of the beep, and thus could put the thought into words, but insisted that neither those words nor any other words or symbols were available to awareness at the moment of the beep, even though the thought itself was easily apprehended at that moment.' (Hurlburt et al. 1994: 386)

people with autism. However, we do not think that the evidence lends any support at all to the TTSA over the MM theory that we advocate. Quite to the contrary, we are inclined to think that if the evidence favours either theory, it favours ours.

What the data do strongly suggest is that the inner lives of autistic individuals differ radically from the inner lives of most of us. Images abound, inner speech is much less salient, and autistic individuals almost certainly devote much less time to thinking or wondering or worrying about *other people's* inner lives. As we read the evidence, however, it indicates that people with autism and Asperger's syndrome *do* have access to their own inner lives. They are aware of, report, and remember their own beliefs and desires as well as their occurrent thoughts and emotions.

Hurlburt, Happé, and Frith (1994) revisited

In the experience sampling study, there were a number of instances in which subjects clearly did report their occurrent thoughts. For example, one of the subjects, Robert, reported that

he was 'thinking about' what he had to do today. This 'thinking about' involved a series of images of the tasks he had set for himself. At the moment of the beep, he was trying to figure out how to find his way to the Cognitive Development Unit, where he had his appointment with us. This 'trying to figure out' was an image of himself walking down the street near Euston station. (Hurlburt et al. 1994: 388)

On another occasion, Robert reported that he was

'trying to figure out' why a key that he had recently had made did not work. This figuring-out involved picturing an image of the key in the door lock, with his left hand holding and turning the key .... The lock itself was seen both from the outside ... and from the inside (he could see the levers inside the lock move as the blades of the key pushed them along). (Hurlburt et al. 1994: 388)

A second subject, Nelson, reported that

he was 'thinking about' an old woman he had seen earlier that day. This thinking-about involved 'picturizing' (Nelson's own term for viewing an image of something) the old woman.... There was also a feeling of 'sympathy' for this woman, who (when he actually saw her earlier) was having difficulty crossing the street. (Hurlburt et al. 1994: 390)

In all three of these cases it seems clear that the subjects are capable of reporting their current thinking and, in the latter case, their feelings. Though, as we suggested earlier, it may well be the case that the inner lives that these people are reporting are rather different from the inner lives of normal people.

Perhaps even more instructive is the fact that Hurlburt and his colleagues claim to have been surprised at how well the subjects did on the experience sampling task. Hurlburt et al. write: 'While we had expected a relative inability to think and talk about inner experience, this was true for only one of the subjects, Peter, who was also the least advanced in terms of understanding mental states in the theory of mind battery' (1994: 393). Moreover, even Peter, although he had difficulty with the experience sampling method, could talk about his current experience. Thus Frith and Happé (1999: 14) report that 'Although Peter was unable to tell us about his past inner experience using the beeper method, it was possible to discuss with him current ongoing inner experience during interviews.' So, far from showing that the theory theory account of self-awareness is correct, these data would seem to count *against* the TTSA. For even Peter, who is likely to have had the most seriously abnormal ToMI, was capable of reporting his inner experiences.

It is true that all of the subjects had some trouble with the experience sampling task, and that one of them could not do it at all. But we think that this should be expected in subjects whose ToMI is functioning poorly, *even if, as we maintain, the ToMI plays no role in self-awareness*.[18] Advocates of TTSA maintain that ToMI plays a central role in detecting mental states in other people and in reasoning about mental states—both their own and others'. And we are in agreement with both of these claims. It follows that people who have poorly functioning ToMI mechanisms will find it difficult to attribute many mental states to other people and will do little or no reasoning about mental states. So thoughts about mental states will not be very useful or salient to them. Given the limited role that thoughts about mental states play in the lives of people with defective ToMI mechanisms, it is hardly surprising that, when asked to describe their experience, they sometimes do not report much. An analogy may help to make the point. Suppose two people are asked to look at a forest scene and report what they notice. One of the two is an expert on the birds of the region and knows a great deal about their habits and distribution. The other knows comparatively little about birds and has little interest in them. Suppose further that there is something quite extraordinary in the forest scene; there is a bird there that is rarely seen in that sort of environment. We would expect that that bird would figure prominently in the expert's description, though it might not be mentioned at all in the novice's description. Now compared to autistic individuals, normal subjects are experts about mental states. They know a lot about them, they think a lot about them, and they care a lot about them. So it is to be expected that autistic subjects—who

---

[18] Though we have been assuming that autism involves a serious ToMI deficit, it is important to note that that assumption plays no substantive role in the argument set out in this paragraph. All we really need to claim is that individuals with autism have serious deficits in the ability to detect and reason about some mental states in other people.

have a comparatively impoverished grasp of mental states—will often fail to spontaneously mention their own mental states even if, like the person who knows little about birds, they *can* detect and report their own mental states if their attention is drawn to them by their interlocutor.

Autobiographies revisited

In the cases of autobiographical reflections, again, we maintain, a number of the examples cited by Frith and Happé are prima facie incompatible with the conclusion they are trying to establish. In the autobiographies, adults with autism or Asperger's syndrome repeatedly claim to recall their own childhood thoughts and other mental states. This is evident in the three quotes from Frith and Happé that we reproduced in Section 4.5.2, and in this respect, the passages from Frith and Happé are not at all unusual. Here are three additional examples of autobiographical comments from adults with Asperger's syndrome:

'I remember being able to understand everything that people said to me, but I could not speak back. . . . One day my mother wanted me to wear a hat when we were in the car. I logically thought to myself that the only way I could tell her that I did not want to wear the hat was to scream and throw it on the car floor.' (Grandin 1984: 145)

'When I was 5 years old I craved deep pressure and would daydream about mechanical devices which I could get into and be held by them. . . . As a child I wanted to feel the comfort of being held, but then I would shrink away for fear of losing control and being engulfed when people hugged me.' (Grandin 1984: 151)

'I didn't talk until I was almost five, you know. Before I started talking I noticed a lot of things, and now when I tell my mother she is amazed I remember them. I remember that the world was really scary and everything was over-stimulating.' (Reported in Dewey 1991: 204)

If these recollections are accurate, then these individuals must have been aware of their own mental states even though, at the time in question, they could not reliably attribute beliefs to other people.

4.6. Double Dissociations and the Monitoring Mechanism Theory

We have argued that the evidence from autism does not support the theory theory of self-awareness over our theory. Indeed, it seems that the evidence provides support for our theory over the TTSA. In this section, we want to strengthen the case for the Monitoring Mechanism theory by arguing that it provides a natural explanation of a pattern of evidence on autism and certain other psychopathologies.

One important difference between our MM theory and all versions of the TTSA is that on our theory there is a theoretically motivated way to divide mindreading tasks and the mechanisms underlying them into two distinct categories. One category includes the Monitoring Mechanisms which are responsible for the detection of one's own mental states. The other category includes a heterogeneous collection of mental mechanisms which subserve detection of other people's mental states, reasoning about other people's mental states, and reasoning about one's own mental states. Thus on our theory it is possible for one or more of the mechanisms in the first category to malfunction, causing a deficit in one or more aspects of first-person mental state detection, while the mechanisms in the second category continue to function normally. It is also possible for the opposite pattern of breakdowns to occur, leading to a deficit in one or more aspects of third-person mental state detection, or in reasoning about mental states, while first-person detection is intact. On the TTSA, by contrast, this sort of 'double dissociation' would be much harder to explain. The central idea of TTSA is that the process of reading one's own mind is largely or entirely parallel to the process of reading someone else's mind, and that ToMI plays a central role in both. Thus any pathology that disrupts first-person mindreading might be expected to disrupt third-person mindreading, and vice versa—particularly if that pathology damaged ToMI. So one way to support our theory over the TTSA would be to find the kind of double dissociation that our theory leads us to expect, but TTSA cannot easily account for.

Do double dissociations of this sort occur? We propose that they do. In autism, we maintain, third-person mindreading is seriously defective, though first-person mental state detection is not significantly impaired. By contrast, in patients exhibiting certain 'first-rank' symptoms of schizophrenia, first-person mental state detection is disrupted while third-person mindreading is not.

4.6.1. Autism: intact first-person detection and impaired third-person mindreading

Much of the case for autism as one-half of the needed double dissociation has already been made. In Chapter 3 we recounted a number of studies indicating that people with autism have considerable difficulty in attributing beliefs and thoughts to other people, though they are much better at attributing desires. And, as we argued in Section 4.5, none of the evidence cited by advocates of TTSA indicates that autism involves a deficit in the ability to detect one's own mental states. Indeed, some of the data suggested just the opposite. The adults with Asperger's syndrome who were asked to recount their immediate experiences did show an appreciation of what was happening in their minds (Hurlburt et al. 1994). Further, in the autobiographical excerpts, the adults claim to recall their own beliefs and thoughts from childhood. Also, there is no evidence that autistic children or adults have any trouble recognizing their thoughts and actions as their own. (The importance of this point will emerge below.)

There is some additional experimental evidence that further confirms our contention that the ability to detect one's own mental states is spared in autism. In a recent set of studies, Farrant and colleagues found that autistic children did remarkably well on 'metamemory' tests (Farrant et al. 1999). In metamemory tasks, subjects are asked to memorize a set of items and subsequently to report on the strategies they used to remember the items. In light of arguments from defenders of the TTSA, the experimenters expected autistic children to perform much worse than non-autistic children on metamemory tasks: 'On the basis of evidence that children with autism are delayed in passing false belief tasks and on the basis of arguments that mentalizing and metacognition involve related processes, we predicted that children with autism would show impaired performance relative to controls on false belief tasks and on metamemory tasks and that children's performances on the two types of task would be related' (Farrant et al. 1999: 108). However, contrary to the researchers' predictions, there was no significant difference between the performance of autistic children and non-autistic children on a range of metamemory tasks. In one task, the subject was asked to remember a set of numbers that were given. The children were subsequently asked, 'What did you do to help you to remember all the numbers that I said?' Like the other children in the study, most of the autistic children answered this question with some explanation that adverted to thinking, listening, or exploiting a strategy. For instance, one autistic child explained that to remember the string of numbers he was given, which included a 6 followed by an 8, 'I did 68, then the rest, instead of being six, eight, you put 68.' Indeed, Farrant et al. claim that it is clear from the data that 'there was no relation between passing/failing false belief tasks and the categories of response given to the metamemory question' (Farrant et al. 1999: 118, 119). Although the results flouted the experimenters' TTSA-based prediction, they fit perfectly with the Monitoring Mechanism theory. For the Monitoring Mechanism can be intact even when the mental mechanisms subserving third-person belief attribution are damaged. While it will of course be important to get further empirical confirmation, these findings and those cited earlier indicate that people afflicted with autism do indeed manifest one of the patterns of dissociation that our theory expects to find.

4.6.2. Passivity experiences in schizophrenia: impaired first-person detection and intact third-person mindreading

Are there cases in which we find the opposite pattern? That is, are there individuals whose ability to detect their own mental states is impaired, but whose third-person mindreading abilities are spared? Although the data are often fragmentary and difficult to interpret, we think there might actually be such cases. Schizophrenia has recently played an important role in the discussion of mindreading, and we think that certain kinds of schizophrenia might involve damage to the Monitoring Mechanism that does not affect other components of the mindreading system.

There is a cluster of symptoms in some cases of schizophrenia sometimes referred to as 'passivity experiences' or 'first rank symptoms' (Schneider 1959) 'in which a patient's own feelings, wishes or acts seem to be alien and under external control' (Frith 1992: 73–4). One first-rank symptom of schizophrenia is delusions of control, in which a patient has difficulty recognizing that certain actions are her own. For example, one patient reported:

'When I reach my hand for the comb it is my hand and arm which move, and my fingers pick up the pen, but I don't control them. . . . I sit there watching them move, and they are quite independent, what they do is nothing to do with me. . . . I am just a puppet that is manipulated by cosmic strings. When the strings are pulled my body moves and I cannot prevent it.' (Mellor 1970: 18)

Another first-rank symptom is 'thought withdrawal', the impression that one's thoughts are extracted from one's mind. One subject reported: 'I am thinking about my mother, and suddenly my thoughts are sucked out of my mind by a phrenological vacuum extractor, and there is nothing in my mind, it is empty' (Mellor 1970: 16–17).

At least some symptomatic schizophrenics have great difficulty in reporting their current thoughts. Russell Hurlburt had four schizophrenic patients participate in a study using Hurlburt's experience sampling method (see Section 4.5.2). Two of these subjects reported experiences and thoughts that were strange or 'goofed up'. One of the patients, who was symptomatic throughout the sampling period (and whose symptoms apparently included first-rank symptoms), seemed incapable of carrying out the task at all. Another patient was able to carry out the task until he became symptomatic, at which point he could no longer carry out the task. Hurlburt argues that these two subjects, while they were symptomatic, did not have access to their inner experience (Hurlburt 1990: 239). Hurlburt writes:

What we had expected to find, with Joe, was that his inner experiences were unusual—perhaps with images that were 'goofed up' as Jennifer had described, or several voices that spoke at once so that none was intelligible, or some other kind of aberrant inner experience that would explain his pressure of speech and delusions. What we found, however, was no such thing; instead, Joe could not describe *any* aspects of his inner experience in ways that we found compelling. (Hurlburt 1990: 207–8)

What is especially striking here is the contrast between this claim and Hurlburt et al.'s finding about the adults with Asperger's syndrome discussed in Section 4.5. Hurlburt (1990) expected the symptomatic schizophrenics to be able to report their inner experiences, and Hurlburt et al. (1994) expected the adults with Asperger's syndrome to be unable to report their inner experiences. What they found, however, was just the opposite. *The symptomatic schizophrenics could not report their inner experiences, and the adults with Asperger's syndrome could.*

These findings on schizophrenia led Christopher Frith to suggest that in schizophrenics with first-rank symptoms, there is a deficit in 'central monitoring' (e.g. Frith 1992: 81–2).[19] Frith's initial account of central monitoring does not specify how the monitoring works, but in recent work, Frith suggests that the way to fill out his proposal on central monitoring is in terms of mechanisms underlying mindreading.

Many of the signs and symptoms of schizophrenia can be understood as arising from impairments in processes underlying 'theory of mind' such as the ability to represent beliefs and intentions. (Frith 1994: 148)

To have a 'theory of mind', we must be able to represent propositions like 'Chris believes that "It is raining"'. Leslie (1987) has proposed that a major requirement for such representations is a mechanism that decouples the content of the proposition (It is raining) from reality ... I propose that, in certain cases of schizophrenia, something goes wrong with this decoupling process.... Failure of this decoupling mechanism would give rise ... to ... the serious consequence ... that the patient would no longer be able to represent mental states, *either their own or those of others.* I have suggested previously (Frith 1987) that patients have passivity experiences (such as delusions of control and thought insertion) because of a defect in central monitoring. Central monitoring depends on our being aware of our intention to make a particular response before the response is made. In the absence of central monitoring, responses and intentions can only be assessed by peripheral feedback. For example, if we were unable to monitor our intentions with regard to speech, we would not know what we were going to say until after we had said it. I now propose that this failure of central

---

[19] Frith used a series of error correction experiments to test the hypothesis that passivity experiences result from a deficit in central monitoring. Frith and colleagues designed simple video games in which subjects had to use a joystick to follow a target around a computer screen. The games were designed so that subjects would make errors, and the researchers were interested in the subjects' ability to correct the errors without external (visual) feedback indicating the error. Normal people are able to rapidly correct these errors even when they don't get feedback. Frith takes this to indicate that normal people can monitor their intended response, so that they don't need to wait for the external feedback. Thus, he suggests, 'If certain patients cannot monitor their own intentions, then they should be unable to make these rapid error corrections' (Frith 1992: 83). Frith and others carried out studies of the performance of schizophrenics on these video game tasks. The researchers found that 'acute schizophrenic patients corrected their errors exactly like normal people when visual feedback was supplied but, unlike normal people often failed to correct errors when there was no feedback. Of particular interest was the observation that this disability was restricted to the patients with passivity experiences: delusions of control, thought insertion and thought blocking. These are precisely the symptoms that can most readily be explained in terms of a defect of self-monitoring' (Frith 1992: 83). Mlakar et al. (1994) found similar results. Thus, there seems to be some evidence supporting Frith's general claim that passivity experiences derive from a defect in central monitoring.

monitoring is the consequence of an inability to represent our own mental states, including our intentions. (Frith 1994: 154, emphasis added)

Hence Frith now views the problem of central monitoring in schizophrenia as a product of a deficit in part of the mindreading system that is also responsible for third-person mindreading (Frith 1994). Indeed, Frith characterizes schizophrenia as late-onset autism (1994: 150).

Although we are intrigued by Frith's initial suggestion that passivity experiences derive from a deficit in central monitoring, we are quite sceptical of his claim that the root problem is a deficit in a part of the mindreading system that is also implicated in third-person mindreading. We think that a better way to fill out Frith's hypothesis is in terms of the Monitoring Mechanism. That is, we suggest that certain first-rank symptoms or passivity experiences might result from a deficit in the Monitoring Mechanism that is quite independent of any deficit in the remainder of the mindreading system. And, indeed, Frith's subsequent empirical work on schizophrenia and mindreading indicates that schizophrenics with passivity experiences do *not* have any special difficulty with standard third-person mindreading tasks. Frith and Corcoran (1996) write, 'It is striking that the patients with passivity features (delusions of control, thought insertion, etc.) could answer the theory of mind questions quite well. This was also found by Corcoran et al. (1995) who used a different kind of task' (Frith and Corcoran 1996: 527). Of course, this is exactly what would be predicted by our theory since we maintain that the mechanism for detecting one's own intentions is independent from the mechanism responsible for detecting the mental states of others. Hence, there's no reason to think that a deficit in detecting one's own intentions would be correlated with a deficit in detecting mental states in others.

We maintain that, as with autism, our theory captures this range of data on schizophrenia comfortably. Contra Frith's proposal, schizophrenia does not seem to be a case, like autism, in which third-person mindreading is damaged; rather, it is more plausible to suppose that in schizophrenic individuals with passivity experiences, it is the Monitoring Mechanism that is not working properly. If this is right, then it is plausible that we have found the sort of double dissociation that our theory predicts. In autism, there is a deficit in third-person mindreading but not in first-person mental state detection. In schizophrenic subjects with first-rank symptoms, first-person mental state detection is severely impaired but third-person mindreading is not. This, we think, provides yet another reason to prefer the MM theory to the theory theory account of self-awareness.[20]

---

[20] The idea that a component of the mindreading system responsible for first-person detection can be selectively damaged while the component of the system responsible for analogous third-person detection remains intact might apply to detection of mental states other than

4.7. The Ascent Routine Theory

Although the TTSA is the most widely accepted account of self-awareness in the recent literature, there are two other accounts that are also quite visible, though neither seems to have gained many advocates. In this section and the next we will briefly consider each of these accounts.

Our MM account appeals to an innate cognitive mechanism (or a cluster of mechanisms) specialized for detecting one's own mental states. One might want to provide an account of self-awareness that is more austere. One familiar suggestion is that when we are asked a question about our own beliefs: 'Do you believe that *p*?' we treat the question as the simple fact-question: '*p*?' This kind of account was proposed by Evans (1982), but in recent years it has been defended most vigorously by Robert Gordon who labels the move from belief-question to fact-question an 'ascent routine'. 'Self-ascription', Gordon maintains, 'relies... on what I call *ascent routines*. For example, the way in which adults ordinarily determine whether or not they believe that p is simply to ask themselves the question whether or not p' (Gordon 1996: 15). Gordon goes on to propose that the account can be extended to other sorts of self-attributions, including even self-attributions of pain (Gordon 1995*b*, 1996).

This account has the virtue of emphasizing that, for both children and adults, questions like 'Do you think that *p*?' and 'Do you believe that *p*?' may not be interpreted as questions about one's mental state, but as questions about *p*. Similarly, statements like 'I believe that *p*' are often guarded assertions of *p*, rather than assertions about the speaker's mental state.[21] These are

propositional attitudes like beliefs and desires. For instance, alexithymia is a clinical condition in which subjects have great difficulty discerning their own emotional states. One researcher characterizes the condition as follows: 'When asked about feelings related to highly charged emotional events, such as the loss of a job or the death of a family member, patients with alexithymia usually respond in one of two ways: either they describe their physical symptoms or they seem not to understand the question' (Lesser 1985: 690). As a result, patients with this condition often need to be given instruction about how to interpret their own somatic sensations. 'For instance, they need to understand that when one is upset or scared, it is normal to feel abdominal discomfort or a rapid heart beat. These sensations can be labeled "anger" or "fear"' (1985: 691). Thus alexithymia might be a case in which subjects have selective damage to a system for monitoring one's own emotions. Of course, to make a persuasive case for this, one would need to explore (among other things) these subjects' ability to attribute emotions to other people. If it turns out that patients with alexithymia can effectively attribute emotions to others but not to themselves, that would indicate that alexithymia might indeed be caused by damage to a monitoring mechanism. We think that these kinds of questions and experiments only become salient when we keep careful track of the distinction between first-person mental state detection and the cluster of mindreading abilities which, according to us, are independent of the Monitoring Mechanism system. (We are grateful to Robert Woolfolk for suggesting this interpretation of alexithymia.)

[21] Claims like this are, of course, commonplace in the philosophical literature on the 'analysis' of belief. For example, Urmson maintains that 'believe' is a 'parenthetical verb' and that such verbs '*are not psychological descriptions*' (Urmson 1956: 194). Rather, 'when a man

facts that must be kept in mind in interpreting the results of experiments on mindreading and self-awareness.

Alongside these virtues, however, the ascent routine also has clear, and we think fatal, shortcomings. As Goldman (2000) points out, the ascent routine story doesn't work well for attitudes other than belief.

Suppose someone is asked the question, 'Do you hope that Team T won their game yesterday?' (Q_1). How is she supposed to answer that question using an ascent routine? Clearly she is not supposed to ask herself the question, 'Did Team T win their game yesterday?' (Q_2), which would only be relevant to belief, not hope. What question is she supposed to ask herself? (Goldman 2000: 183)

The ascent routine strategy doesn't work any better for lots of other important cases of self-attribution. In addition to questions like 'Do you believe that p?', we can answer questions about current mental states like 'What are you thinking about?' But in this case, it is hard to see how to rework the question into an ascent routine. Similarly, as we noted in Section 4.2.1, people can give accurate retrospective reports in response to questions like 'How did you figure that out?' We can see no way of transforming these questions into fact-questions of the sort that Gordon's theory requires. This also holds for questions about current desires, intentions, and imaginings, questions like: 'What do you want to do?'; 'What are you going to do?'; 'What are you imagining?' Our ability to answer these questions suggests that the ascent routine strategy simply cannot accommodate many central cases of self-awareness. There is no plausible way of recasting these questions so that they are questions about the world rather than about one's mental state. As a result, the ascent routine account strikes us as clearly inadequate as a general theory of self-awareness.

4.8. The Phenomenological Theory

For the last decade, Alvin Goldman has been advocating a 'phenomenological model for the attitudes' (Goldman 1993b: 23; see also Goldman 1997, 2000). According to Goldman, in order to detect one's own mental states, 'the cognitive system [must] use...information about the *intrinsic* (nonrelational) and *categorical* (nondispositional) properties of the target state' (1993a: 87). Goldman then goes on to ask 'which intrinsic and categorical properties might be detected in the case of mental states?' His answer is as follows: 'The best candidates, it would seem, are so-called *qualitative properties* of mental states—their

says, "I believe that he is at home" or "He is, I believe, at home", he both implies a (guarded) claim of the truth, and also implies a claim of the reasonableness of the statement that he is at home' (Urmson 1956: 202).

phenomenological or subjective *feelings* (often called "qualia")' (1993*a*: 87).[22] So, on this view, one detects one's own mental states by discerning the phenomenological properties of the mental states—the way those mental states feel.

Goldman is most confident of this phenomenological approach when the mental states being detected are not propositional attitudes but rather what he calls 'sensations'. 'Certainly,' he argues, 'it is highly plausible that one classifies such sensations as headaches or itches on the basis of their qualitative feel' (1993*a*: 87). Goldman suggests that this account might also be extended to propositional attitudes, though he is rather more tentative about this application.

Whether the qualitative or phenomenological approach to mental concepts could be extended from sensations to attitudes is an open question. Even this prospect, though, is not beyond the bounds of credibility. There is no reason why phenomenological characteristics should be restricted to sensory characteristics, and it does indeed seem to 'feel' a particular way to experience doubt, surprise, or disappointment, all of which are forms of propositional attitudes. (1993*a*: 88; see also 1993*b*: 25, 104)

We are inclined to think that the idea of extending the phenomenological approach from sensations to propositional attitudes is much less of an 'open question' than Goldman suggests. Indeed, as a general theory of the self-attribution of propositional attitudes, we think that it is quite hopeless.

4.8.1. Two versions of Goldman's proposal

To explain our scepticsm, let us begin by noting that there are two quite different ways in which Goldman's proposal might be elaborated:

1. *The Weaker Version* claims that we (or our cognitive systems) detect or classify the *type* of a given mental state by the qualitative or phenomenological properties of the mental state in question. It is the qualitative character of a state that tells us that it is a belief or a desire or a doubt. On the weaker version, however, the qualitative properties of propositional attitudes do not play a role in detecting the *content* of propositional attitudes.

2. *The Stronger Version* claims that we (or our cognitive systems) detect or classify *both* the *type* and *the content* of a given mental state by the qualitative or phenomenological properties of the mental state in question. So it is the qualitative character of a state that tells us that it is a belief or a desire

---

[22] Since Goldman regards these phenomenological properties as 'intrinsic', he rejects the higher-order account of consciousness advocated by Rosenthal (1992), Carruthers (2000), and others (see Goldman 2000: 179).

and it is also the qualitative character that tells us that it is the belief *that there is no greatest prime number* or the desire *that the Democrats win the next election.*

If one speaks, as we just did, of qualitative or phenomenological qualities 'telling us' that a state is a belief or that its content is *that there is no greatest prime number*, it is easy to ignore the fact that this is a metaphor. Qualitative states don't literally 'tell' anybody anything. What is really needed, to make a proposal like Goldman's work, is a mental mechanism (or a pair of mental mechanisms) which can be thought of as transducers: they are acted upon by the qualitative properties in question and produce, as output, *representations* of these qualitative properties (or, perhaps more accurately, representations of the kind of state that *has* the qualitative property). So, for example, on the Weaker Version of the theory, what is needed is a mechanism that goes from the qualitative property associated with belief or doubt to a representation that the state in question is a belief or doubt. On the Stronger Version, the transducer must do this for the content of the state as well. So, for instance, on the Stronger Version, the transducer must go from the qualitative property of the content *there is no greatest prime number* to a representation that the state in question has the content *there is no greatest prime number*. Figure 4.8 is an attempt to depict the mechanisms and processes required by Goldman's theory.

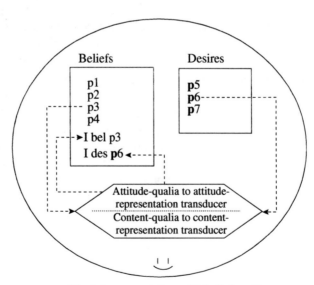

p Mental representation with belief-qualia
p Mental representation with desire-qualia

Fig. 4.8   Phenomenological model of self-awareness

4.8.2. Critique of Goldman's theory

As we see it, the Weaker Version of Goldman's proposal is not a serious competitor for our MM theory, since the Weaker Version does not really explain some of the crucial facts about self-awareness. At best, it explains how, if I know that I have a mental state with the content *p*, I can come to know that it is a belief and not a hope or desire. But the Weaker Version doesn't even try to explain how I know that I have a mental state with the content *p* in the first place. So as a full account of self-awareness of propositional attitudes, the Weaker Version is a non-starter.

The Stronger Version of Goldman's model *does* attempt to provide a full account of self-awareness of propositional attitudes. However, we think that there is no reason to believe the account, and there is good reason to doubt it. The Stronger Version of Goldman's theory requires a phenomenological account of the awareness of content as well as a phenomenological account of the awareness of attitude type. Goldman does not provide a detailed defence of the phenomenological account of content awareness, but he does sketch one argument in its favour. The argument draws on an example proposed by Keith Gunderson (1993). Goldman discusses the example as follows:

> If I overhear Brown say to Jones, 'I'm off to the bank,' I may wish to know whether he means a spot for fishing or a place to do financial transactions. But if *I* say to someone, 'I'm off to the bank,' I cannot query my own remark: 'To go fishing or to make a deposit?' I virtually always already know.... The target article mainly supported a distinctive phenomenology for the attitude types. Gunderson's example supports distinctive phenomenology for different *contents*. (Goldman 1993*b*: 104)

We think this argument is wholly unconvincing. It is true that we typically know the interpretation of our own ambiguous sentences. However, this doesn't even begin to show that belief contents have distinctive phenomenologies. At best it shows that we must have *some* mechanism or strategy for obtaining this knowledge. The MM theory can quite comfortably capture the fact that we typically know the interpretations of our own ambiguous sentences, and it does so without resorting to phenomenological features of content. As far as we can tell, then, there is no reason to adopt the phenomenological account of content. Moreover, there are two rather obvious reasons to prefer the MM account to the Stronger Version of the Phenomenological Theory.

On an account like Goldman's there must be mechanisms in the mind that are sensitive to phenomenological or qualitative properties—i.e. mechanisms that *are causally affected by* these qualitative properties in a highly sensitive and discriminating way. The qualia of a belief must lead the mechanism to produce a representation of belief. The qualitative properties of states with the content *Socrates is wise* must cause the mechanism to produce representations with the content *Socrates is wise*. Now we don't wish to claim that there are no mechanisms of this sort or that there couldn't be. But what is clear is that no one has a clue about how such mechanisms would work. No one has even the beginning of a serious idea about how a mechanism could be built that would be differentially sensitive to the (putative) qualitative properties of the contents of propositional attitude states. So, for the moment, at least, the mechanisms that Goldman needs are quite mysterious. The mechanism that *our* theory needs, by contrast, is simple and straightforward. To generate representations of one's own beliefs, all that the Monitoring Mechanism has to do is copy representations in the Belief Box, embed them in a representation schema of the form *I believe that* ___, and then place this new representation back in the Belief Box. The analogous sort of transformation for representations in a computer memory could be performed by a simple and utterly *un*mysterious mechanism.[23]

The preceding argument is simply that it would be trivial to implement a mechanism like the MM whereas no one has the faintest idea how to implement the mechanisms required for Goldman's account or how such mechanisms could work. Of course, this is hardly a knock-down argument against Goldman's account. If it were independently plausible that phenomenology is the basis for awareness of one's own propositional attitudes, then the mysteriousness of the transducers would simply pose a challenge for cognitive scientists to figure out how such a mechanism could work. However, far from being independently plausible, it seems to us that the phenomenological account is *phenomenologically implausible*—to say the least! To take the Stronger Version of Goldman's proposal seriously, one would have to assume that there is a distinct feel or qualia for every *type* of propositional attitude, *and* a distinct qualia for every *content* (or at least for every content we can detect). Now perhaps others have mental lives that are very different from ours. But from our perspective this seems to be (as Jerry Fodor might say) *crazy*. As best we can tell, believing that 17 is a prime number doesn't feel any different from believing that 19 is a prime number. Indeed, as best we can tell, neither of these states has any distinctive qualitative properties. Neither of them feels like much at all. If this is right, then the Strong Version of the Phenomenological Theory is every bit as much a non-starter as the Weak Version.

---

[23] It might be argued that the PMM that we posit in Section 4.3.2 is just as mysterious as the mechanism that Goldman's theory requires. However, nothing in our account of the PMM requires that it is sensitive to *qualitative* properties of percepts. But even if it turns out that the PMM is sensitive to qualitative properties, we are inclined to think that the objection that we are proposing in this paragraph still has some force, since Goldman's account invokes a rather mysterious mechanism for generating beliefs about one's own *beliefs* and *desires* when a very unmysterious one would do the job.

4.9. Conclusion

The empirical work on mindreading provides an invaluable resource for characterizing the cognitive mechanisms underlying our capacity for self-awareness. However, we think that other authors have drawn the wrong conclusions from the data. Contrary to the claims of those who advocate the TTSA, the evidence indicates that the capacity for self-awareness is not subserved by the same mental mechanisms that are responsible for third-person mindreading. It is much more plausible, we have argued, to suppose that self-awareness derives from a Monitoring Mechanism that is independent of the mechanisms that enable us to detect other people's mental states and to reason about mental states. Other authors have attempted to use the intriguing evidence from autism and young children to support the TTSA. But we have argued that the evidence from psychopathologies and from developmental studies actually suggests the opposite. The available evidence indicates that the capacity for understanding other minds can be dissociated from the capacity to detect one's own mental states and that the dissociation can go in either direction. If this is right, it poses a serious challenge to the TTSA, but it fits neatly with our suggestion that the Monitoring Mechanism is independent of third-person mindreading. Like our Monitoring Mechanism theory, the ascent routine and the phenomenological accounts are also alternatives to the TTSA; but these theories, we have argued, are either obviously implausible or patently insufficient to capture central cases of self-awareness. Hence, we think that at this juncture in cognitive science, the most plausible account of self-awareness is that the mind comes pre-packaged with a set of special-purpose mechanisms for reading one's own mind.

5

Objections, Replies, and Philosophical Implications

The account of mindreading that we have presented in the preceding chapters is ambitiously detailed, and this is no accident. Throughout the book it has been a recurrent theme that other theories of mindreading are often hard to evaluate since they tell us too little about the mental mechanisms they are positing and how these mechanisms are supposed to explain one or another aspect of mindreading. Thus providing a clear and richly detailed theory was one of our principal goals. Inevitably, some of those details will turn out to be mistaken. But, as we noted in the first chapter, we think the best way to make progress in the study of mindreading is to construct the sort of explicit and systematic theory that can be clearly seen to be mistaken, if it is, and with a bit of luck can be repaired, when confronted with new evidence and sharply focused criticism. Since we have presented much of this material at conferences and shared drafts of earlier chapters with many colleagues—including most of the people whose work we have criticized—it is no surprise that a number of objections have already been raised. In this chapter, we will begin by addressing what we think are four of the most important of these. We will then conclude the volume where our own interest in mindreading began, well over a decade ago, by asking what implications the theory we've offered has for philosophical debate over functionalism and eliminativism.

5.1. Objections and Replies

5.1.1. How do first-person and third-person mentalistic concepts get unified?

Objection

On the account of mindreading we have sketched, the mechanisms that subserve introspection are largely independent of the mechanisms that produce beliefs about the mental states of others. But it seems quite likely that in adult mindreading the same mental state concepts are used in both first- and third-person mental state attributions. Several critics have suggested that there is a problem lurking here. For if first-person and third-person mindreading are the result of quite different mechanisms, how does it come about that the outputs of these mechanisms are representations which invoke the same mental state concepts? How, for example, can we explain the fact that when the Monitoring Mechanism generates the belief that *I desire some vanilla ice cream*, and the Desire Detection Mechanisms generate the belief that *You desire some vanilla ice cream*, these beliefs invoke the very same concept of *desire*? We will call this *the problem of concept unity*.

Reply

Though the theory we have presented thus far does not address the problem of concept unity, there are, as we will see shortly, a number of different approaches to the problem that are perfectly consistent with our account. However, the task of assessing these options is complicated by the fact that there are no generally accepted answers to a pair of more fundamental questions: what, exactly, *are* concepts? And how are concepts *individuated*? And without answers to these questions—particularly the second—it is far from clear what the problem of concept unity *is*, or what would count as an acceptable solution. Actually, it is a bit misleading to say there is no agreement on how concepts are individuated, for there seems to be widespread agreement that *content* identity is at least a necessary condition for *concept* identity. Or, to put the point a bit more transparently, if two concept tokens are of the same type, then they have the same content. The shouting starts when we ask what it is that determines the content of a concept token, or what conditions have to obtain for two concept tokens to have the same content. Nor is this the only major point of disagreement. Some theorists suggest that content identity is also *sufficient* for concept type identity, and thus that concept tokens are type identical *if and only if* they have the same content. Others maintain that more is needed, since concepts with the same content can differ in their 'mode of presentation' or the way they are represented in the mind.

To see why these disagreements make it difficult to assess solutions to the problem of concept unity, let's begin by considering Jerry Fodor's widely discussed account of the factors that determine conceptual content. According to Fodor, concepts are *atomic*: they have no internal structure, or at least none that is relevant to their content. And if that's right then, of course, a concept's content cannot be determined by its internal structure (Fodor 1998). Moreover, Fodor also maintains that the conceptual role of a concept—the pattern of its causal interactions with other mental states and processes (including other concept tokens) is not what determines its content. Rather, on Fodor's account, a concept's content is determined by the pattern of causal connections between the concept and the properties that cause it to be invoked or 'tokened'. A bit more accurately, two concept tokens have the same content if and only if they both stand in the appropriate (and rather complex!) nomological relation to the same property. Now notice that if Fodor's theory, or something like it, is correct, and if content identity is both necessary and sufficient for concept identity, then it is far from clear that there *is* any serious problem of concept unity, since the answer to the question:

> How can we explain the fact that when the Monitoring Mechanism generates the belief that *I desire some vanilla ice cream*, and the Desire Detection Mechanisms generate the belief that *You desire some vanilla ice cream*, these beliefs invoke the very same concept of *desire*?

might be as simple as:

> They are both caused by (or stand in the appropriate nomological relation to) *desires* (i.e. mental states that have the property of being a desire).

Though, of course, the belief that *I desire some vanilla ice cream* is typically caused by one of *my* desires, while the belief that *You desire some vanilla ice cream* is typically caused by one of *your* desires. So if something like Fodor's theory gives the right account of conceptual content, and if content identity is both necessary and sufficient for concept identity, then the fact that two *desire* concept tokens are produced by two quite different mechanisms, like those proposed in our theory, provides no reason to think that the tokens differ in concept *type*.

There are other accounts of conceptual content on which the problem of content unity cannot be dismissed so easily, however. Many philosophers and psychologists have suggested that the content of a concept is a function of its conceptual role—or perhaps some part of its conceptual role, for example, the pattern of inferential interactions that the concept would exhibit with other concepts (Block 1986; Murphy and Medin 1985). According to these theorists, concept tokens have the same content if they have the same (or approximately the same) inferential or conceptual roles. It is plausible to suppose that the token of the *desire* concept produced by the first-person mindreading system when it leads me to believe that *I desire some vanilla ice cream*, and the token produced by the third-person system when it leads me to believe that *You desire some vanilla ice cream* have the same inferential role, near enough. But if that's right, then some explanation seems to be called for. Why do these two distinct mindreading systems generate representation tokens exhibiting the same pattern of inferences? Even those who are attracted to Fodor's theory of conceptual content might see a puzzle here if they allow that concept tokens with the same content might nonetheless have different modes of presentation. For, in theories which allow that content-identical concepts can have different modes of presentation, it is natural to suppose that the mode of presentation of a concept token plays a major role in determining its conceptual role. So how does it happen that the *desire* tokens generated by the first-person mechanism and those generated by the third-person mechanism have the same conceptual roles?

We think that there are a number of possible answers to this question, all of which are compatible with the account of mindreading we have offered. We will present brief sketches of three of these, though we will not endorse any of them, since we know of no data that favours one over the others. Rather, our theme will be that there are many ways in which the problem of concept identity *might* be resolved, and that none of them poses any significant problem for our theory.

The first option is what might be called the 'pre-established harmony' hypothesis, according to which it is an *innate* feature of the first-person and third-person mindreading mechanisms that they produce mental state concept tokens with the same content and the same conceptual role or mode of presentation. It is, after all, a matter of some importance that we understand that other people have the same sorts of mental states that we do, and thus it is not at all far-fetched to speculate that natural selection might have favoured genes that led to this sort of conceptual pre-established harmony. The possibility that natural selection can bring it about that distinct mental systems generate concepts of the same type is, we think, supported by some ingenious findings on one-month-old infants reported by Meltzoff and Borton (1979). In their study, Meltzoff and Borton used two pacifiers (baby's dummies) mounted with distinct shapes: attached to one pacifier was a smooth sphere, and attached to the other was a sphere with pronounced bumps on it. For half of the infants in the study, the smooth sphere was put in their mouths; for the other half, the bumpy sphere was put in their mouths. The infants had no visual access to the pacifiers during this procedure. (The experimenter used his hand to hide the pacifier as it was put in and retrieved from the infant's mouth.) All infants were then shown both the smooth sphere and the bumpy sphere pacifiers. Meltzoff and Borton predicted that if infants could relate the shape they *felt* to one of the shapes they *saw*, they would look longer at that shape. The prediction was borne out. Infants did tend to look longer at the shape they had just felt. Evidently, Mother Nature thought it important to have these two modalities pre-mapped. Though there are various ways in which the Meltzoff and Borton findings might be interpreted, we think it is plausible to view them as indicating that the tactile system and the visual system are innately constructed so that, given the appropriate input, they will both generate concept tokens (like *bumpy* or *smooth*) which are of the same type.

A second possible solution to the concept unity problem is that, though the first- and third-person systems initially generate mentalistic concepts with different conceptual roles or modes of representation, normal people all ultimately *learn* that desires detected by the first-person system and desires detected by the third-person system are states of the same type, and similarly for other sorts of mental states. A bit fancifully, we might imagine that the first-person system initially produces *desire* concept tokens whose mode of presentation is $desire_{1p}$ and that the third-person system initially produces tokens whose mode of presentation is $desire_{3p}$, but that at some point in development the child learns that all $desires_{1p}$ are $desires_{3p}$ and conversely. Once this belief is well entrenched, tokens of $desire_{1p}$ and tokens of $desire_{3p}$ will have all but identical conceptual roles. How this learning takes place is a further issue that might be resolved in a variety of ways. One obvious route to explore would be a suitably psychologized version of the venerable argument from analogy. The learning option is also broadly compatible with the hypothesis, defended by Goldman (1993*b*, 2000) and others, which maintains that we acquire a great deal of information about mental states via introspection. It is certainly *possible* that children learn a fair amount about $desires_{1p}$ by noting how desires feel and how they interact with other mental states and with behaviour *in their own case*. When they come upon evidence suggesting that $desires_{3p}$ are the same type of mental state as $desires_{1p}$, they will then readily infer that $desires_{3p}$ have the same qualitative properties and patterns of interaction as $desires_{1p}$.[1]

A third approach to the concept unity problem rejects both pre-established harmony and the suggestion that people simply learn that $desires_{1p}$ and $desires_{3p}$ are the same. Rather it proposes that concept unity is achieved via *conceptual change*. The central idea of a conceptual change account is that first-person mindreading mechanisms and third-person mindreading mechanisms initially produce type distinct mental state concepts, but then, at some point in ontogeny, the child develops a *new* concept that encompasses both first-person and third-person mental states, and that both first-person and third-person systems start generating representations involving this new concept. Again, there are precedents for this kind of model in recent cognitive science. Research on the mathematical concepts of infants and children indicates that there are two quite different systems that produce mathematical concepts, a system for approximating large numerosities, and a system for detecting small exact numerosities (see e.g. Carey and Spelke forthcoming). On some accounts, these two systems form the basis from which the child develops the

---

[1] The introspection hypothesis is also comfortably compatible with a pre-established harmony solution to the concept unity problem. For even if the first-person and third-person mind-reading systems are innately structured to generate mental state concept tokens of the same type, it is entirely possible that children learn much about desires and other mental states by attending to how these states interact in their own case. They might also acquire beliefs about 'what it's like' for other people to have mental states in this way. Though, as we noted in Chapter 4, we are quite sceptical about the claim that basic propositional attitudes like beliefs and desires *have* a rich phenomenological profile.

distinctive and new concept of *number*, which applies both to small and large numerosities (see e.g. Spelke and Tsivkin 2001). Thus, the idea that first-person and third-person concepts provide the basis for new, inclusive, mental state concepts has some important cognitive models on which to draw.

If the reader is puzzled about *how* the child goes about developing a new concept, or about what it means to say that the initial first- and third-person concepts 'provide the basis for a new concept', we're afraid we can't be of much help, since we share that puzzlement. But these are issues which arise, *mutatis mutandis*, for every theory that postulates genuine conceptual change either in development or in the course of theory revision in science.[2] And since it is hard to deny that conceptual change does occur, at least in some domains, we assume that ultimately some satisfactory story will be told about how it happens. There are some philosophers—Fodor is the most notorious—who *do* deny that conceptual change can occur, and who insist that, with a few theoretically uninteresting exceptions, all concepts are innate. If it turns out that they are right, then we will have to scratch conceptual change from our list of possible solutions to the concept unity problem.

What we have been arguing in this section is that pre-established harmony, conceptual change, and learning that does not involve conceptual change all offer distinctive solutions to the problem of concept unity. And each of these accounts is entirely consistent with the account of mindreading we have offered in this volume. Currently, there is little evidence to help sort out which solution is most plausible. Indeed, we think it is possible that a pluralist approach may ultimately prevail: some mental state concepts might be unified via conceptual change, some might be innately tracked to converge, and for some, children might have to learn that the mental states detected by the first-person system and those detected by the third-person system are of the same type. This kind of pluralism would also be consistent with the account of mindreading that we have presented. So the concept unity problem, though it raises some interesting and unresolved questions, does not pose a serious challenge for our theory.

5.1.2. The account neglects the attribution of 'thick' mental states

Objection

At several points (see e.g. Sections 3.1.5 and 4.3.1), we have emphasized that the mental state concepts delivered by various mechanisms we posit for detecting mental states are not rich concepts from which a wide array of

---

[2] For some insightful criticism of the account of conceptual change offered by Spelke, Carey, and others in the domain of numerical concepts, see Laurence and Margolis (forthcoming).

inferences can be drawn. Indeed, in Chapter 4, we suggested that it might be advisable to use the technical terms '*bel*' and '*des*' in place of '*belief*' and '*desire*' because the concepts produced by the detection mechanisms really are quite thin—they do not come loaded with a rich set of inferential connections. However, many mental state concepts we exploit as adults clearly are inferentially rich and sophisticated. For instance, we can attribute *Schadenfreude* to a colleague or dread to a logic student. Our theory, as it stands, has no explanation for the attribution of such inferentially rich or 'thick' mental state concepts. None of our proposed mechanisms for detecting mental states will detect *Schadenfreude*. Yet the capacity to attribute such thick mental state concepts is an important part of people's mindreading skill, and not just for academics. So our account neglects an important aspect of everyday mindreading.

Reply

How can we extend our theory to accommodate the deployment of thick mental state concepts? Our strategy in Chapters 3 and 4 was to posit special purpose mechanisms for detecting beliefs, desires, and perceptions. But we are hardly inclined to continue that practice for thick mental state concepts. We think it is highly unlikely that there is a special purpose mechanism for detecting *Schadenfreude*. We don't think that this presents us with a serious problem, however. The obvious way to extend the account is to maintain that thick mental state attribution is a product of inference in which a great deal of additional information—often culturally local information—plays an important role. The account we set out in Chapters 3 and 4 tries to capture what we take to be the universal mechanisms of mindreading, including universal mechanisms for detecting beliefs and desires. Once these universal mechanisms are up and running, we maintain, the culture in which the mindreader is embedded supplies additional information that plays an essential role in the acquisition of thick mental state concepts and inferential strategies for attribution of these concepts. Little is known about the processes that enable people to internalize the information about thick mental states that prevails in their culture. However, we think it is plausible to suppose that, in most cases, the acquisition and deployment of these concepts depends crucially on previously acquired thinner mental state concepts. So, for instance, the concept of *disappointment* presumably can't be acquired without the concept of *desire*, and the concept of *doubt* can't be acquired without the concept of *belief*.

The claim that the acquisition and deployment of thick mental state concepts depends on additional, culturally supplied informational resources gains some support from two kinds of empirical findings. First, there is developmental evidence that thick mental state concepts are acquired later than thin mental state concepts. Second, there is cross-cultural work indicating that different cultures invoke remarkably different thick mental state concepts.

One source of developmental evidence on thick mental state concepts derives from work on children's understanding of emotion. The bulk of the work in that area focuses on simple emotions like happiness and sadness. But there is also some research on emotions like guilt, pride, and shame, which seem to be inferentially richer than simple emotions like happiness and sadness. Pride, for instance, is a positive affective state like happiness, but pride is an emotion one has *in response to one's own traits or actions or those of some person or group one identifies with*. There are no such restrictions imposed on a simple emotion like happiness. The findings indicate that thicker emotion concepts like *guilt* and *pride* are acquired significantly later than the simple emotion concepts. For instance, although children understand emotions like sadness and happiness at a very young age (before the third birthday), children apparently aren't able to identify emotions like guilt, pride, and shame until the age of 6 or 7 (see e.g. Nunner-Winkler and Sodian 1988). A study by Paul Harris and colleagues indicates that younger children aren't able to describe situations that would cause such complex emotions. Harris and colleagues presented Dutch and British children with a range of emotion terms and asked them to describe situations that would cause the emotion (Harris et al. 1987). They found exactly what they expected. Five-year-old children successfully described situations that would produce emotions like fear, sadness, and anger, which have characteristic facial expressions. But they were unable to describe situations that would produce the more complex emotions like pride, guilt, or gratefulness. Seven-year-olds were able to describe situations that would produce all of those emotions, but they were unable to describe situations that would lead to relief or disappointment. Ten-year-old children, however, were able to describe situations that would elicit even these more complex emotions. These findings fit nicely with our proposal that the use of thick mental state concepts requires additional informational resources. Since thick emotion concepts like *pride* and *relief* require additional informational resources, it is no surprise that children take longer to acquire these concepts.

The cross-cultural evidence on mindreading suggests that, at least in many cases, the surrounding culture supplies information that leads to the acquisition of thick mental state concepts, since there seems to be substantial variation in the thick mental state concepts invoked in different cultures. One particularly illuminating example of this phenomenon is described in great detail by Catherine Lutz (1988). Among the Ifaluk, inhabitants of a Micronesian atoll, there is a thick emotion, called *song*, which is built on anger. But, according to Lutz, there is a strong moral component to *song*. In order to count as being or feeling *song*, an Ifaluk must be *justifiably* angry at another person who has engaged in certain sorts of morally inappropriate behaviour. It is, Lutz maintains, part of the concept of *song* that one *cannot* be *song* unless one's anger is justified. And, according to the prevailing moral views, if two people are involved in a dispute, only one can *really* be *song*, regardless of what the other person may think about the emotion he or she is experiencing (1988: 173). In light of these facts, it is not surprising that 'daily negotiations over who is *song* and over the proper reasons for that anger lie at the heart of the politics of everyday life' (1988: 170).[3] Obviously, attributions of *song* require much more than the mere capacity to detect that the target is angry. One must know that real *song* can only be provoked by certain sorts of moral transgressions, and one must know a fair amount about the prevailing moral code as well.

One important category of transgression that can provoke *song* is the violation of a taboo, and among the Ifaluk taboos are not in short supply. There are taboos that apply only to women (they are forbidden to enter the canoe houses or work in the taro gardens when they are menstruating) and others that apply only to men (they are not to enter birth houses). Other taboos apply to everyone. Violation of these taboos provokes *song* among the chiefs who may impose fines or other punishments. On a less public level, *song* is often provoked when people fail to live up to their obligation to share (Lutz 1988: 160) or when they are lazy, loud, or disrespectful (1988: 165). From a Western perspective, one of the stranger features of *song* is that it can be provoked by a sort of excited happiness that the Ifaluk call *ker*. 'Happiness/excitement', Lutz reports, 'is an emotion people see as pleasant but amoral. It is often, in fact, *im*moral because someone who is happy/ excited is more likely to be unafraid of other people. While this lack of fear may lead them to laugh and talk with other people, it may also make them misbehave or walk around showing off...' (1988: 167). So, on the sort of account that we favour, when an Ifaluk mindreader detects an anger-like response—either in another person or in herself—and when she believes that the response is provoked by a taboo violation or by *ker*, she will infer that the target is *song*, though of course the inference may be largely or entirely unconscious.

We think that this example provides a model for dealing with the full range of 'thick' mental state attributions. The mindreading systems we have described in Chapters 3 and 4 explain the mindreader's capacity to detect a range of 'thin' mental states including belief, desire, and a small number of

---

[3] The Ifaluk have an array of other terms for types of anger that do not involve this moral dimension—*tipmochmoch* for the irritability that often accompanies sickness, *lingeringer* for anger that builds up slowly when one is confronted with a series of minor annoyances, etc. (Lutz 1988: 157). But, intriguingly, they have no generic term that picks out all and only these various sorts of anger (Lutz, personal communication).

basic (and presumably universal) emotions.[4] When the adult mindreader's cognitive system forms the belief that the target is in one of these thin mental states, it then uses this belief, along with a large body of (mostly tacit) culturally local knowledge about the thick mental states recognized in the culture to draw inferences about the thick mental states of the target. This sort of account, we believe, explains the ability of the Ifaluk to attribute mental states like *song*, and the ability of people in our culture to attribute mental states like pride, dread, and *Schadenfreude*. While this account of the attribution of thick mental states further complicates our picture of the processes underlying mindreading, we think that this additional complexity is amply warranted by the phenomena. People clearly do attribute thick mental states, and these attributions seem to require a great deal of culturally local information.

5.1.3. The theory doesn't really explain, it just posits 'boxes'

Objection

At many junctures in the development of our theory we have maintained that one or another aspect of mindreading requires a mental mechanism that performs a certain task, and then simply posited the existence of such a mechanism and added a box to our increasingly elaborate 'boxology'. A number of critics have complained that this strategy doesn't really explain mindreading, since we offer no account of how the mechanism accomplishes its task.

Reply

Though we tried to anticipate this objection in our introductory chapter, we think that it is worth revisiting the issue now that the details of our theory have been set out. The explanatory strategy we have adopted in this volume is a version of 'functional analysis' which, as writers like Fodor (1968), Cummins (1975, 2000), Dennett (1978*b*), and Lycan (1981, 1988) have argued, is the dominant explanatory strategy in much of cognitive science. Cummins, who has made a persuasive case that the strategy is also widely used in biology and engineering, has suggested that the 'explanatory interest'

---

[4] Lutz and others who adopt a 'social constructionist' approach to the emotions sometimes insist that there are no universal emotions. However, we don't think that we have any *empirical* disagreements with the social constructionists on this issue. Rather, we believe, the social constructionists' claim that there are no universal emotions can be traced to their acceptance of a very dubious account of the meaning and reference of mental state terms. For much more detail on all this, see Mallon and Stich (2000).

of an 'analytical account' of this sort is 'roughly proportional to':

   (i) the extent to which the analyzing capacities are less sophisticated than the
        analyzed capacities,
  (ii) the extent to which the analyzing capacities are different in type from the
        analyzed capacities, and
 (iii) the relative sophistication of the program appealed to, i.e., the relative complex-
        ity of the organization of component parts / processes which is attributed to the
        system. (Cummins 1975: 66)

By these criteria, we think that our theory does reasonably well. The capacities
of the mechanisms (or boxes) we have posited in Figures like 3.6 and 4.6 are significantly less sophisticated than the mindreading capacity they are helping to
explain. And, though the notion of a 'type' of capacity could do with some
unpacking, many of our boxes perform functions that are, intuitively, quite
different from mindreading. As for complexity, we take it that Figures 3.6 and
4.6 speak for themselves. Of course our critics are right to point out that we have
said very little about how the mechanisms we have proposed carry out the task
assigned to them. Our entire theory has been elaborated at Marr's task-analytic
'computational' level, and we've said nothing about algorithms or physical imple-
mentations. So we agree with the critics that there is much work left to be done.
But we reject the suggestion that functional analyses like the one we have elaborated make no explanatory progress. If this were the case, then *all* of the competing theories of mindreading that we have discussed would be subject to the
same criticism, as would much of cognitive science and large parts of biology!

5.1.4. The theory is too complex

Objection

A final objection that we have encountered on a number of occasions is that
our account is too complicated. Mindreading, on our theory, looks like an
extremely complex and ungainly collection of processes. Surely, one
commentator remarked, our capacity for mindreading isn't *that* kludgy.

Reply

We are happy to plead guilty to the charge of having produced an extremely
complex model of mindreading. However, we don't think that this counts as
an *objection* to our theory. Quite the opposite. For, as Cummins has pointed
out, *ceteris paribus*, complexity is a virtue in theories that aim to explain
sophisticated skills by decomposing them into a system of interacting sub-
components. Of course, simplicity also plays an important role in evaluating
scientific theories. But we believe that appeals to simplicity are only relevant

in comparing theories that are approximately equally in their capacity to explain the phenomena that need to be explained. It is true that monolithic accounts which insist that all of mindreading can be explained by simulation or by the scientific-theory theory are significantly simpler than the bristling bricolages depicted in Figures 3.6 and 4.6. But, as we argued at length in Chapters 3 and 4, those theories simply cannot explain the range of facts that our theory can, and in many cases the advocates of monolithic accounts don't even *try*. So the greater simplicity of monolithic theories hardly counts as an argument against our theory.

To those who insist, as some critics have, that the processes underlying mindreading just *can't* be that complicated since Mother Nature is not *that much* of a tinkerer, we recommend a crash course in contemporary biology, where even what were once thought of as relatively simple phenomena, like regulation of protein construction by DNA, have turned out to be subserved by interacting processes of astounding complexity (Alberts et al. 2002; or for a useful brief overview, see Sterelny and Griffiths 1999: ch. 6). In putting together organisms and enabling them to survive and reproduce, Mother Nature has shown an almost boundless exuberance. We see no reason to suspect that when she got around to designing systems for mindreading she suddenly developed a taste for austerity.

5.2. Functionalism, Eliminativism, and Mindreading

In the introduction to this volume, we set out some of the reasons why mindreading and the processes that underlie it have become increasingly important for people working in a wide range of disciplines. For philosophers, we argued, determining the nature of mindreading is especially important in evaluating the prospects of functionalism and eliminativism. Since we came to this debate through philosophy, it is fitting to close by reflecting briefly on these issues.

Functionalists, it will be recalled, propose that the meaning of mental state terms is determined by a commonsense psychological theory often called 'folk psychology'. Eliminativists typically endorse the functionalist account of the meaning of mental state terms, but they go on to argue that folk psychology is a seriously mistaken theory—indeed it is so profoundly mistaken that the commonsense mental states the theory invokes do not exist. But what exactly is folk psychology? In Section 1.1 we suggested that the most natural answer, for both functionalists and eliminativists, is that *folk psychology is a rich body of information about the mind that is utilized by the mental mechanisms responsible for mindreading.* If that's right, then simulation theory appears to pose a threat to both functionalism and eliminativism. For according to simulation theory, there is no rich body of information underlying mindreading, and obviously the meaning of mental state terms cannot be determined by the body of information underlying mindreading if there is no such body of information. Moreover, the folk theory underlying mindreading can't be radically mistaken, as eliminativists insist, if there is no folk theory underlying mindreading.

In the early days of the simulation / theory theory debate, the issue was characterized as dichotomous—either mindreading derives from a theory or from simulation. Thus the threat to functionalism and eliminativism seemed crisp and clear. If simulation theory is right, functionalism and eliminativism are off the mark. We have gone to some lengths to argue that this picture is far too simple. On our account, mindreading depends on a motley array of mechanisms. Some aspects of mindreading are best explained by appeal to an information-rich theory, while other mindreading abilities are best explained by simulation, and still others are explained by processes like default attribution, which are not comfortably classified as either theory driven or simulation based. If this is correct, it presents both functionalists and eliminativists with some rather awkward choices. Since only *parts* of mindreading rely on an information-rich theory, should functionalists insist that the theory underlying these aspects of mindreading fixes the meaning of mental state terms? Or should they embrace some other account of folk psychology?

As our philosophical readers know well, there are other accounts on offer. For David Lewis, and for many of those who followed his lead, folk psychology is closely tied to the *platitudes* about mental states that almost everyone would agree with and take to be obvious. Here is one well-known passage in which Lewis develops the idea.

Collect all the platitudes you can think of regarding the causal relations of mental states, sensory stimuli, and motor responses.... Add also the platitudes to the effect that one mental state falls under another—'toothache is a kind of pain' and the like. Perhaps there are platitudes of other forms as well. Include only platitudes that are common knowledge among us—everyone knows them, everyone knows that everyone else knows them, and so on. For the meanings of our words are common knowledge, and I am going to claim that *names of mental states derive their meaning from these platitudes*. (Lewis 1972: 212, emphasis added)

So, on this account, folk psychology is just a collection of platitudes, or perhaps, since that set of platitudes is bound to be large and ungainly, we might think of folk psychology as a set of generalizations that systematizes the platitudes in a perspicuous way. We can call this the *platitude account* of folk psychology. When Lewis first introduced this idea, many philosophers apparently believed that folk psychology, unpacked along the lines of the platitude account, could explain how we actually go about the business of attributing mental states to others (and perhaps to ourselves). But we take it that this book, and the many studies we've cited, constitute a definitive refutation of that rather naïve view. The platitudes about the mind 'that are common knowledge among us' would hardly scratch the surface in explaining how people go about attributing beliefs, desires, and basic emotions, not to mention 'thicker' mental states like *song* and *Schadenfreude*.

We are inclined to think that neither the platitude account of folk psychology nor the account which identifies folk psychology with the information-rich theory (or theories!) underlying a scattered fragment of mindreading should be particularly attractive to functionalists. Nor do we know of any plausible *argument* for the view that ordinary mental state terms derive their meaning from either of these bodies of information. So perhaps the main philosophical conclusion to be drawn from this book is that both functionalists and eliminativists have their work cut out for them. The reason is not, as simulationists suggest, that there is no theory being invoked when we attribute and reason about mental states, but that the theory which is utilized in mindreading is only one component in a very complicated story.

REFERENCES

ABELSON, R. (1981). 'Psychological status of the script concept', *American Psychologist*, 36: 715–29.

ALBERTS, B., JOHNSON, A., LEWIS, J., RAFF, M., ROBERTS, K., and WALTER, P. (2002). *Molecular Biology of the Cell*. New York: Garland Publishing.

ARMSTRONG, D. (1968). *A Materialist Theory of the Mind*. New York: Humanities Press.

ASTINGTON, J., and GOPNIK, A. (1991). 'Understanding desire and intention', in A. Whiten (ed.), *Natural Theories of Mind*. Cambridge: Basil Blackwell.

BARON, J. (2000). *Thinking and Deciding*, 3rd edn. Cambridge: Cambridge University Press.

BARON-COHEN, S. (1989). 'Are autistic children "behaviorists"?', *Journal of Autism and Developmental Disorders*, 19: 579–600.

—— (1991a). 'The development of a theory of mind in autism: deviance and delay?', *Psychiatric Clinics of North America*, 14: 33–51.

—— (1991b). 'Do people with autism understand what causes emotion', *Child Development*, 62: 385–95.

—— (1995). *Mindblindness*. Cambridge, Mass.: Bradford Books/MIT Press.

—— and BOLTON, P. (1993). *Autism: The Facts*. Oxford: Oxford University Press.

—— and GOODHART, F. (1994). 'The "seeing leads to knowing" deficit in autism: the Pratt and Bryant probe', *British Journal of Developmental Psychology*, 12: 397–402.

—— LESLIE, A., and FRITH, U. (1985). 'Does the autistic child have a "theory of mind"?', *Cognition*, 21: 37–46.

—————— (1986). 'Mechanical, behavioral and intentional understanding of picture stories in autistic children', *British Journal of Developmental Psychology*, 4: 113–25.

—— TAGER-FLUSBERG, H., and COHEN, D. (eds.) (2000). *Understanding Other Minds*, 2nd edn. Oxford: Oxford University Press.

BARTSCH, K., and WELLMAN, H. (1989). 'Young children's attribution of action to belief and desires', *Child Development*, 60: 946–64.

—————— (1995). *Children Talk about the Mind*. Oxford: Oxford University Press.

BIERBRAUER, G. (1973). 'Effect of Set, Perspective, and Temporal Factors in Attribution', unpublished doctoral dissertation, Stanford University.

BLOCK, N. (1986). 'Advertisement for a semantics for psychology', in P. A. French, T Uehling Jr., and H. Wettstein (eds.), *Midwest Studies in Philosophy*, vol. x: *Studies in the Philosophy of Mind*. Minneapolis: University of Minnesota Press, 73–121.

—— (1994). 'Functionalism', in S. Guttenplan (ed.), *A Companion to the Philosophy of Mind*. Oxford: Blackwell, 323–32.

—— (2003). 'Mental paint', in M. Hahn and B. Ramberg (eds.), *Reflections and Replies*. Cambridge, Mass.: MIT Press.

BLOOM, P. (2000). *How Children Learn the Meaning of Words*. Cambridge, Mass.: Bradford Books/MIT Press.

—— and GERMAN, T. (2000). 'Two reasons to abandon the false belief task as a test of theory of mind', *Cognition*, 77: B25–B31.

BOESCH, C., and BOESCH, H. (1989). 'Hunting behavior of wild chimpanzees in the Tai Forest National Park', *American Journal of Physical Anthropology*, 78: 547–73.

BOTTERILL, G., and CARRUTHERS, P. (1999). *The Philosophy of Psychology*. Cambridge: Cambridge University Press.

BRAINE, M. (1994). 'Mental logic and how to discover it', in J. Macnamara and G. Reyes (eds.), *The Logical Foundations of Cognition*. Oxford: Oxford University Press.

BRANDON, R. (1990). *Adaptation and Environment*. Princeton: Princeton University Press.

BRETHERTON, I. (1989). 'Pretense: the form and function of make-believe play', *Developmental Review*, 9: 383–401.

BROWN, R. (1973). *A First Language: The Early Stages*. Cambridge, Mass.: Harvard University Press.

BUSS, D., LARSEN, R., WESTEN, D., and SEMMELROTH, J. (1992). 'Sex differences in jealousy: evolution, physiology, and psychology', *Psychological Science*, 3: 251–5.

BYRNE, A., and WHITEN, R. (1988). *Machiavellian Intelligence*. Cambridge: Cambridge University Press.

CALL, J., and TOMASELLO, M. (1998). 'Distinguishing intentional from accidental actions in orangutans, chimpanzees, and human children', *Journal of Comparative Psychology*, 112: 192–206.

———— (1999). 'A nonverbal false belief task: the performance of children and great apes', *Child Development*, 70: 381–95.

—— HARE, B., and TOMASELLO, M. (1998). 'Chimpanzee gaze following in an object choice task', *Animal Cognition*, 1: 89–99.

CAREY, S. (1985). *Conceptual Change in Childhood*. Cambridge, Mass.: Bradford Books/MIT Press.

—— and SPELKE, E. (forthcoming). 'Constructing the integer list representation of number', in L. Bonatti, J. Mehler, and S. Carey (eds.), *Developmental Cognitive Science*. Cambridge, Mass.: Bradford Books/MIT Press.

CARRUTHERS, P. (1996). 'Autism as mind-blindness: an elaboration and partial defence', in P. Carruthers and P. Smith (eds.), *Theories of Theories of Mind*. Cambridge: Cambridge University Press.

—— (2000). *Phenomenal Consciousness*. Cambridge: Cambridge University Press.

—— and SMITH, P. (1996). *Theories of Theories of Mind*. Cambridge: Cambridge University Press.

CHERNIAK, C. (1986). *Minimal Rationality*. Cambridge, Mass.: Bradford Books/MIT Press.

CHOMSKY, N. (1965). *Aspects of the Theory of Syntax*. Cambridge, Mass.: MIT Press.

CHURCHLAND, P. (1981). 'Eliminative materialism and propositional attitudes', *Journal of Philosophy*, 78: 67–90; repr. in W. Lycan (ed.), *Mind and Cognition* (Oxford: Blackwell, 1990), 206–23. Page reference is to the Lycan volume.

CLEMENTS, W., and PERNER, J. (1994). 'Implicit understanding of belief', *Cognitive Development*, 9: 377–95.

CORCORAN, R., FRITH, C., and MERCER, G. (1995). 'Schizophrenia, symptomatology and social inference: investigating "theory of mind" in people with schizophrenia', *Schizophrenia Research*, 17: 5–13.

CSIBRA, G., GERGELY, G., BIRO, S., KOOS, O., BROCKBANK, M. (1999). 'Goal attribution without agency cues: the perception of "pure reason" in infancy', *Cognition* 72: 237–67.

CUMMINS, R. (1975). 'Functional analysis', *Journal of Philosophy*, 72: 741–64; repr. in E. Sober (ed.), *Conceptual Issues in Evolutionary Biology*, 2nd edn. (Cambridge, Mass.: MIT Press, 1994), 49–69. Page reference is to the Sober volume.

——(2000). ' "How does it work?" versus "What are the laws?": two conceptions of psychological explanation', in F. Keil and R. Wilson (eds.), *Explanation and Cognition*. Cambridge, Mass.: Bradford Books/MIT Press.

CURRIE, G. (1990). *The Nature of Fiction*. Cambridge: Cambridge University Press.

——(1995a). *Image and Mind*. Cambridge: Cambridge University Press.

——(1995b). 'Imagination and simulation: aesthetics meets cognitive science', in A. Stone and M. Davies (eds.), *Mental Simulation: Evaluations and Applications*. Oxford: Basil Blackwell.

——(1995c). 'The moral psychology of fiction', *Australasian Journal of Philosophy*, 73: 250–9.

——(1995d). 'Visual imagery as the simulation of vision', *Mind and Language*, 10: 25–44.

——(1996). 'Simulation-theory, theory-theory, and the evidence from autism', in P. Carruthers and P. Smith (eds.), *Theories of Theories of Mind*. Cambridge: Cambridge University Press.

——(1997). 'The paradox of caring', in M. Hjort and S. Laver (eds.), *Emotion and the Arts*. Oxford: Oxford University Press.

——(1998). 'Pretence, pretending and metarepresenting', *Mind and Language*, 13: 35–55.

——and RAVENSCROFT, I. (1997). 'Mental simulation and motor imagery', *Philosophy of Science*, 64: 161–80.

DASSER, V., ULBAEK, I., and PREMACK, D. (1989). 'The perception of intention', *Science*, 243: 365–7.

DAVIDSON, D. (1980). *Essays on Action and Events*. Oxford: Oxford University Press.

DAVIES, M., and STONE, T. (1995a). *Folk Psychology: The Theory of Mind Debate*. Oxford: Blackwell.

————(1995b). *Mental Simulation: Evaluations and Applications*. Oxford: Blackwell.

DENNETT, D. (1978a). *Brainstorms: Philosophical Essays on Mind and Psychology*. Cambridge, Mass.: Bradford Books/MIT Press.

——(1978b). 'Artificial intelligence as philosophy and as psychology', in Dennett 1978a: 109–26.

——(1987). *The Intentional Stance*. Cambridge, Mass.: Bradford Books/MIT Press.

——(1991). *Consciousness Explained*. Boston, Mass.: Little Brown.

DE WAAL, F. (1986). 'Deception in the natural communication of chimpanzees', in R. Mitchell and N. Thompson (eds.), *Deception: Perspectives on Human and Nonhuman Deceit*. Albany, NY: SUNY Press.

DEWEY, M. (1991). 'Living with Asperger's syndrome', in U. Frith (ed.), *Autism and Asperger Syndrome*. Cambridge: Cambridge University Press.

EKMAN, P. (1985). *Telling Lies: Clues to Deceit in the Marketplace, Politics, and Marriage*. New York: W. W. Norton & Co.

——(1992). 'Facial expression and emotion', *American Psychologist*, 48: 384–92.

ERICSSON, K., and SIMON, H. (1993). *Protocol Analysis: Verbal Reports as Data*. Cambridge, Mass.: Bradford Books/MIT Press.

EVANS, G. (1982). *The Varieties of Reference*. Oxford: Oxford University Press.

FARRANT, A., BOUCHER, J., and BLADES, M. (1999). 'Metamemory in children with autism', *Child Development*, 70: 107–31.

FEIN, G. (1981). 'Pretend play in childhood: an integrative review', *Child Development*, 52: 1095–118.

——and KINNEY, P. (1994). 'He's a nice alligator: observations on the affective organization of pretense', in A. Slade and D. Wolf (eds.), *Children at Play: Clinical and Developmental Approaches to Meaning and Representation*. New York: Oxford University Press.

FIRST, E. (1994). 'The leaving game, or I'll play you and you play me: the emergence of dramatic role play in 2-year-olds', in A. Slade and D. Wolf (eds.), *Children at Play: Clinical and Developmental Approaches to Meaning and Representation*. New York: Oxford University Press.

FLAVELL, J. (1978). 'The development of knowledge about visual perception', in C. B. Keasey (ed.), *Nebraska Symposium on Motivation*, xxv. 43–76. Lincoln: University of Nebraska Press.

——(1988). 'The development of children's knowledge about the mind: from cognitive connections to mental representations', in J. Astington, P. Harris, and D. Olson (eds.), *Developing Theories of Mind*. Cambridge: Cambridge University Press.

——and MILLER, P. (1998). 'Social cognition', in D. Kuhn and R. Siegler (eds.), *Handbook of Child Psychology*, 5th edn. ii. 851–98.

——EVERETT, B., CROFT, K., and FLAVELL, E. (1981). 'Young children's knowledge about visual perception', *Developmental Psychology*, 17: 99–103.

——GREEN, F., and FLAVELL, E. (1986). *Development of Knowledge about the Appearance-Reality Distinction*. Chicago: Society for Research in Child Development.

——FLAVELL, E., and GREEN, F. (1987). 'Young children's knowledge about the apparent-real and pretend-real distinctions', *Developmental Psychology*, 23: 816–22.

———— and MOSES, L. (1990). 'Young children's understanding of fact beliefs versus value beliefs', *Child Development*, 61: 915–28.

FODOR, J. (1968). 'The appeal to tacit knowledge in psychological explanation', *Journal of Philosophy*, 65: 627–40.

——(1981). *Representations*. Cambridge, Mass.: Bradford Books/MIT Press.

——(1983). *The Modularity of Mind*. Cambridge, Mass.: Bradford Books/MIT Press.

——(1987). *Psychosemantics*. Cambridge, Mass.: Bradford Books/MIT Press.

——(1992). 'A theory of the child's theory of mind', *Cognition*, 44: 283–96.

——(1998). *Concepts*. Oxford: Oxford University Press.

——and CHIHARA, C. (1965). 'Operationalism and ordinary language', *American Philosophical Quarterly*, 2/4; repr. in J. Fodor, *Representations* (Cambridge, Mass.: Bradford Books/MIT Press, 1981), 35–62.

FREGE, G. (1892/1970). 'On sense and reference', in P. Geach and M. Black (eds.), *Translations from the Philosophical Writings of Gottlob Frege*. Oxford: Basil Blackwell.

FRITH, C. (1987). 'The positive and negative symptoms of schizophrenia reflect impairment in the perception and initiation of action', *Psychological Medicine*, 17: 631–48.

—— (1992). *The Cognitive Neuropsychology of Schizophrenia*. Hillsdale, NJ: LEA.

—— (1994). 'Theory of mind in schizophrenia', in A. David and J. Cutting (eds.), *The Neuropsychology of Schizophrenia*. Hillsdale, NJ: LEA.

—— and CORCORAN, R. (1996). 'Exploring "theory of mind" in people with schizophrenia', *Psychological Medicine*, 26: 521–30.

FRITH, U. (1991). *Autism and Asperger Syndrome*. Cambridge: Cambridge University Press.

—— and HAPPÉ, F. (1999). 'Theory of mind and self consciousness: what is it like to be autistic?', *Mind and Language*, 14: 1–22.

GALLESE, V., and GOLDMAN, A. (1998). 'Motor neurons and the simulation theory of mind-reading', *Trends in Cognitive Science*, 2/12: 493–501.

GARVEY, C. (1979). 'An approach to the study of children's role play', *Quarterly Newsletter of the Laboratory of Comparative Human Cognition*, 12: 69–73.

GERGELY, G., NADASDY, Z., CSIBRA, G., and BIRO, S. (1995). 'Taking the intentional stance at 12 months of age', *Cognition*, 56: 165–93.

GERLAND, G. (1997). *A Real Person: Life on the Outside*, trans. from the Swedish by J. Tate. London: Souvenir Press.

GERMAN, T., and LESLIE, A. (2001). 'Children's inferences from *knowing* to *pretending* and *believing*', *British Journal of Developmental Psychology*, 19: 59–83.

—— —— (forthcoming). 'Self-other differences in false belief: recall versus reconstruction'.

GIGERENZER, G. (2000). *Adaptive Thinking: Rationality in the Real World*. New York: Oxford University Press.

GOLDMAN, A. (1989). 'Interpretation psychologized', *Mind and Language*, 4: 161–85.

—— (1992a). 'Empathy, mind, and morals', *Proceedings and Addresses of the American Philosophical Association*, 66/3: 17–41.

—— (1992b). 'In defense of the simulation theory', *Mind and Language*, 7: 104–19.

—— (1993a). *Philosophical Applications of Cognitive Science*. Boulder, Colo.: Westview Press.

—— (1993b). 'The psychology of folk psychology', *Behavioral and Brain Sciences*, 16: 15–28.

—— (1997). 'Science, publicity, and consciousness', *Philosophy of Science*, 64: 525–46.

—— (2000). 'The mentalizing folk', in D. Sperber (ed.), *Metarepresentation*. Oxford: Oxford University Press, 171–96.

GOODMAN, N. (1983). *Fact, Fiction and Forecast*, 4th edn. Cambridge, Mass.: Harvard University Press.

GOPNIK, A. (1993). 'How we know our own minds: the illusion of first-person knowledge of intentionality', *Behavioral and Brain Sciences*, 16: 1–14.

—— and ASTINGTON, J. (1988). 'Children's understanding of representational change and its relation to the understanding of false belief and the appearance-reality distinction', *Child Development*, 59: 26–37.

—— and GRAF, P. (1988). 'Knowing how you know: young children's ability to identify and remember the sources of their beliefs', *Child Development*, 59: 1366–71.

—— and MELTZOFF, A. (1994). 'Minds, bodies, and persons: young children's understanding of the self and others as reflected in imitation and theory of mind research', in S. Parker, R. Mitchell, and M. Boccia (eds.), *Self-awareness in Animals and Humans*. New York: Cambridge University Press.

—————— (1997). *Words, Thoughts and Theories*. Cambridge, Mass.: Bradford Books/MIT Press.

—— and SLAUGHTER, V. (1991). 'Young children's understanding of changes in their mental states', *Child Development*, 62: 98–110.

—— and WELLMAN H. (1992). 'Why the child's theory of mind really *is* a theory', *Mind and Language*, 7: 145–71.

—————— (1994). 'The theory theory', in L. Hirschfeld and S. Gelman (eds.), *Mapping the Mind: Domain Specificity in Cognition and Culture*. New York: Cambridge University Press, 257–93.

—— CAPPS, L., and MELTZOFF, A. (2000). 'Early theories of mind: what the theory theory can tell us about autism', in Baron-Cohen et al. 2000: 50–72.

—— MELTZOFF, A., ESTERLY, J., and RUBENSTEIN, J. (1995). 'Young children's understanding of visual perspective-taking'. Paper presented at the First Annual West Coast Conference on Theory of Mind, Eugene, Ore.

GORDON, R. (1986). 'Folk psychology as simulation', *Mind and Language*, 1: 158–70.

—— (1995*a*). 'Reply to Stich and Nichols', in M. Davies and T. Stone (eds.), *Folk Psychology*. Oxford: Blackwell Publishers, 174–84.

—— (1995*b*). 'Simulation without introspection or inference from me to you', in T. Stone and M. Davies (eds.), *Mental Simulation: Evaluations and Applications*. Oxford: Blackwell.

—— (1996). '"Radical" simulation', in Carruthers and Smith 1996: 11–21.

—— (2000). 'Sellars's Ryleans revisited', *Protosociology*, 14: 102–14.

—— and BARKER, J. (1994). 'Autism and the "theory of mind" debate', in G. Graham and G. L. Stephens (eds.), *Philosophical Psychopathology: A Book of Readings*. Cambridge, Mass.: Bradford Books/MIT Press.

GOULD, R. (1972). *Child Studies through Fantasy*. New York: Quadrangle Books.

GOULD, S. (1992). *Bully for Brontosaurus: Further Reflections in Natural History*. London: Penguin Books.

—— and VRBA, E. (1982). 'Exaptation: a missing term in the science of form', *Paleobiology*, 8: 4–15.

GRANDIN, T. (1984). 'My experiences as an autistic child and review of selected literature', *Journal of Orthomolecular Psychiatry*, 13: 144–75.

—— (1995). *Thinking in Pictures*. New York: Doubleday.

GREGORY, R. (1997). 'Visual illusions classified', *Trends in Cognitive Science*, 190–4.

GROSS, A., and BALLIF, B. (1991). 'Children's understanding of emotion from facial expressions and situations: a review', *Developmental Review*, 11/4: 368–98.

GUNDERSON, K. (1993). 'On behalf of phenomenological parity for the attitudes', *Behavioral and Brain Sciences*, 16: 46–7.

HALLE, M., and STEVENS, K. (1962). 'Speech recognition: a model and a program for research', in J. Fodor and J. Katz (eds.), *The Structure of Language: Readings in the Philosophy of Language*. Englewood Cliffs, NJ: Prentice-Hall.

HARE, B., CALL, J., AGNETTA, B., and TOMASELLO, M. (2000). 'Chimpanzees know what conspecifics do and do not see', *Animal Behaviour*, 59: 771–85.

HARRIS, P. (1989). *Children and Emotion*. Oxford: Blackwell.

——(1991). 'The work of the imagination', in A. Whiten (ed.), *Natural Theories of Mind*. Oxford: Blackwell.

——(1992). 'From simulation to folk psychology: the case for development', *Mind and Language*, 7: 120–44.

——(1993). 'Pretending and planning', in S. Baron-Cohen, H. Tager-Flusberg, and D. Cohen (eds.), *Understanding Other Minds: Perspectives from Autism*. Oxford: Oxford University Press.

——(1994a). 'Thinking by children and scientists: false analogies and neglected similarities', in L. Hirschfeld and S. Gelman (eds.), *Mapping the Mind: Domain Specificity in Cognition and Culture*. New York: Cambridge University Press.

——(1994b). 'Understanding pretense', in Lewis and Mitchell 1994: 235–59.

——(1995). 'Imagining and pretending', in M. Davies and T. Stone (eds.), *Mental Simulation*. Oxford: Blackwell.

——(1996). 'Desires, beliefs, and language', in Carruthers and Smith 1996: 200–20.

——(2000). *The Work of the Imagination*. Oxford: Blackwell Publishers.

——and KAVANAUGH, R. D. (1993). 'Young children's understanding of pretense', *Monographs of the Society for Research in Child Development*, 58/1.

——OLTHOF, T., MEERUM TERWOGT, M., and HARDMAN, C. (1987). 'Children's knowledge of the situations that provoke emotions', *International Journal of Behavioral Development*, 10: 319–44.

HEAL, J. (1986). 'Replication and functionalism', in J. Butterfield (ed.), *Language, Mind and Logic*. Cambridge: Cambridge University Press.

——(1996). 'Simulation and cognitive penetrability', *Mind and Language*, 11: 44–67.

——(1998). 'Co-cognition and off-line simulation', *Mind and Language*, 13: 477–98.

HEIDER, F., and SIMMEL, M. (1944). 'An experimental study of apparent behavior', *American Journal of Psychology*, 57: 243–59.

HEMPEL, C. (1964). 'The theoretician's dilemma: a study in the logic of theory construction', in C. Hempel, *Aspects of Scientific Explanation*. New York: The Free Press, 173–226.

HIGGINBOTHAM, J. (1995). 'Tensed thoughts', *Mind and Language*, 10: 226–49.

HOGREFE, G., WIMMER, H., and PERNER, J. (1986). 'Ignorance versus false belief: a developmental lag in attribution of epistemic states', *Child Development*, 57: 567–82.

HOWLIN, P., BARON-COHEN, S., HADWIN, J. (1999). *Teaching Children with Autism to Mind-Read: A Practical Guide for Teachers and Parents*. New York: J. Wiley & Sons.

HUMPHREY, N. (1976). 'The social function of intellect', in P. Bateson and R. Hinde (eds.), *Growing Points in Ethology*. Cambridge: Cambridge University Press.

HURLBURT, R. (1990). *Sampling Normal and Schizophrenic Inner Experience*. New York: Plenum Press.

—— HAPPÉ, F., and FRITH, U. (1994). 'Sampling the form of inner experience in three adults with Asperger syndrome', *Psychological Medicine*, 24: 385–95.

IZARD, C. (1991). *Psychology of Emotion*. New York: Plenum Press.

JARROLD, C., CARRUTHERS, P., SMITH, P., and BOUCHER, J. (1994). 'Pretend play: is it metarepresentational?', *Mind and Language*, 9: 445–68.

JOHNSON, S. (2000). 'The recognition of mentalistic agents in infants', *Trends in Cognitive Sciences*, 4: 22–8.

—— SLAUGHTER, V., and CAREY, S. (1998). 'Whose gaze will infants follow? features that elicit gaze-following in 12-month-olds', *Developmental Science*, 1: 233–8.

JOLLIFFE, T., LANSDOWN, R., and ROBINSON, C. (1992). 'Autism: a personal account', *Communication*, 26: 12–19.

KAHNEMAN, D., and TVERSKY, A. (1982*a*). 'The psychology of preferences', *Scientific American*, 246/1: 160–73.

—————— (1982*b*). 'The simulation heuristic', in Kahneman et al. 1982: 201–8.

—— SLOVIC, P., and TVERSKY, A. (eds.) (1982). *Judgment under Uncertainty*. Cambridge: Cambridge University Press.

—— KNETSCH, J., and THALER, R. (1990). 'Experimental tests of the endowment effect and the Coase theorem', *Journal of Political Economy*, 98: 1325–48.

KREBS, J., and DAWKINS, R. (1984). 'Animal signals: mind-reading and manipulation', in J. Krebs and N. Davies (eds.), *Behavioural Ecology: An Evolutionary Approach*, 2nd edn. Oxford: Blackwell Scientific Publications.

KUCZAJ, S., and MARATSOS, M. (1975). 'What children *can* say before they *will*', *Merrill-Palmer Quarterly*, 21: 87–111.

KUNDA, Z. (1987). 'Motivated inference', *Journal of Personality and Social Psychology*, 53: 636–47.

LANGER, E. (1975). 'The illusion of control', *Journal of Personality and Social Psychology*, 32: 311–28.

LAURENCE, S., and MARGOLIS, E. (forthcoming). 'Acquiring number concepts: language, object, and number', in P. Carruthers, S. Laurence, and S. Stich (eds.), *The Structure of the Innate Mind*. Cambridge: Cambridge University Press.

LEMPERS, J., FLAVELL, E., and FLAVELL, J. (1977). 'The development in very young children of tacit knowledge concerning visual perception', *Genetic Psychology Monographs*, 95: 3–53.

LESLIE, A. (1987). 'Pretense and representation: the origins of "theory of mind"', *Psychological Review*, 94: 412–26.

—— (1991). 'The theory of mind impairment in autism: evidence for a modular mechanism of development?', in A. Whiten (ed.), *Natural Theories of Mind: Evolution, Development and Simulation of Everyday Mindreading*. Oxford: Blackwell, 63–78.

—— (1994*a*). 'Pretending and believing: issues in the theory of ToMM', *Cognition*, 50: 211–38.

—— (1994*b*). 'ToMM, ToBY and Agency: core architecture and domain specificity', in L. Hirschfeld and S. Gelman (eds.), *Mapping the Mind*. Cambridge: Cambridge University Press, 119–48.

—— (1995). 'A theory of agency', in D. Sperber, D. Premack, and A. Premack (eds.), *Causal Cognition*. Oxford: Oxford University Press.

LESLIE, A. (2000). ' "Theory of mind" as a mechanism of selective attention', in M. Gazzaniga (ed.), *The New Cognitive Neurosciences*. Cambridge, Mass.: MIT Press.

—— and GERMAN, T. (1994). 'Knowledge and ability in "theory of mind": one-eyed overview of a debate', in M. Davies and T. Stone (eds.), *Mental Simulation: Philosophical and Psychological Essays*. Oxford: Blackwell.

—— and ROTH, D. (1993). 'What autism teaches us about metarepresentation', in S. Baron-Cohen, H. Tager-Flusberg, and D. Cohen (eds.), *Understanding Other Minds: Perspectives from Autism*. Oxford: Oxford University Press.

—— and THAISS, L. (1992). 'Domain specificity in conceptual development: neuro-psychological evidence from autism', *Cognition*, 43: 225–51.

—— XU, F., TREMOULET, P., and SCHOLL, B. (1998). 'Indexing and the object concept: developing "what" and "where" systems', *Trends in Cognitive Sciences*, 2: 10–18.

LESSER, I. (1985). 'Current concepts in psychiatry', *New England Journal of Medicine*, 312: 690–2.

LEVIN, D., MOMEN, N., DRIVDAHL, S., and SIMONS, D. (2000). 'Change blindness blindness: the metacognitive error of overestimating change-detection ability', *Visual Cognition*, 7/1–3: 397–412.

LEWIS, C., and MITCHELL, P. (1994). *Children's Early Understanding of Mind: Origins and Development*. Hillsdale, NJ: Lawrence Erlbaum Associates.

LEWIS, D. (1970). 'How to define theoretical terms'. *Journal of Philosophy*, 67: 17–25.

—— (1972). 'Psychophysical and theoretical identifications', *Australasian Journal of Philosophy*, 50: 249–58; repr. in N. Block (ed.), *Readings in the Philosophy of Psychology*, vol. i. Cambridge, Mass.: Harvard University Press. 207–15. Page references are to the Block volume.

—— (1986). *On the Plurality of Worlds*. NY: Basil Blackwell.

LILLARD, A. (1993). 'Young children's conceptualization of pretense: action or mental representational state?', *Child Development*, 64: 372–86.

—— (1994). 'Making sense of pretense', in Lewis and Mitchell 1994: 211–34.

—— (1996). 'Body or mind: children's categorizing of pretense', *Child Development*, 67: 1717–34.

—— and FLAVELL, J. (1992). 'Young children's understanding of different mental states', *Developmental Psychology*, 28: 626–34.

LOEWENSTEIN, G., and ADLER, D. (1995). 'A bias in the prediction of tastes', *Economic Journal: The Quarterly Journal of the Royal Economic Society*, 105: 929–37.

LOFTUS, E. (1979). *Eyewitness Testimony*. Cambridge, Mass.: Harvard University Press.

LUTZ, C. (1985). 'Ethnopsychology compared to what? Explaining behavior and consciousness among the Ifaluk', in G. White and J. Kirkpatrick (eds.), *Person, Self, and Experience: Exploring Pacific Ethnopsychologies*. Berkeley: University of California Press, 35–79.

—— (1988). *Unnatural Emotions: Everyday Sentiments on a Micronesian Atoll and Their Challenge to Western Theory*. Chicago: The University of Chicago Press.

LYCAN, W. (1981). 'Form, function and feel', *Journal of Philosophy*, 78: 24–50.

—— (1987). *Consciousness*. Cambridge, Mass.: Bradford Books/MIT Press.

—— (1988). *Judgement and Justification*. Cambridge: Cambridge University Press.

—— (1994). 'Functionalism', in S. Guttenplan (ed.), *A Companion to the Philosophy of Mind*. Oxford: Blackwell, 317–23.

McCLOSKY, M. (1983). 'Naïve theories of motion', in D. Gentner and A. Stevens (eds.), *Mental Models*. Hillsdale, NJ: Erlbaum.

McLAUGHLIN, B., and TYE, M. (1998). 'Is content externalism compatible with privileged access?', *Philosophical Review*, 107: 349–80.

MacWHINNEY, B., and SNOW, C. (1990). 'The child language data exchange system: an update', *Journal of Child Language*, 17: 457–72.

MALLON, R., and STICH, S. (2000). 'The odd couple: the compatibility of social construction and evolutionary psychology', *Philosophy of Science*, 67: 133–54.

MARKS, J. (ed.) (1986). *The Ways of Desire: New Essays in Philosophical Psychology on the Concept of Wanting*. Chicago: Precedent Publishing.

MARR, D. (1982). *Vision*. San Francisco: W. H. Freeman.

MASANGKAY, Z., McCLUSKEY, K., McINTYRE, C., SIMS-KNIGHT, J., VAUGHAN, B., and FLAVELL, J. (1974). 'The early development of inferences about the visual percepts of others', *Child Development*, 45: 357–66.

MELLOR, C. (1970). 'First rank symptoms of schizophrenia', *British Journal of Psychiatry*, 117: 15–23.

MELTZOFF, A. (1993). 'Molyneux's babies: cross-modal perception, imitation, and the mind of the preverbal infant', in N. Eilan, R. McCarthy, and B. Brewer (eds.), *Spatial Representation*. Oxford: Blackwell.

—— (1995). 'Understanding the intentions of others: re-enactment of intended acts by 18-month-old children', *Developmental Psychology*, 31: 838–50.

—— and BORTON, R. (1979). 'Intermodal matching by human neonates', *Nature*, 282: 403–4.

—— GOPNIK, A., and REPACHOLI, B. (1999). 'Toddlers' understanding of intentions, desires, and emotions: explorations of the dark ages', in P. Zelazo (ed.), *Developing Intentions in a Social World*. NJ: Erlbaum.

MILGRAM, S. (1963). 'Behavioral study of obedience', *Journal of Abnormal and Social Psychology*, 67: 371–8.

MILLER, J. (1984). 'Culture and the development of everyday social explanation', *Journal of Personality and Social Psychology*, 46: 961–78.

MILLIKAN, R. (1984). *Language, Thought, and other Biological Categories*. Cambridge, Mass.: Bradford Books/MIT Press.

MLAKAR, J., JENSTERLE, J., and FRITH, C. (1994). 'Central monitoring deficiency and schizophrenic symptoms', *Psychological Medicine*, 24: 557–64.

MORTON, A. (1980). *Frames of Mind: Constraints on the Common-Sense Conception of the Mental*. Oxford: Clarendon Press.

MOSES, L. (1993). 'Young children's understanding of belief constraints on intention', *Cognitive Development*, 6: 1–25.

MOSHER, D., BARTON-HENRY, M., and GREEN, S. (1989). 'Subjective sexual arousal and involvement: development of multiple indicators', *Journal of Sex Research*, 25: 412–25.

MURPHY, G., and MEDIN, D. (1985). 'The role of theories in conceptual coherence', *Psychological Review*, 92: 289–316.

NICHOLS, S. (1993). 'Developmental evidence and introspection', *Behavioral and Brain Sciences*, 16/1: 64–5.

——(2001). 'The mind's "I" and the *Theory of Mind*'s "I": Introspection and two concepts of self', *Philosophical Topics*, 28: 171–99.

——(2002). 'Folk psychology', in L. Nadel (ed.), *Encyclopedia of Cognitive Science*. London: Nature Publishing Group.

——and STICH, S. (1998). 'Rethinking co-cognition', *Mind and Language*, 13: 499–512.

————(2000). 'A cognitive theory of pretense', *Cognition*, 74: 115–47.

————(2002). 'How to read your own mind: a cognitive theory of self-consciousness', in Q. Smith and A. Jokic (eds.), *Aspects of Consciousness*. Oxford: Oxford University Press, 157–200.

————and LESLIE, A. (1995). 'Choice effects and the ineffectiveness of simulation', *Mind and Language*, 10/4: 437–45.

——————and KLEIN, D. (1996). 'Varieties of off-line simulation', in P. Carruthers and P. Smith (eds.), *Theories of Theories of Mind*. Cambridge: Cambridge University Press, 39–74.

NISBETT, R., and ROSS, L. (1980). *Human Inference*. Englewood Cliffs, NJ: Prentice-Hall.

——and SCHACTER, S. (1966). 'Cognitive manipulation of pain', *Journal of Experimental Social Psychology*, 21: 227–36.

——and WILSON, T. (1977). 'Telling more than we can know', *Psychological Review*, 84: 231–59.

——PENG, K., CHOI, I., and NORENZAYAN, A. (2001). 'Culture and systems of thought: holistic versus analytic cognition', *Psychological Review*, 108: 291–310.

NUNNER-WINKLER, G., and SODIAN, B. (1988). 'Children's understanding of moral emotions', *Child Development*, 59: 1323–38.

NUTTIN, J., and BECKERS, A. (1975). *The Illusion of Attitude Change: Toward a Response Contagion Theory of Persuasion*. London: Academic Press.

O'NEILL, D., and GOPNIK, A. (1991). 'Young children's understanding of the sources of their beliefs', *Developmental Psychology*, 27: 390–7.

——ASTINGTON, J., and FLAVELL, J. (1992). 'Young children's understanding of the role that sensory experiences play in knowledge acquisition', *Child Development*, 63: 474–91.

PAPINEAU, D. (2000). 'The evolution of knowledge', in P. Carruthers and A. Chamberlain (eds.), *Evolution and the Human Mind*. Cambridge: Cambridge University Press, 170–206.

PEACOCKE, C. (1983). *Sense and Content*. Oxford: Clarendon Press.

PERNER, J. (1988). 'Developing semantics for theories of mind: from propositional attitudes to mental representation', in J. Astington, P. Harris, and D. Olson (eds.), *Developing Theories of Mind*. Cambridge: Cambridge University Press, 141–72.

——(1991). *Understanding the Representational Mind*. Cambridge, Mass.: Bradford Books/MIT Press.

——(1993). 'Rethinking the metarepresentation theory', in S. Baron-Cohen, H. Tager-Flusberg, and D. Cohen (eds.), *Understanding Other Minds: Perspectives from Autism*. Oxford: Oxford University Press.

——LEEKAM, S., and WIMMER, H. (1987). 'Three-year olds' difficulty with false belief: the case for a conceptual deficit', *British Journal of Experimental Child Psychology*, 39: 437–71.

——FRITH, U., LESLIE A., and LEEKAM, S. (1989). 'Exploration of the autistic child's theory of mind: knowledge, belief and communication', *Child Development*, 60: 689–700.

——BARKER, S., and HUTTON, D. (1994). '*Prelief:* the conceptual origins of belief and pretense', in Lewis and Mitchell 1994: 261–86.

PERRY, J. (1993). *The Problem of the Essential Indexical and Other Essays*. New York: Oxford University Press.

——(1994). 'Intentionality', in S. Guttenplan (ed.), *A Companion to the Philosophy of Mind*. Oxford: Basil Blackwell, 386–95.

PHILLIPS, W., BARON-COHEN, S., and RUTTER, M. (1995). 'To what extent can children with autism understand desire?', *Development and Psychopathology*, 7: 151–69.

PIAGET, J. (1962). *Play, Dreams, and Imitation in Childhood*, trans. C. Gattegno and F. M. Hodgson. New York: Norton.

——(1967). *The Child's Conception of Space*. New York: Norton.

PINKER, S. (1994). *The Language Instinct*. New York: William Morrow.

POVINELLI, D. (1996). 'Chimpanzee theory of mind? The long road to strong inference', in Carruthers and Smith 1996: 293–329.

——and EDDY, T. (1996). 'What young chimpanzees know about seeing', *Monograph of the Society for Research in Child Development*, 61/2.

——PERILLOUX, H., REAUX, J., and BIERSCHWALE, D. (1998). 'Young and juvenile chimpanzees' reactions to intentional versus accidental and inadvertent actions', *Behavioral Processes*, 42: 205–18.

PRATT, C., and BRYANT, P. (1990). 'Young children understand that looking leads to knowing (so long as they are looking into a single barrel)', *Child Development*, 61: 973–83.

PREMACK, D., and PREMACK, A. (1997). 'Motor competence as integral to attribution of goal', *Cognition*, 63: 235–42.

——and WOODRUFF, G. (1978). 'Does the chimpanzee have a theory of mind?', *Behavioral and Brain Sciences*, 1: 516–26.

PUTNAM, H. (1960). 'Minds and machines', in S. Hook (ed.), *Dimensions of Mind*. New York: New York University Press, 138–64.

——(1975). 'The meaning of "meaning"', in Putnam, *Mind, Language and Reality: Philosophical Papers*, vol. ii. Cambridge: Cambridge University Press.

PYLYSHYN, Z. (1978). 'When is attribution of beliefs justified?', *Behavioral and Brain Sciences*, 1: 592–3.

——(1987). *The Robot's Dilemma: The Frame Problem in Artificial Intelligence*. Norwood, NJ: Ablex.

QUINE, W. (1960). *Word and Object*. Cambridge, Mass.: MIT Press.

REPACHOLI, B., and GOPNIK, A. (1997). 'Early understanding of desires: evidence from 14 and 18 month olds', *Developmental Psychology*, 33: 12–21.

RESNICK, R., O'REGAN, J., CLARKE, J. (1997). 'To see or not to see: the need for attention to perceive changes in scenes', *Psychological Science*, 8: 369–73.

RICE, C., KOINIS, D., SULLIVAN, K., TAGER-FLUSBERG, H., and WINNER, E. (1997). 'When 3-year-olds pass the appearance-reality test', *Developmental Psychology*, 33: 54–61.

ROBINSON, E., and MITCHELL, P. (1995). 'Masking of children's early understanding of the representational mind: backwards explanation versus prediction', *Child Development*, 66: 1022–39.

ROSEN, C., SCHWEBEL, D., and SINGER, J. (1997). 'Preschoolers' attributions of mental states in pretense', *Child Development*, 68: 1133–42.

ROSENTHAL, D. (1992). 'Thinking that one thinks', in M. Davies and G. Humphreys (eds.), *Consciousness*. Oxford: Blackwell.

ROSS, L., and NISBETT, R. (1991). *The Person and the Situation: Perspectives of Social Psychology*. Philadelphia: Temple University Press.

ROTH, D., and LESLIE, A. (1991). 'The recognition of attitude conveyed by utterance: a study of preschool and autistic children', *British Journal of Developmental Psychology*, 9: 315–30.

——— (1998). 'Solving belief problems: a task analysis', *Cognition*, 66: 1–31.

RUFFMAN, T. (1996). 'Do children understand the mind by means of simulation or a theory: evidence from their understanding of inference', *Mind and Language*, 11: 388–414.

RYLE, G. (1949). *The Concept of Mind*. London: Hutchinson.

SACKS, O. (1995). *An Anthropologist on Mars*. New York: Alfred A. Knopf.

SAMUELS, R. (2000). 'Massively modular minds: evolutionary psychology and cognitive architecture', in P. Carruthers and A. Chamberlain (eds.), *Evolution and the Human Mind*. Cambridge: Cambridge University Press.

—— STICH, S., and FAUCHER, L. (2003). 'Reasoning and rationality', in I. Niiniluoto, M. Sintonen, and J. Wolenski (eds.), *Handbook of Epistemology*. Dordrecht: Kluwer, 1–50.

SCHANK, R., and ABELSON, R. (1977). *Scripts, Plans, Goals, and Understanding: An Inquiry Into Human Knowledge Structures*. Hillsdale, N.J.: L. Erlbaum Associates.

SCHNEIDER, K. (1959). *Clinical Psychopathology*, trans. M. Hamilton. New York: Grune & Stratton.

SCHOLL, B., and LESLIE, A. (1999). 'Modularity, development, and "theory of mind"', *Mind and Language*, 14: 131–53.

—— SIMONS, D., and LEVIN, D. (forthcoming). 'Change blindness blindness: an implicit measure of a metacognitive error', in D. Levin (ed.), *Visual Metacognition: Thinking about seeing*. Wesport, Conn.: Greenwood Press.

SCHUELER, G. (1995). *Desire: Its Role in Practical Reason and the Explanation of Action*. Cambridge, Mass.: MIT Press.

SCHWARTZ, R. (1994). 'Representation', in S. Guttenplan (ed.), *A Companion to the Philosophy of Mind*. Oxford: Basil Blackwell, 536–41.

SCHWITZGEBEL, E. (1999). 'Representation and desire: a philosophical error with consequences for theory-of-mind research', *Philosophical Psychology*, 12: 157–80.

SEARLE, J. (1994). 'Intentionality', in S. Guttenplan (ed.), *A Companion to the Philosophy of Mind*. Oxford: Basil Blackwell, 379–86.

SEGAL, G. (1996). 'The modularity of theory of mind', in Carruthers and Smith 1996: 141–57.

SELLARS, W. (1956). 'Empiricism and the philosophy of mind', in H. Feigl and M. Scriven (eds.), *The Foundations of Science and the Concepts of Psychology and Psychoanalysis* (Minnesota Studies in the Philosophy of Science, 1). Minneapolis: University of Minnesota Press, 253–329.

SHALLICE, T. (1988). *From Neuropsychology to Mental Structure*. Cambridge: Cambridge University Press.

SIEGAL, M., and BEATTIE, K. (1991). 'Where to look first for children's knowledge of false beliefs', *Cognition*, 38: 1–12.

SIMONS, D. (2000). 'Current approaches to change blindness', *Visual Cognition*, 7: 1–15.

—— and LEVIN, D. (1997). 'Change blindness', *Trends in Cognitive Sciences*, 1: 261–7.

SMITH, D., and OVER, R. (1987). 'Correlates of fantasy-induced and film-induced male sexual arousal', *Archives of Sexual Behavior*, 16: 395–409.

—— —— (1990). 'Enhancement of fantasy-induced sexual arousal in men through training in sexual imagery', *Archives of Sexual Behavior*, 19: 477–90.

SORENSEN, R. (1998). 'Self-strengthening empathy', *Philosophy and Phenomenological Research*, 58: 75–98.

SPELKE, E., and TSIVKIN, S. (2001). 'Language and number: a bilingual training study', *Cognition*, 78: 45–88.

—— PHILLIPS, A., and WOODWARD, A. (1995). 'Infants' knowledge about object motion and human action', in D. Sperber, D. Premack, A. Premack (eds.), *Causal Cognition: A Multidisciplinary Debate*. Oxford: Clarendon Press, 44–78.

STERELNY, K. (1990). *The Representational Theory of the Mind: An Introduction*. Oxford: Blackwell.

—— and GRIFFITHS, P. (1999). *Sex and Death: An Introduction to Philosophy of Biology*. Chicago: University of Chicago Press.

STICH, S. (1981). 'Dennett on intentional systems', *Philosophical Topics*, 12: 39–62.

—— (1983). *From Folk Psychology to Cognitive Science*. Cambridge, Mass.: Bradford Books/MIT Press.

—— (1992). 'What is a theory of mental representation?', *Mind*, 101: 243–61.

—— (1996). *Deconstructing the Mind*. Oxford: Oxford University Press.

—— and NICHOLS, S. (1992). 'Folk psychology: simulation or tacit theory', *Mind and Language*, 71: 35–71.

—— —— (1995). 'Second thoughts on simulation', in A. Stone and M. Darier (eds.), *Mental Simulation: Evaluations and Applications*. Oxford: Basil Blackwell, 87–108.

—— —— (1997). 'Cognitive penetrability, rationality and restricted simulation', *Mind and Language*, 12: 297–326.

—— —— (1998). 'Theory theory to the max: a critical notice of Gopnik and Meltzoff's *Words, thoughts, and theories*', *Mind and Language*, 13: 421–49.

—— —— (2003). 'Folk psychology', in T. Warfield and S. Stich (eds.), *The Blackwell Guide to Philosophy of Mind*. Oxford: Basil Blackwell.

—— and RAVENSCROFT, I. (1994). 'What *is* folk psychology?', *Cognition*, 50: 447–68. repr. in Stich 1996.

—— and WARFIELD, T. (1994). *Mental Representation*. Oxford: Basil Blackwell.

SURIAN, L., and LESLIE, A. (1999). 'Competence and performance in false belief understanding: a comparison of autistic and three-year-old children', *British Journal of Developmental Psychology*, 17: 141–55.

TAGER-FLUSBERG, H. (1993). 'What language reveals about the understanding of minds in children with autism', in S. Baron-Cohen, H. Tager-Flusberg, and Donald Cohen (eds.) *Understanding Other Minds: Perspectives from Autism*, 1st edn. Oxford: Oxford University Press, 138–57.

—— SULLIVAN, K., and BOSHART, J. (1997). 'Executive functions and performance on false belief tasks', *Developmental Neurobiology*, 13: 487–93.

TAN, J., and HARRIS, P. (1991). 'Autistic children understand seeing and wanting', *Development and Psychopathology*, 3: 163–74.

THALER, R. (1980). 'Toward a positive theory of consumer choice', *Journal of Economic Behavior and Organization*, 1: 39–60.

TOMASELLO, M., and CALL, J. (1997). *Primate Cognition*. Oxford: Oxford University Press.

TYE, M. (1995). *Ten Problems of Consciousness: A Representational Theory of the Phenomenal Mind*. Cambridge, Mass.: Bradford Books/MIT Press.

URMSON, J. (1956). 'Parenthetical verbs', in A. Flew (ed.), *Essays in Conceptual Analysis*. London: MacMillan.

VON ECKARDT, B. (1999). 'Mental representation', in R. Wilson and F. Keil (eds.), *The MIT Encyclopedia of Cognitive Science*. Cambridge, Mass.: MIT Press, 527–9.

VRANA, S., CUTHBURT, B., and LANG, P. (1989). 'Processing fearful and neutral sentences: memory and heart rate change', *Cognition and Emotion*, 3: 179–95.

VRBA, E. (1989). 'Levels of selection and sorting with special reference to the species level', in R. Dawkins and M. Ridley (eds.), *Oxford Surveys in Evolutionary Biology*. New York: Oxford University Press.

VYGOTSKY, L. (1967). 'Play and its role in the mental development of the child', *Soviet Psychology*, 5: 6–18.

WALTON, K. (1990). *Mimesis as Make-Believe: On the Foundations of the Representational Arts*. Cambridge, Mass.: Harvard University Press.

—— (1997). 'Spelunking, simulation and slime: on being moved by fiction', in M. Hjort and S. Laver (eds.), *Emotion and the Arts*. Oxford: Oxford University Press.

WEBB, S. (1994). 'Witnessed behavior and Dennett's intentional stance', *Philosophical Topics*, 22: 457–70.

WELLMAN, H. (1990). *The Child's Theory of Mind*. Cambridge, Mass.: Bradford Books/MIT Press.

—— and BARTSCH, K. (1988). 'Young children's reasoning about beliefs', *Cognition*, 30: 239–77.

—— and ESTES, D. (1986). 'Early understanding of mental entities: a reexamination of childhood realism', *Child Development*, 57: 910–23.

—— and WOOLLEY, J. (1990). 'From simple desires to ordinary beliefs: the early development of everyday psychology', *Cognition*, 35: 245–75.

—— HARRIS, P., BANERJEE, M., and SINCLAIR, A. (1995). 'Early understanding of emotion: evidence from natural language', *Cognition and Emotion*, 9: 117–79.

—— PHILLIPS, A., and RODRIGUEZ, T. (2000). 'Young children's understanding of perception, desire, and emotion', *Child Development*, 71: 895–912.

—— CROSS, D., and WATSON, J. (2001). 'Meta-analysis of theory-of-mind development: the truth about false belief', *Child Development*, 72: 655–84.

WHITEN, A., and BYRNE, R. (1991). *Natural Theories of Mind*. Oxford: Blackwell.

——— (1997). *Machiavellian Intelligence II*. Cambridge: Cambridge University Press.

WIMMER, H., and HARTL, M. (1991). 'The Cartesian view and the theory view of mind: developmental evidence from understanding false belief in self and other', *British Journal of Developmental Psychology*, 9: 125–8.

—— and PERNER, J. (1983). 'Beliefs about beliefs: representation and constraining function of wrong beliefs in young children's understanding of deception', *Cognition*, 13: 103–28.

—— HOGREFE, G., and PERNER, J. (1988). 'Children's understanding of informational access as a source of knowledge', *Child Development*, 59: 386–96.

WING, L., and GOULD, J. (1979). 'Severe impairments of social interaction and associated abnormalities in children: epidemiology and classification', *Journal of Autism and Developmental Disorders*, 9: 11–29.

WOODWARD, A. (1998). 'Infants selectively encode the goal object of an actor's reach', *Cognition*, 69: 1–34.

WRIGHT, C., SMITH, B., and MACDONALD, C. (eds.) (1998). *Knowing Our Own Minds*. New York : Oxford University Press.

YOUNG, A. (1994). 'Neuropsychology of Awareness', in A. Revonsou and M. Kamppinen (eds.), *Consciousness in Philosophy and Cognitive Neuroscience*. Hillsdale, NJ: LEA.

—— (1998). *Face and Mind*. Oxford: Oxford University Press.

INDEX